Learning OpenStack Networking (Neutron)

Architect and build a network infrastructure for your cloud using OpenStack Neutron networking

James Denton

[PACKT]
PUBLISHING

open source*
community experience distilled

BIRMINGHAM - MUMBAI

Learning OpenStack Networking (Neutron)

First published: October 2014

Production reference: 1071014

Published by Packt Publishing Ltd.
Livery Place
35 Livery Street
Birmingham B3 2PB, UK.

ISBN 978-1-78398-330-8

www.packtpub.com

Cover image by Suyog Gharat (yogiee@me.com)

Credits

Author
James Denton

Reviewers
Kevin Jackson
Jorge Armin Garcia Lopez
Jacob Walcik

Commissioning Editor
Kartikey Pandey

Acquisition Editor
Richard Harvey

Content Development Editor
Susmita Panda

Technical Editor
Shiny Poojary

Copy Editors
Roshni Banerjee
Sarang Chari
Karuna Narayanan

Project Coordinator
Kartik Vedam

Proofreaders
Martin Diver
Ameesha Green
Samantha Lyon

Indexers
Hemangini Bari
Monica Ajmera Mehta
Tejal Soni

Graphics
Sheetal Aute
Ronak Dhruv
Valentina D'silva
Disha Haria
Abhinash Sahu

Production Coordinators
Aparna Bhagat
Shantanu N. Zagade

Cover Work
Aparna Bhagat

About the Author

James Denton lives with his beautiful wife, Amanda, and son, Wyatt, in San Antonio, Texas. He is an experienced IT professional with extensive experience in application networking technologies and OpenStack networking. He specializes in OpenStack for Rackspace in San Antonio, Texas. He is a Network Architect for the Rackspace Private Cloud team. He can be found on Twitter @jimmdenton and on Freenode IRC as busterswt.

I'd like to thank my wife, Amanda, for providing encouragement and patience throughout the writing of this book. In addition, I would like to thank my team at Rackspace for reviewing many rough drafts and providing excellent feedback.

Without OpenStack and Rackspace, the opportunity to write this book would not have been possible. A big thanks goes out to the OpenStack community for developing, and continuing to improve on, the product. It has been an amazing experience to be involved in this open source movement, and I look forward to the future.

About the Reviewers

Kevin Jackson is married and has three children. He is an experienced IT professional working with a range of clients, from small businesses to online enterprises. He has extensive experience of various flavors of Linux and Unix. He works as Principal Cloud Architect for Rackspace UK, specializing in OpenStack and covering the international market for the DevOps & Automation Advisory Services team. He is a co-author of *OpenStack Cloud Computing Cookbook, Packt Publishing* and *OpenStack Architecture Design Guide, OpenStack Foundation*. He can be found on Twitter @itarchitectkev.

Jorge Armin Garcia Lopez is a very passionate information security consultant from Mexico with more than 6 years of experience in computer security, penetration testing, intrusion detection/prevention, malware analysis, and incident response. He is the leader of a tiger team at one of the most important security companies placed in Latin America and Spain. He is also a security researcher at Cipher Storm Ltd Group and is the cofounder and CEO of the most important security conference in Mexico, BugCON. He holds important security industry certifications, such as OSCP, GCIA, GPEN, FireEye Specialist.

He has reviewed the following books:

- *Penetration Testing with BackBox, Packt Publishing*
- *Django Essentials, Packt Publishing*
- *Penetration Testing with the Bash shell, Packt Publishing*

Thanks to all my friends for supporting me. Special thanks to my grandmother, Margarita, and my sister, Abril. I would also like to thank Krangel, Shakeel Ali, Mada, Hector Garcia Posadas, and Belindo.

Jacob Walcik works as Principal Solutions Architect for Rackspace (http://rackspace.com). Over the last 18 years, he has worked as a software developer, systems administrator, and general technologist. In recent years, he has specialized in helping companies design and build their OpenStack-based private clouds. In his spare time, he enjoys hiking, playing soccer, and riding British motorcycles.

www.PacktPub.com

Support files, eBooks, discount offers, and more

You might want to visit www.PacktPub.com for support files and downloads related to your book.

Did you know that Packt offers eBook versions of every book published, with PDF and ePub files available? You can upgrade to the eBook version at www.PacktPub.com and as a print book customer, you are entitled to a discount on the eBook copy. Get in touch with us at service@packtpub.com for more details.

At www.PacktPub.com, you can also read a collection of free technical articles, sign up for a range of free newsletters and receive exclusive discounts and offers on Packt books and eBooks.

http://PacktLib.PacktPub.com

Do you need instant solutions to your IT questions? PacktLib is Packt's online digital book library. Here, you can access, read and search across Packt's entire library of books.

Why subscribe?

- Fully searchable across every book published by Packt
- Copy and paste, print and bookmark content
- On demand and accessible via web browser

Free access for Packt account holders

If you have an account with Packt at www.PacktPub.com, you can use this to access PacktLib today and view nine entirely free books. Simply use your login credentials for immediate access.

I dedicate this book to the memory of my grandfather, a proud Aggie whose curiosity in all things, including technology, helped form my identity and career. This book also goes to our friend, Alejandro Martinez, a great teammate and Racker.

Table of Contents

Preface

The latest release of OpenStack, code-named Icehouse, was released in April 2014 and includes the networking service known as Neutron (formerly Quantum). First introduced in the Folsom release of OpenStack, Neutron provides cloud operators and users with an API to create and manage networks in the cloud. An extension framework allows for additional network services, such as load balancing, firewalls, and virtual private networks, to be deployed and managed.

It is important to note that OpenStack Networking in this book refers only to Neutron and should not be confused with the legacy networking service known as nova-network built in Nova (Compute). While nova-network has slipped its deprecation date in the last two releases, support for the technology is limited in the future.

What this book covers

Chapter 1, Preparing the Network for OpenStack, will provide an introduction to OpenStack Networking that includes a description of the different supported networking technologies, and it will explain how to architect the physical network to support an OpenStack cloud.

Chapter 2, Installing OpenStack, will cover how to install the base components of the Havana release of OpenStack on the CentOS 6.5 operating system.

Chapter 3, Installing Neutron, will explain how to install the Neutron networking components of OpenStack and will help us to understand the internal architecture of Neutron, including the use of agents and plugins to orchestrate network connectivity.

Chapter 4, Building a Virtual Switching Infrastructure, will help us to install and configure the LinuxBridge plugin for Neutron to provide layer 2 connectivity to instances. We will also cover the architectural differences between the LinuxBridge and Open vSwitch plugins and how they connect instances to the network.

Chapter 5, Creating Networks with Neutron, will create networks and subnets in Neutron, boot and attach instances to networks, and explore the process of obtaining DHCP leases and metadata.

Chapter 6, Creating Routers with Neutron, will create Neutron routers and attach them to networks, follow traffic from an instance through a router, and explore the process of applying floating IPs to instances.

Chapter 7, Load Balancing Traffic in Neutron, will explore the fundamental components of a load balancer in Neutron, including virtual IPs, pools, pool members, and monitors. It will also help us to create and integrate a load balancer into the network.

Chapter 8, Protecting Instances on the Network, will cover the creation and management of security-group rules to secure instance traffic. In addition, it will help us create and integrate a firewall into the network using the firewall-as-a-service API.

Appendix A, Additional Neutron Commands, will briefly cover additional Neutron functionality that is outside the scope of this book. It will also acquaint us with VPN-as-a-service, Cisco 1000V integration, and VMWare/Nicera integration.

Appendix B, ML2 Configuration, will briefly cover the configuration of the ML2 plugin as a replacement for the deprecated LinuxBridge and Open Switch plugins.

What you need for this book

This book assumes a moderate level of networking experience, including experience with Linux networking configurations as well as physical switch and router configurations. While this book will walk the reader through a basic installation of OpenStack, little time will be spent on services other than Neutron. Therefore, it is important that the reader has a basic understanding of OpenStack and its general configuration prior to configuring OpenStack Networking.

In this book, the following software is required:

- Operating system
    - CentOS 6.5

- Software
    - OpenStack Havana

Internet connectivity will be required to install OpenStack packages and to make use of the example architectures in the book. While virtualization software, such as VMware or VirtualBox, can be used to simulate the servers and the network infrastructure, this book assumes that OpenStack will be installed on physical hardware and that a physical network infrastructure is in place.

Who this book is for

This book is for the novice-to-intermediate OpenStack cloud administrators who are looking to build or enhance their cloud using the networking service known as Neutron. By laying down a basic installation of OpenStack, the reader should be able to follow the examples laid out in the book to receive a functional understanding of the various components of OpenStack Networking. This book is focused on the usage of OpenStack Networking services rather than its development, and it uses free and open source software rather than commercial solutions.

Conventions

In this book, you will find a number of styles of text that distinguish between different kinds of information. Here are some examples of these styles, and an explanation of their meaning.

Code words in text, database table names, folder names, filenames, file extensions, pathnames, dummy URLs, user input, and Twitter handles are shown as follows: "OpenStack services can be installed either as root or as a user with sudo permissions."

Any command-line input or output is written as follows:

```
# nano /etc/sysconfig/network-scripts/ifcfg-eth0
```

New terms and **important words** are shown in bold. Words that you see on the screen, in menus or dialog boxes for example, appear in the text like this: "To view the status of Nova (Compute) services, click on the **Compute Services** tab."

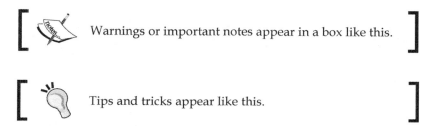

Warnings or important notes appear in a box like this.

Tips and tricks appear like this.

Reader feedback

Feedback from our readers is always welcome. Let us know what you think about this book—what you liked or may have disliked. Reader feedback is important for us to develop titles that you really get the most out of.

To send us general feedback, simply send an e-mail to feedback@packtpub.com, and mention the book title via the subject of your message.

If there is a topic that you have expertise in and you are interested in either writing or contributing to a book, see our author guide on www.packtpub.com/authors.

Customer support

Now that you are the proud owner of a Packt book, we have a number of things to help you to get the most from your purchase.

Downloading the example code

You can download the example code files for all Packt books you have purchased from your account at http://www.packtpub.com. If you purchased this book elsewhere, you can visit http://www.packtpub.com/support and register to have the files e-mailed directly to you.

Downloading the color images of this book

We also provide you with a PDF file that has color images of the screenshots/ diagrams used in this book. The color images will help you better understand the changes in the output. You can download this file from: https://www.packtpub.com/sites/default/files/downloads/3308OS_ColoredImages.pdf.

Errata

Although we have taken every care to ensure the accuracy of our content, mistakes do happen. If you find a mistake in one of our books—maybe a mistake in the text or the code—we would be grateful if you would report this to us. By doing so, you can save other readers from frustration and help us improve subsequent versions of this book. If you find any errata, please report them by visiting http://www.packtpub.com/submit-errata, selecting your book, clicking on the **errata submission form** link, and entering the details of your errata. Once your errata are verified, your submission will be accepted and the errata will be uploaded on our website, or added to any list of existing errata, under the Errata section of that title. Any existing errata can be viewed by selecting your title from http://www.packtpub.com/support.

Piracy

Piracy of copyright material on the Internet is an ongoing problem across all media. At Packt, we take the protection of our copyright and licenses very seriously. If you come across any illegal copies of our works, in any form, on the Internet, please provide us with the location address or website name immediately so that we can pursue a remedy.

Please contact us at copyright@packtpub.com with a link to the suspected pirated material.

We appreciate your help in protecting our authors, and our ability to bring you valuable content.

Questions

You can contact us at questions@packtpub.com if you are having a problem with any aspect of the book, and we will do our best to address it.

1

Preparing the Network for OpenStack

Enterprises, both large and small, run their clouds using OpenStack software. While the clouds themselves may vary in complexity, one thing is common: they are made possible by the scalability and flexibility of OpenStack Compute and Networking services.

Modern cloud computing platforms, such as OpenStack, rely on a method of networking known as software-defined networking, or SDN. Traditional network administration relies heavily on the administrator to manually configure and maintain physical network hardware and connectivity. SDN, on the other hand, allows network administrators to manage network services in an abstract and automated manner. Software-defined networking, and the software-defined data center as a whole, is often regarded as a necessary foundation for scalable and efficient cloud computing.

In this chapter, you will be introduced to the different components and features of OpenStack Networking, codenamed Neutron, as well as various methods in which Neutron can be deployed and configured from both software and hardware perspectives. Throughout the book, the Neutron moniker will often be used in place of the official name.

What is OpenStack Networking?

OpenStack Networking is a standalone service that can be installed independently of other OpenStack services. Other OpenStack services that fall under this category include Compute (Nova), Image (Glance), Identity (Keystone), Block Storage (Cinder), and Dashboard (Horizon). OpenStack Networking services can be split amongst multiple hosts to provide resilience and redundancy, or can be configured to operate on a single node.

OpenStack Networking uses a service called neutron-server to expose an application programmable interface, or API, to users and to pass requests to the configured network plugins for additional processing. Users are able to define network connectivity in the cloud, and cloud operators are allowed to leverage different networking technologies to enhance and power the cloud.

Like many other OpenStack services, Networking requires access to a database for persistent storage of the network configuration.

Features of OpenStack Networking

OpenStack Networking in Havana includes many technologies one would find in the data center, including switching, routing, load balancing, firewalling, and virtual private networks. These features can be configured to leverage open source or commercial software, and provide a cloud operator with all of the tools necessary to build a functional and self-contained cloud. OpenStack Networking also provides a framework for third-party vendors to build on and enhance the capabilities of the cloud.

Switching

Virtual switches are defined as software applications that connect virtual machines to virtual networks at layer 2, or the data-link layer of the OSI model. Neutron supports multiple virtual switching platforms, including built-in Linux bridging and Open vSwitch. Open vSwitch, also known as OVS, is an open source virtual switch that supports standard management interfaces and protocols, including NetFlow, SPAN, RSPAN, LACP, and 802.1q, though many of these features are not exposed to the user through the OpenStack API. In addition to VLAN tagging, users can build overlay networks in software using L2-in-L3 tunneling protocols, such as GRE or VXLAN. Open vSwitch can be used to facilitate communication between instances and devices outside the control of OpenStack, which include hardware switches, network firewalls, storage devices, dedicated servers, and more. Additional information on the use of Linux bridges and Open vSwitch as switching platforms for OpenStack can be found in *Chapter 4, Building a Virtual Switching Infrastructure*.

Routing

OpenStack Networking provides routing and NAT capabilities through the use of IP forwarding, iptables, and network namespaces. A network namespace is analogous to `chroot` for the network stack. Inside a network namespace, you can find sockets, bound ports, and interfaces that were created in the namespace. Each network namespace has its own routing table and iptables process that provide filtering and network address translation, also known as NAT. Network namespaces are comparable to VRFs in Cisco, routing instances in Juniper JunOS, or route domains in F5 BIG-IP. With network namespaces, there is no concern of overlapping subnets between networks created by tenants. Configuring a router within Neutron enables instances to interact and communicate with outside networks. More information on routing within OpenStack can be found in *Chapter 6, Creating Routers with Neutron*.

Load balancing

First introduced in the Grizzly release of OpenStack, **Load-Balancing-as-a-Service**, also known as **LBaaS**, provides users the ability to distribute client requests across multiple instances or servers. Havana is equipped with a plugin for LBaaS that utilizes HAProxy as the load balancer. More information on the use of load balancers within Neutron can be found in *Chapter 7, Load Balancing Traffic in Neutron*.

Firewalling

In Havana, there are two methods of providing security to instances or networks: security groups and firewalls. Security group functionality was originally found in nova-network in OpenStack Compute and has since migrated to OpenStack Networking. This is a method of securing traffic to and from instances through the use of iptables on the compute node. With the introduction of **Firewall-as-a-Service**, also known as **FWaaS**, security is handled at the router rather than at the compute node. In the Havana release of OpenStack, FWaaS is an experimental extension with no guaranteed backwards compatibility in future releases. More information on securing instances can be found in *Chapter 8, Protecting Instances on the Network*.

Virtual private networks

A **virtual private network (VPN)**, extends a private network across a public network such as the Internet. A VPN enables a computer to send and receive data across public networks as if it were directly connected to the private network. Neutron provides a set of APIs to allow tenants to create IPSec-based VPN tunnels to remote gateways. In the Havana release of OpenStack, VPNaaS is an experimental extension with no guaranteed backwards compatibility in future releases; it will not be covered in this book.

Preparing the physical infrastructure

When architecting the network, it is important to first determine the purpose of the cloud. Is the goal to build a highly scalable environment with multiple levels of network redundancy? Or is the goal to provide a sandbox for developers with little thought given to the resilience of the network or compute platform? Do you want an environment that leverages everything OpenStack Networking has to offer in terms of routing, switching, and application networking? Is the environment intended to be an extension of an existing physical network?

OpenStack Networking can serve many roles within different clouds but is better at some technologies than others. The purpose of the cloud itself, along with security requirements and available hardware, will play a big part in determining the architecture of the network and OpenStack's role in the network.

The OpenStack portal www.openstack.org provides reference architectures for Neutron-based clouds that involve a combination of the following nodes:

- Controller node
- Network node
- Compute node(s)

Prior to the installation of OpenStack, the physical network infrastructure must be configured to support the networks needed for an operational cloud. In the following diagram, I have highlighted the area of responsibility for the network administrator:

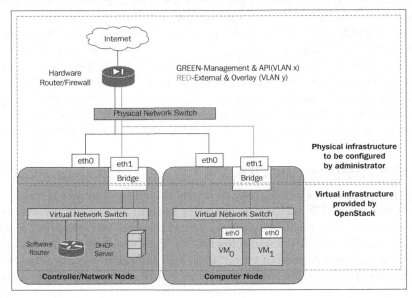

Figure 1.1

The physical network infrastructure must be configured to support OpenStack Networking. In this diagram, the area marked in red is the responsibility of the network administrator. That may include the need to configure physical switches, firewalls, or routers, as well as interfaces on the servers themselves.

In the next few chapters, I have defined networks and VLANs that will be used throughout the book to demonstrate the various components of OpenStack Networking. Generic information on the configuration of switch ports, routers, or firewalls can be found in upcoming chapters as well.

Types of network traffic

The reference architecture for OpenStack Networking defines at least four distinct types of network traffic:

- Management
- API
- External
- Guest

These distinct types of network traffic do not require dedicated interfaces and are often collapsed onto single interfaces. Depending on the chosen deployment model, the cloud architecture may spread networking services across multiple nodes. The security requirements of the enterprise deploying the cloud will often dictate how the cloud is built.

Management network

The management network is used for internal communication between hosts for services, such as the messaging service and database service. All hosts will communicate with each other over this network. The management network can be configured as an isolated network on a dedicated interface or combined with another network as described below.

API network

The API network is used to expose OpenStack APIs to users of the cloud and services within the cloud. Endpoint addresses for services, such as Keystone, Neutron, Glance, and Horizon, are procured from the API network.

It is common practice to configure a single IP address on a dedicated interface that will serve as the listener address for the various services as well as the management address for the host itself. A diagram of this configuration is provided later in this chapter.

External network

An external network provides Neutron routers with network access. Once a router has been configured, this network becomes the source of floating IP addresses for instances and load balancer VIPs. IP addresses in this network should be reachable by any client on the Internet.

Guest network

The guest network is a network dedicated to instance traffic. Options for guest networks include local networks restricted to a particular node, flat or VLAN tagged networks, or the use of virtual overlay networks made possible with GRE or VXLAN encapsulation. For more information on guest networks, please refer to *Chapter 5, Creating Networks with Neutron*.

The interfaces used for the external and guest networks can be dedicated interfaces or ones that are shared with other types of traffic. Each approach has its benefits and caveats, and those are described in more detail as we progress in the chapter.

Physical server connections

The number of interfaces needed per host is dependent on the type of cloud being built and the security and performance requirements of the organization.

A single interface per server that results in a combined control and data plane is all that is needed for a fully functional OpenStack cloud. Many organizations choose to deploy their cloud this way, especially when port density is at a premium or the environment is simply used for testing. In production clouds, however, separate control and data interfaces are recommended.

Single interface

For hosts using a single interface, all traffic to and from instances as well as internal OpenStack, SSH management, and API traffic traverses the same interface. This configuration can result in severe performance degradation, as a guest can create a denial of service attack against its host by consuming the total available bandwidth. Not recommended for production environments, this type of configuration should only be used for testing or proof-of-concept.

The following diagram demonstrates the use of a single physical interface for all traffic using the Open vSwitch plugin. A physical interface resides in the network bridge and handles external, guest, management, and API service traffic:

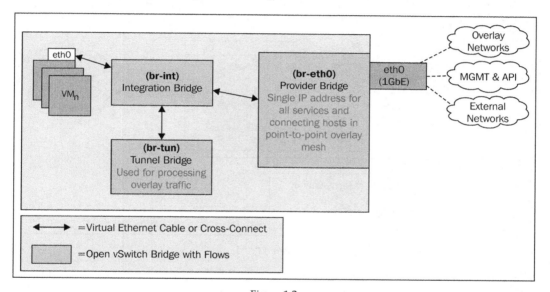

Figure 1.2

In this diagram, all OpenStack service and management traffic traverses the same physical interface as guest traffic.

Multiple interfaces

To reduce the likelihood of guest network bandwidth consumption affecting management of traffic and to maintain a proper security posture, segregation of traffic between multiple physical interfaces is recommended. At a minimum, two interfaces should be used: one that serves as the management and API interface and another that serves as the external and guest interface. If required, additional interfaces can be used to further segregate traffic. The following diagram demonstrates the use of two physical interfaces using the Open vSwitch plugin:

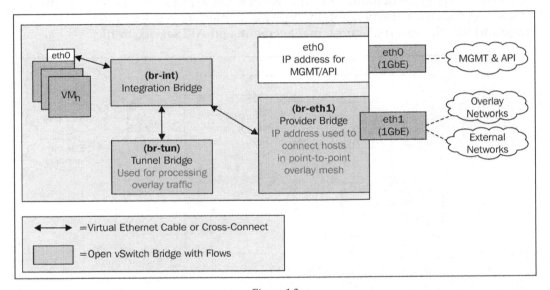

Figure 1.3

In this diagram, a dedicated physical interface handles all traffic directed to and from instances or other OpenStack Networking services, such as LBaaS and FWaaS, while another interface handles OpenStack API and management traffic.

Bonding

NIC bonding offers users the ability to multiply available bandwidth by aggregating links. Two or more physical interfaces can be combined to create a single virtual interface, or bond, which can then be placed in the bridge. The physical switching infrastructure, however, must be capable of supporting this type of bond. In addition to aggregating links, bonding can also refer to the ability to create redundant links in an active/passive manner. Both links are simultaneously cabled to a switch or pair of switches, but only one interface is active at any given time. Both types of bonds can be created within CentOS or Ubuntu when the appropriate kernel module is installed. In lieu of built-in bonding techniques, bonding can be configured in Open vSwitch if desired.

Bonding is an inexpensive way to provide hardware-level network redundancy to the cloud. If you are interested in configuring NIC bonding on your hosts, please refer to the following sites:

- **CentOS 6.5**: `https://access.redhat.com/documentation/en-US/Red_Hat_Enterprise_Linux/6/html/Deployment_Guide/s2-networkscripts-interfaces-chan.html`

- **Ubuntu 12.04 LTS**: `https://help.ubuntu.com/community/UbuntuBonding`

Separating services across nodes

Like other OpenStack services, cloud operators can split OpenStack Networking services across multiple nodes. Small deployments may use a single node to host all services, including networking, compute, database, and messaging, while others might find benefit in using a dedicated network node to handle guest traffic routed through software routers and to offload Neutron DHCP and metadata services. The following diagrams reflect a few common service deployment models.

A single controller with one or more compute nodes

In an environment consisting of a single controller and one or more compute nodes, the controller will likely handle all networking services and other OpenStack services, while the compute nodes strictly provide compute resources.

The following diagram demonstrates a controller node hosting all OpenStack management and networking services where the layer 3 agent is not utilized. Two physical interfaces are used to provide separate control and data planes:

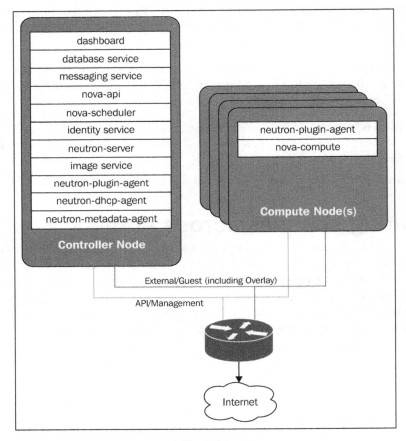

Figure 1.4

This diagram reflects the use of a single controller and one or more compute nodes where Neutron provides only layer 2 connectivity to instances. An external router is needed to handle routing between network segments.

The following diagram demonstrates a controller node hosting all OpenStack management and networking services, including the Neutron L3 agent. Two physical interfaces are used to provide separate control and data planes:

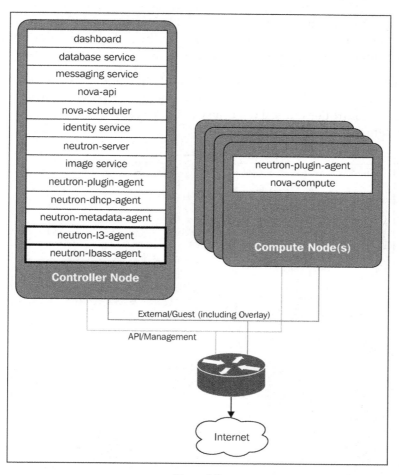

Figure 1.5

This diagram reflects the use of a single controller node and one or more compute nodes in a network configuration that utilizes the Neutron L3 agent. Software routers created with Neutron reside on the controller node and handle routing between connected tenant networks

A single controller plus network node with one or more compute nodes

A network node is one that is dedicated to handling most or all OpenStack networking services, including the L3 agent, DHCP agent, metadata agent, and more. The use of a dedicated network node provides additional security and resilience, as the controller node will be at less risk of network and resource saturation.

The following figure demonstrates a network node hosting all OpenStack networking services, including the Neutron L3 agent. The Neutron API, however, is installed on the controller node. Two physical interfaces are used to provide separate control and data planes:

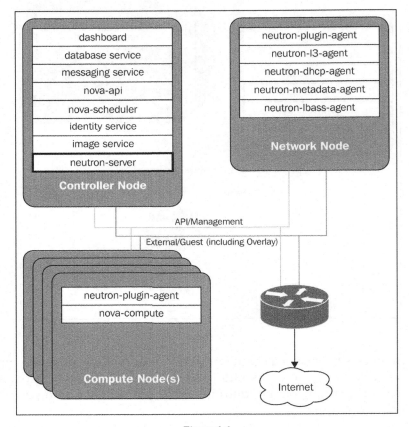

Figure 1.6

This diagram reflects the use of a dedicated network node in a network configuration that utilizes the Neutron L3 agent. Software routers created with Neutron reside on the network node and handle routing between connected tenant networks. The API service, neutron-server, remains on the controller node.

Summary

OpenStack Networking offers the ability to leverage the different technologies found in a data center in a virtualized and programmable manner. If the built-in features are not enough, the plugin architecture of OpenStack Networking allows for additional functionality to be provided by third parties, whether it be a commercial entity or the open source community. The security requirements of the enterprise building the cloud, as well as the use cases of the cloud, will ultimately dictate the physical layout and separation of services across the infrastructure nodes.

Throughout this book, you will learn how to build a functional OpenStack cloud utilizing advanced networking features available in the Havana release. In the next chapter, you will be guided through a package-based installation of OpenStack on the CentOS operating system. Topics covered include the installation, configuration, and verification of database, messaging, and OpenStack Identity, Image, Compute, and Dashboard services. The installation and configuration of OpenStack Networking services can be found in *Chapter 3, Installing Neutron*.

2
Installing OpenStack

Installing, configuring, and maintaining OpenStack clouds can be an arduous task when performed by hand. Many third-party vendors offer downloadable cloud software based on OpenStack that provide deployment and management strategies using Chef, Puppet, Fuel, Ansible, and other tools.

This chapter will guide you through a package-based installation of the following OpenStack components on the CentOS operating system:

- Keystone
- Glance
- Nova Compute
- Horizon

The installation process documented within this chapter is based on the *OpenStack Installation Guide* for Red Hat Enterprise Linux, CentOS, and Fedora, that is found at http://docs.openstack.org/.

If you'd rather download a third-party cloud distribution based on OpenStack, try one of the following:

- **Rackspace Private Cloud**: http://www.rackspace.com/cloud/private/
- **RedHat RDO**: http://openstack.redhat.com/
- **Mirantis OpenStack**: http://software.mirantis.com/
- **Piston Cloud**: http://www.pistoncloud.com/

Once installed, many of the concepts and examples used throughout the book should still apply but may require extra effort to implement.

System requirements

OpenStack components are intended to run on standard hardware that range from desktop machines to enterprise-grade servers. The processors of the compute nodes need to support virtualization technologies, such as Intel's VT-x or AMD's AMD-v technologies.

This book assumes that OpenStack will be installed on physical hardware that meets the following minimum requirements:

Server	Recommended hardware	Notes
Controller node (runs network, volume, API, scheduler, and image services)	Processor: 64-bit x86 Memory: 8 GB RAM Disk space: 80 GB Network: Two 1 Gbps network interface cards (NICs)	While a single NIC can be used, it is not recommended, and therefore not addressed in this build.
Compute node (runs virtual instances)	Processor: 64-bit x86 Memory: 16 GB RAM Disk space: 80 GB Network: Two 1 Gbps network interface cards (NICs)	While a single NIC can be used, it is not recommended and therefore not addressed in this build.

While machines that fail to meet the minimum requirements may be capable of installation, based on the documentation included herein, these requirements are there to ensure a successful experience.

Operating system requirements

OpenStack currently has packages for the following distributions: CentOS, Debian, Fedora, RHEL, openSUSE, SLES, and Ubuntu. This book assumes that the CentOS 6.5 operating system has been installed on all hosts prior to the installation of OpenStack:

- **CentOS 6.5**: http://www.centos.org/

At the time of writing, the following minimum kernel version is recommended:

- **Kernel version**: 2.6.32-431.20.3.el6.x86_64

Prior kernel versions may experience a lack of support for network namespaces that are used throughout various Neutron services.

Initial network configuration

To understand how networking should initially be configured on each host, please refer to the following diagram:

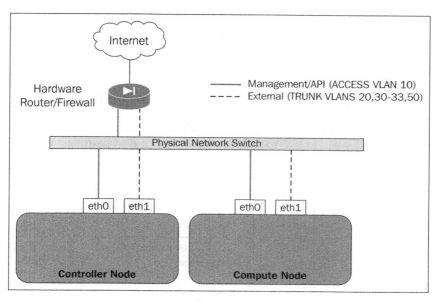

Figure 2.1

In the preceding diagram, two interfaces are cabled to each host. The `eth0` interface will serve as the management interface for OpenStack services and API access, and `eth1` will serve as the provider bridge and tunnel interface for external and tenant traffic.

At a minimum, the management interface should be configured with an IP address that has outbound access to the Internet. Internet access is required to download OpenStack packages from the package repository. Inbound access to the management address of the servers from a trusted network via SSH (TCP port 22) is recommended.

Throughout the book, there will be examples on configuring and using various OpenStack services. The following table provides the VLANs and associated networks used for those services:

VLAN name	VLAN ID	Network
MGMT_NET	10	10.254.254.0/24
OVERLAY_NET	20	172.18.0.0/24
GATEWAY_NET	50	10.50.0.0/24
TENANT_NET30	30	10.30.0.0/24
TENANT_NET31	31	10.31.0.0/24
TENANT_NET32	32	10.32.0.0/24
TENANT_NET33	33	10.33.0.0/24

The following table provides IP addresses and VLAN IDs recommended for each host interface, should you choose to follow along with the examples:

Hostname	Interface	IP address	Switchport
controller. learningneutron.com	eth0	10.254.254.100	Access port (VLAN 10, Untagged)
	eth1	Cabled, but unconfigured at this time	Trunk port (VLAN 20, 30-33, 50)
compute01. learningneutron.com	eth0	10.254.254.101	Access port (VLAN 10, untagged)
	eth1	Cabled, but unconfigured at this time	Trunk port (VLAN 20, 30-33, 50)

The eth1 interface of each server will be configured in *Chapter 4, Building a Virtual Switching Infrastructure*. For now, the interface should be cabled and the corresponding switch port configured as a trunk. In the event of connectivity loss, out-of-band management access to the servers via DRAC, iLo, or some other mechanism, is highly recommended.

Interface configuration

CentOS uses individual interface files to describe the configuration of an interface. As the system boots, these files are used to determine which interfaces to bring up and how they should be configured. The interface configuration files can be found in /etc/sysconfig/network-scripts/.

> **Downloading the example code**
>
> You can download the example code files for all Packt books you have purchased from your account at http://www.packtpub.com. If you purchased this book elsewhere, you can visit http://www.packtpub.com/support and register to have the files e-mailed directly to you.

Using a text editor, update the corresponding interface file for eth0 on each host as follows:

```
# nano /etc/sysconfig/network-scripts/ifcfg-eth0
```

The following is the configuration of eth0 on the controller node:

```
DEVICE=eth0

TYPE=Ethernet

ONBOOT=yes

NM_CONTROLLED=yes

BOOTPROTO=static

IPADDR=10.254.254.100

NETMASK=255.255.255.0

GATEWAY=10.254.254.1
```

The following is the configuration of eth0 on the compute node:

```
DEVICE=eth0
TYPE=Ethernet
ONBOOT=yes
NM_CONTROLLED=yes
BOOTPROTO=static
IPADDR=10.254.254.101
NETMASK=255.255.255.0
GATEWAY=10.254.254.1
```

To activate the changes, cycle the interface using the `ifdown` and `ifup` commands on each node:

```
# ifdown eth0; ifup eth0
```

Before you begin

Before you can install OpenStack, some work must be done to prepare the system for a successful installation.

Permissions

OpenStack services can be installed either as root or as a user with `sudo` permissions. The latter may require that the user be added to the `sudoers` file on each host. For tips on configuring `sudoers`, please visit the following URL:

```
http://wiki.centos.org/TipsAndTricks/BecomingRoot
```

For this installation, all commands should be run as root unless specified otherwise.

Configuring the OpenStack repository

Installation of OpenStack on CentOS uses packages from the RedHat RDO repository. To enable the RDO repository, download and install the `rdo-release-havana` package on all hosts:

```
# rpm -ivh http://repos.fedorapeople.org/repos/openstack/openstack-
havana/rdo-release-havana-8.noarch.rpm
```

The EPEL package includes GPG keys to aid in signing packages and repository information and should be installed on all hosts:

```
# rpm -ivh http://dl.fedoraproject.org/pub/epel/6/x86_64/epel-
release-6-8.noarch.rpm
```

Installing OpenStack utilities

The `crudini` utility is used throughout this book to make the configuration of various services easier and consistent. Crudini overwrites or adds individual configuration settings without overwriting the entire file. The following command installs `crudini` and another useful OpenStack configuration package, `openstack-utils`:

```
# yum -y install crudini openstack-utils
```

Setting the hostnames

Before installing OpenStack, be sure that each node in the environment has been configured with its proper hostname. Using a text editor, change the HOSTNAME value in the /etc/sysconfig/network file on each host:

- Controller node: HOSTNAME=controller.learningneutron.com
- Compute node: HOSTNAME=compute01.learningneutron.com

To simplify communication between hosts, it is recommended that DNS or a local name resolver be used to resolve hostnames. Using a text editor, update the /etc/hosts file on each node to include the management IP address and hostname of all nodes:

```
10.254.254.100 controller.learningneutron.com controller
10.254.254.101 compute01.learningneutron.com compute01
```

Disabling SELinux

To avoid issues with communication among services, it is advised that the SELinux security policy be disabled on all nodes for the duration of this installation and subsequent test use.

SELinux can be set to one of the following three states:

- enforcing: SELinux security policy is enforced
- permissive: SELinux prints warnings instead of enforcing
- disabled: No SELinux policy is loaded

To disable SELinux, edit the /etc/selinux/config file, and change the SELINUX value to disabled. For your convenience, the following command will make the appropriate change:

```
# sed -i "/SELINUX=enforcing/c\SELINUX=disabled" /etc/selinux/config
```

Removing iptables rules

CentOS ships with rather restrictive iptables rules by default. Edit the iptables firewall service to allow all incoming traffic with the following commands:

```
# iptables -D INPUT -j REJECT --reject-with icmp-host-prohibited
# iptables -D FORWARD -j REJECT --reject-with icmp-host-prohibited
# service iptables save
```

The rule changes are meant to reduce possible issues with this installation guide and are not meant for production use. Consult the OpenStack security guide at http://docs.openstack.org/sec/ for more information on securing an OpenStack environment.

Installing and configuring Network Time Protocol

A time synchronization program, such as NTP, is a requirement, as OpenStack services depend on consistent and synchronized time between hosts. For Nova (Compute), having synchronized time helps to avoid problems when scheduling VM launches on compute nodes. Other services can experience similar issues when the time is not synchronized.

To install NTP, issue the following commands on all nodes in the environment:

```
# yum -y install ntp
# service ntpd start
```

Unlike Ubuntu, the RHEL and CentOS operating systems do not automatically start services upon installation. To configure NTP to start at boot, use the chkconfig command as follows:

```
# chkconfig ntpd on
```

Additional services will be configured to start in a similar manner throughout this book.

Upgrading the system

Before installing OpenStack, it is imperative that the kernel and other system packages on each node be upgraded to the latest version supported by CentOS 6.5. Issue the following yum command on each node, followed by a reboot to allow the changes to take effect:

```
# yum -y upgrade
# reboot
```

Installation of OpenStack

The steps in the later part of the chapter document the installation of OpenStack services, including Keystone, Glance, Nova Compute, and Horizon, on a single controller and compute node. Neutron, the OpenStack Networking service, will be installed in the next chapter.

Installing and configuring the MySQL database server

On the controller node, use yum to install the MySQL database server:

```
# yum -y install mysql mysql-server MySQL-python
```

Once installed, set the IP address that MySQL will bind to by editing the /etc/my.cnf configuration file and adding the bind-address definition. Doing so will allow connectivity to MySQL from other hosts in the environment. The value for bind-address should be the management IP of the controller node:

```
# crudini --set /etc/my.cnf mysqld bind-address 10.254.254.100
```

Start the mysqld process, and configure it to start at boot:

```
# service mysqld start
# chkconfig mysqld on
```

The MySQL secure installation utility is used to build the default MySQL database and set a password for the MySQL root user. The following command will begin the MySQL installation and configuration process:

```
# mysql_secure_installation
```

During the MySQL installation process, you will be prompted to enter a password and change various settings. For this installation, the chosen root password is openstack. A more secure password suitable for your environment is highly recommended.

Answer [Y]es to the remaining questions to exit the configuration process. At this point, MySQL server has been successfully installed on the controller node.

Installing the MySQL database client

The compute nodes in the environment should be configured as MySQL clients rather than as MySQL servers. On `compute01`, install the MySQL client as follows:

```
# yum -y install mysql MySQL-python
```

Installing and configuring the messaging server

Advanced Message Queue Protocol (AMQP) is the messaging technology chosen for use with an OpenStack-based cloud. Components such as Nova, Cinder, and Neutron communicate internally via AMQP and to each other using API calls. The following are instructions to install Qpid, an AMQP broker. Popular alternatives include RabbitMQ and ZeroMQ.

On the controller node, install the messaging server:

```
# yum -y install qpid-cpp-server memcached
```

To simplify this installation, disable Qpid authentication by editing the `/etc/qpidd.conf` file and changing the `auth` option to `no`, as follows:

```
# sed -i "/^auth/s/auth=yes/auth=no/" /etc/qpidd.conf
```

> While disabling authentication is acceptable for this test environment, authentication should be enabled on a production deployment. Consult Qpid documentation for further instructions on how to enable authentication.

Start the `qpid` service, and set it to automatically start at boot:

```
# service qpidd start
# chkconfig qpidd on
```

Installing and configuring the Identity service

Keystone is the Identity service for OpenStack and is used to authenticate and authorize users and services in the OpenStack cloud. Keystone should only be installed on the controller node along with `python-keystoneclient`:

```
# yum -y install openstack-keystone python-keystoneclient
```

Using `crudini`, configure Keystone to use MySQL as its database. In this installation, the username and password will be `keystone`:

```
# crudini --set /etc/keystone/keystone.conf sql connection mysql://
keystone:keystone@controller/keystone
```

 Insecure passwords are used throughout the book to simplify the configuration and are not recommended for production use. Visit `http://www.strongpasswordgenerator.org` to generate strong passwords for your environment.

Use the `openstack-db` command to create the Keystone database, related tables, and a database user named `keystone` that will be used by the Keystone service to connect to the database:

```
# openstack-db --init --service keystone --password keystone
```

You may be prompted to enter the password for the MySQL `root` user. Unless it has been changed, this installation set the MySQL `root` password to `openstack`.

Define an authorization token to use as a shared secret between Keystone and other OpenStack services. When defined, the authorization token, `admin_token`, can be used to make changes to Keystone in the event an administrative user has not been configured or the password has been forgotten. Clients making calls to Keystone can pass the authorization token, which is then validated by Keystone before actions are taken.

OpenSSL can be used to generate a random token and store it in the configuration file:

```
# ADMIN_TOKEN=$(openssl rand -hex 10)
```
```
# crudini --set /etc/keystone/keystone.conf DEFAULT admin_token $ADMIN_
TOKEN
```

By default, Keystone uses PKI tokens for authentication. The following steps will create the signing keys and certificates:

```
# keystone-manage pki_setup --keystone-user keystone --keystone-group
keystone
```
```
# chown -R keystone:keystone /etc/keystone/* /var/log/keystone/keystone.
log
```

Using `crudini`, edit `/etc/keystone/keystone.conf`, and set the `provider` value to PKI:

```
# crudini --set /etc/keystone/keystone.conf token provider keystone.
token.providers.pki.Provider
```

Start the Keystone service and enable it to start at boot time by entering the following command:

```
# service openstack-keystone start
# chkconfig openstack-keystone on
```

Defining users, tenants, and roles in Keystone

Once the installation of Keystone is complete, it is necessary to set up users, tenants, roles, and endpoints that will be used by various OpenStack services.

Typically, a username and password are used to authenticate against Keystone. But because users have not yet been created, it is necessary to use the authorization token created earlier. The token can be passed using the `--os-token` option of the `keystone` command or by setting the `OS_SERVICE_TOKEN` environment variable. We will use both the `OS_SERVICE_TOKEN` and `OS_SERVICE_ENDPOINT` environment variables to provide the authorization token and to specify where the Keystone service is running.

Use the `export` command to export the variables and their values to your environment. `OS_SERVICE_TOKEN` should be set to the `$ADMIN_TOKEN` value determined earlier:

```
# export OS_SERVICE_TOKEN=$ADMIN_TOKEN
# export OS_SERVICE_ENDPOINT=http://controller:35357/v2.0
```

In Keystone, a tenant represents a logical group of users to which resources are assigned. Resources are assigned to tenants and not directly to users. Create an `admin` tenant for the administrative user and a `service` tenant for other OpenStack services to use as follows:

```
# keystone tenant-create --name=admin --description="Admin Tenant"
# keystone tenant-create --name=service --description="Service Tenant"
```

Additional tenants can be created later for other users of the cloud. Next, create an administrative user called `admin`. Specify a secure password and an email address for the `admin` user as follows:

```
# keystone user-create --name=admin --pass=secrete --email=admin@
learningneutron.com
```

Once the `admin` user has been created, create a role for administrative tasks called `admin`:

```
# keystone role-create --name=admin
```

Any roles that are created should map to roles specified in the `policy.json` files of the corresponding OpenStack services. The default policy files use the `admin` role to allow access to services. For more information on user management in Keystone, please refer to the following URL: `http://docs.openstack.org/admin-guide-cloud/content/keystone-user-management.html`.

Finally, associate the `admin` role to the `admin` user when logging in with the `admin` tenant as follows:

```
# keystone user-role-add --user=admin --tenant=admin --role=admin
```

Define services and API endpoints in Keystone

Each OpenStack service that is installed should be registered with Keystone, so its location on the network can be tracked. There are two commands involved in registering a service:

- `keystone service-create`: This describes the service that is being created
- `keystone endpoint-create`: This associates API endpoints with the service

Keystone itself is among the services that must be registered. You can create a service entry for Keystone with the following command:

```
# keystone service-create --name=keystone --type=identity
--description="Keystone Identity Service"
```

The resulting output will be in table format and will include a unique ID that will be used in the subsequent command:

```
+-------------+----------------------------------+
|  Property   |              Value               |
+-------------+----------------------------------+
| description | Keystone Identity Service        |
| id          | 47b36f2684e94cfdbd78ba912e6091ec |
| name        | keystone                         |
| type        | identity                         |
+-------------+----------------------------------+
```

Next, you can specify an API endpoint for the Identity service using the returned ID. When specifying an endpoint, you must provide URLs for the public API, internal API, and the admin API. The three URLs can potentially be on three different IP networks depending on your network setup and if NAT is used. The short name of the controller will be used to populate the URLs. Each host can reference the other based on hostname via DNS or the local `/etc/hosts` entries created earlier. Have a look at the following commands:

```
# keystone endpoint-create \
  --service-id=`keystone service-get keystone | awk '/ id / { print $4
}'` \
  --publicurl=http://controller:5000/v2.0 \
  --internalurl=http://controller:5000/v2.0 \
  --adminurl=http://controller:35357/v2.0
```

The resulting output is as follows:

```
+-------------+-----------------------------------+
|  Property   |             Value                 |
+-------------+-----------------------------------+
| adminurl    | http://controller:35357/v2.0      |
| id          | 7c1112c14cd8494fbd8dadb09581926f  |
| internalurl | http://controller:5000/v2.0       |
| publicurl   | http://controller:5000/v2.0       |
| region      | regionOne                         |
| service_id  | 47b36f2684e94cfdbd78ba912e6091ec  |
+-------------+-----------------------------------+
```

Verify the Keystone installation

To verify that Keystone was installed and configured properly, use the unset command to unset the OS_SERVICE_TOKEN and OS_SERVICE_ENDPOINT environment variables. Those variables are only needed to bootstrap the administrative user and to register the Keystone service. Have a look at the following command:

```
# unset OS_SERVICE_TOKEN OS_SERVICE_ENDPOINT
```

Once the environment variables are unset, it should be possible to use username-based authentication. You can request an authentication token using the admin user and the password specified earlier:

```
# keystone --os-username=admin --os-password=secrete --os-auth-
url=http://controller:35357/v2.0 token-get
```

Keystone should respond with a token that is paired with the specified user ID. This verifies that the user account is established in Keystone with the expected credentials. The resulting output is as follows:

```
+-----------+-----------------------------------+
|  Property |              Value                |
+-----------+-----------------------------------+
|  expires  |        2014-07-25T00:45:46Z       |
|    id     | <Base64-encoded Token>            |
|  user_id  | 6d8b854881ff4568a22342fae7cc4df6  |
+-----------+-----------------------------------+
```

Next, you can verify that authorization is working as expected by requesting authorization for a tenant:

```
# keystone --os-username=admin --os-password=secrete --os-tenant-name=admin --os-auth-url=http://controller:35357/v2.0 token-get
```

You should receive a new token in response, this time including the tenant ID of the admin tenant. This verifies that your user account has an explicitly defined role in the specified tenant and that the tenant exists as expected.

Setting environment variables

To avoid having to provide credentials every time you run an OpenStack command, create a file containing environment variables that can be loaded at any time:

```
# mkdir ~/credentials

# cat >> ~/credentials/admin <<EOF
export OS_USERNAME=admin
export OS_PASSWORD=secrete
export OS_TENANT_NAME=admin
export OS_AUTH_URL=http://controller:35357/v2.0
EOF
```

Use the source command to load the environment variables from the file. To test Keystone, issue the following commands:

```
# source ~/credentials/admin
# keystone token-get
# keystone user-list
```

Keystone should return the token and user list as requested as follows:

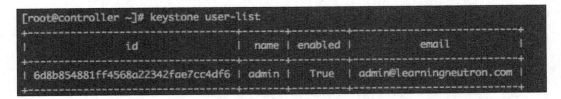

```
[root@controller ~]# keystone user-list
+----------------------------------+-------+---------+----------------------------+
|                id                |  name | enabled |            email           |
+----------------------------------+-------+---------+----------------------------+
| 6d8b854881ff4568a22342fae7cc4df6 | admin |   True  | admin@learningneutron.com  |
+----------------------------------+-------+---------+----------------------------+
```

Installing and configuring the image service

Glance is the image service for OpenStack. It is responsible for storing images and snapshots of instances and for providing images to compute nodes when instances are created.

To install Glance, run the following command from the controller node:

```
# yum -y install openstack-glance
```

You can use openstack-db to initialize the Glance database and add the glance user to MySQL:

```
# openstack-db --init --service glance --password glance
```

Use crudini to set the SQL connection string in the Glance configuration files:

```
# crudini --set /etc/glance/glance-api.conf DEFAULT sql_connection
mysql://glance:glance@controller/glance
```

```
# crudini --set /etc/glance/glance-registry.conf DEFAULT sql_connection
mysql://glance:glance@controller/glance
```

You can then add the glance user to Keystone and create the appropriate role:

```
# keystone user-create --name=glance --pass=glance --email=glance@
learningneutron.com
```

```
# keystone user-role-add --user=glance --tenant=service --role=admin
```

Use crudini to set Keystone attributes in the Glance configuration files:

```
# crudini --set /etc/glance/glance-api.conf keystone_authtoken auth_host
controller
```

```
# crudini --set /etc/glance/glance-api.conf  keystone_authtoken admin_
user glance
```

```
# crudini --set /etc/glance/glance-api.conf keystone_authtoken admin_
tenant_name service
```

```
# crudini --set /etc/glance/glance-api.conf keystone_authtoken admin_
password glance
```

```
# crudini --set /etc/glance/glance-registry.conf keystone_authtoken auth_
host controller
```

```
# crudini --set /etc/glance/glance-registry.conf keystone_authtoken
admin_user glance
```

```
# crudini --set /etc/glance/glance-registry.conf keystone_authtoken
admin_tenant_name service
```

```
# crudini --set /etc/glance/glance-registry.conf keystone_authtoken
admin_password glance
```

Glance includes default configuration files that should be copied and modified as follows:

```
# cp /usr/share/glance/glance-api-dist-paste.ini /etc/glance/glance-api-
paste.ini
```

```
# cp /usr/share/glance/glance-registry-dist-paste.ini /etc/glance/glance-
registry-paste.ini
```

Each of the files mentioned in the preceding commands must then be edited to add the following options:

```
# crudini --set /etc/glance/glance-api-paste.ini filter:authtoken auth_
host controller
```

```
# crudini --set /etc/glance/glance-api-paste.ini filter:authtoken admin_
user glance
```

```
# crudini --set /etc/glance/glance-api-paste.ini filter:authtoken admin_
tenant_name service
```

```
# crudini --set /etc/glance/glance-api-paste.ini filter:authtoken admin_
password glance
```

```
# crudini --set /etc/glance/glance-api-paste.ini filter:authtoken flavor
keystone
```

```
# crudini --set /etc/glance/glance-registry-paste.ini filter:authtoken
auth_host controller
```

```
# crudini --set /etc/glance/glance-registry-paste.ini filter:authtoken
admin_user glance
```

```
# crudini --set /etc/glance/glance-registry-paste.ini filter:authtoken
admin_tenant_name service
```

```
# crudini --set /etc/glance/glance-registry-paste.ini filter:authtoken
admin_password glance
```

```
# crudini --set /etc/glance/glance-registry-paste.ini filter:authtoken
flavor keystone
```

You can start the Glance services and enable them to start at boot time with the following command:

```
# service openstack-glance-api start
# service openstack-glance-registry start
# chkconfig openstack-glance-api on
# chkconfig openstack-glance-registry on
```

Define the Glance service and API endpoints in Keystone

Like other OpenStack services, Glance should be added to the Keystone database using the `service-create` and `endpoint-create` commands:

```
# keystone service-create --name=glance --type=image
--description="Glance Image Service"
```

The resulting output is as follows:

```
+-------------+----------------------------------+
|  Property   |              Value               |
+-------------+----------------------------------+
| description |       Glance Image Service       |
|     id      | bbbacfbe630341b181659f00a2ef6a90|
|    name     |              glance              |
|    type     |              image               |
+-------------+----------------------------------+
```

The `id` value here should be used to populate the `service-id` value as follows:

```
# keystone endpoint-create \
  --service-id=`keystone service-get glance | awk '/ id / { print $4 }'`
\
  --publicurl=http://controller:9292 \
  --internalurl=http://controller:9292 \
  --adminurl=http://controller:9292
```

The resulting output is as follows:

```
+-------------+----------------------------------+
|  Property   |               Value              |
+-------------+----------------------------------+
|   adminurl  |       http://controller:9292     |
|      id     | 32504596c4cc4661a04adbf1dfb97c08 |
| internalurl |       http://controller:9292     |
|  publicurl  |       http://controller:9292     |
|    region   |             regionOne            |
|  service_id | bbbacfbe630341b181659f00a2ef6a90 |
+-------------+----------------------------------+
```

Verify the Glance image service installation

To verify that Glance was installed and configured properly, download a test image from the Internet, and verify that it can be uploaded to the image server:

```
# mkdir /var/tmp/images ; cd /var/tmp/images/
```

```
# wget http://cdn.download.cirros-cloud.net/0.3.1/cirros-0.3.1-x86_64-disk.img
```

Upload the image to Glance using the following command:

```
# glance image-create --name=CirrOS-0.3.1 --disk-format=qcow2
--container-format=bare --is-public=true --file /var/tmp/images/cirros-
0.3.1-x86_64-disk.img
```

Verify that the image exists in Glance using the `image-list` command. Have a look at the following screenshot:

The CirrOS image is very limited in functionality and is recommended only for testing connectivity and operational Compute functionality. Multiple vendors provide cloud-ready images for use with OpenStack as follows:

- **Ubuntu cloud images**: http://cloud-images.ubuntu.com/
- **Red Hat-based images**: http://openstack.redhat.com/Image_resources

To install an image from a remote location, use the `--location` parameter instead of `--file` as follows:

```
# glance image-create --name=Ubuntu-14.04 --disk-format=qcow2
--container-format=bare --is-public=true --location http://cloud-images.
ubuntu.com/trusty/current/trusty-server-cloudimg-amd64-disk1.img
```

Another look at the image list (in the following screenshot) shows the new images are available for use:

```
[root@controller openstack-dashboard]# glance image-list
+--------------------------------------+--------------+-------------+------------------+-----------+--------+
| ID                                   | Name         | Disk Format | Container Format | Size      | Status |
+--------------------------------------+--------------+-------------+------------------+-----------+--------+
| 1a8afdd0-4d23-4c31-873c-72abbd947501 | CentOS-6.5   | qcow2       | bare             | 344457216 | active |
| ed78e8ef-0884-4d2d-bc02-c1df09a4cd6e | CirrOS-0.3.1 | qcow2       | bare             | 13147648  | active |
| f496e19d-e074-4308-a9f2-548b4880a119 | Ubuntu-14.04 | qcow2       | bare             | 254870016 | active |
+--------------------------------------+--------------+-------------+------------------+-----------+--------+
```

Installing and configuring the Compute service

OpenStack Compute is a collection of services that enable cloud operators and tenants to launch virtual machine instances. Most services run on the controller node, with the exception of the `openstack-nova-compute` service, which runs on the compute nodes and is responsible for launching the virtual machine instances.

Installing and configuring controller node components

Install the `openstack-nova` package, which installs various Nova (Compute) services that are used on the controller node, as follows:

```
# yum -y install openstack-nova python-novaclient
```

Run the `openstack-db` command to initialize and create the Nova (Compute) service database, related tables, and MySQL user as follows:

```
# openstack-db --init --service nova --password nova
```

Use `crudini` to configure Nova Compute to use MySQL as its database as follows:

```
# crudini --set /etc/nova/nova.conf database connection mysql://
nova:nova@controller/nova
```

Set these configuration keys to configure Nova (Compute) to use the Qpid message broker:

```
# crudini --set /etc/nova/nova.conf DEFAULT rpc_backend nova.openstack.
common.rpc.impl_qpid
```

```
# crudini --set /etc/nova/nova.conf DEFAULT qpid_hostname controller
```

The VNC Proxy is an OpenStack component that allows users to access their instances through VNC clients. **VNC** stands for **Virtual Network Computing**, and is a graphical desktop sharing system that uses the Remote Frame Buffer protocol to control another computer over a network. The controller must be able to communicate with compute nodes for VNC services to work properly through the Horizon dashboard or other VNC clients.

Use crudini to set the my_ip, vncserver_listen and vncserver_proxyclient_address configuration options to the management IP address of the controller node:

```
# crudini --set /etc/nova/nova.conf DEFAULT my_ip 10.254.254.100
```

```
# crudini --set /etc/nova/nova.conf DEFAULT vncserver_listen
10.254.254.100
```

```
# crudini --set /etc/nova/nova.conf DEFAULT vncserver_proxyclient_address
10.254.254.100
```

Create a user called nova in Keystone that the Nova (Compute) service will use for authentication. After this, place the user in the service tenant, and give the user the admin role:

```
# keystone user-create --name=nova --pass=nova --email=nova@
learningneutron.com
```

```
# keystone user-role-add --user=nova --tenant=service --role=admin
```

Configure Nova (Compute) to use the following Keystone credentials:

```
# crudini --set /etc/nova/nova.conf DEFAULT auth_strategy keystone
```

```
# crudini --set /etc/nova/nova.conf keystone_authtoken auth_host
controller
```

```
# crudini --set /etc/nova/nova.conf keystone_authtoken auth_protocol http
```

```
# crudini --set /etc/nova/nova.conf keystone_authtoken auth_port 35357
```

```
# crudini --set /etc/nova/nova.conf keystone_authtoken admin_user nova
```

```
# crudini --set /etc/nova/nova.conf keystone_authtoken admin_tenant_name
service
```

```
# crudini --set /etc/nova/nova.conf keystone_authtoken admin_password
nova
```

Credentials must be added to the /etc/nova/api-paste.ini file that corresponds to the details of this build. These options should be added to the [filter:authtoken] section of the ini file:

```
# crudini --set /etc/nova/api-paste.ini filter:authtoken auth_host
controller

# crudini --set /etc/nova/api-paste.ini filter:authtoken auth_port 35357

# crudini --set /etc/nova/api-paste.ini filter:authtoken auth_protocol
http

# crudini --set /etc/nova/api-paste.ini filter:authtoken auth_uri http://
controller:5000/v2.0

# crudini --set /etc/nova/api-paste.ini filter:authtoken admin_tenant_
name service

# crudini --set /etc/nova/api-paste.ini filter:authtoken admin_user nova

# crudini --set /etc/nova/api-paste.ini filter:authtoken admin_password
nova
```

You can ensure that the api_paste_config=/etc/nova/api-paste.ini option is set in the /etc/nova/nova.conf file using the following command:

```
# crudini --set /etc/nova/nova.conf DEFAULT api_paste_config /etc/nova/
api-paste.ini
```

You should then register Nova (Compute) with the Identity service so that other OpenStack services can locate it. Register the service and specify the endpoint:

```
# keystone service-create --name=nova --type=compute --description="Nova
Compute service"
```

The resulting output should resemble the following:

```
+-------------+------------------------------------+
|  Property   |               Value                |
+-------------+------------------------------------+
| description |         Nova Compute service       |
|     id      |  a946cbd06a124ec39662622cc2d6e4ec  |
|    name     |                nova                |
|    type     |               compute              |
+-------------+------------------------------------+
```

Use the `id` property that is returned to create the endpoint:

```
# keystone endpoint-create \
  --service-id=`keystone service-get nova | awk '/ id / { print $4 }'` \
  --publicurl=http://controller:8774/v2/%\(tenant_id\)s \
  --internalurl=http://controller:8774/v2/%\(tenant_id\)s \
  --adminurl=http://controller:8774/v2/%\(tenant_id\)s
```

Start the Nova (Compute) services, and configure them to start when the system boots:

```
# service openstack-nova-api start
# service openstack-nova-cert start
# service openstack-nova-consoleauth start
# service openstack-nova-scheduler start
# service openstack-nova-conductor start
# service openstack-nova-novncproxy start
# service openstack-nova-console start
# chkconfig openstack-nova-api on
# chkconfig openstack-nova-cert on
# chkconfig openstack-nova-consoleauth on
# chkconfig openstack-nova-scheduler on
# chkconfig openstack-nova-conductor on
# chkconfig openstack-nova-novncproxy on
# chkconfig openstack-nova-console on
```

> The `openstack-nova-network` service will be installed as part of the `openstack-nova` package but should not be started. The `openstack-nova-network` service is the legacy networking service replaced by Neutron. Neutron will be installed in *Chapter 3, Installing Neutron*.

Installing and configuring compute node components

Once the Nova (Compute) services have been configured on the controller node, another host must be configured as a compute node. The compute node receives requests from the controller node to host virtual machine instances. Separating the services by running dedicated compute nodes means that Nova (Compute) can be scaled horizontally by adding additional compute nodes once all available resources have been utilized.

On the compute node, install the `openstack-nova-compute` package. This package provides virtualization services to the compute node:

```
# yum -y install openstack-nova-compute
```

Using `crudini`, edit the `/etc/nova/nova.conf` configuration file to specify MySQL as the database and configure various Keystone authentication settings. The `nova` keystone user was configured in the previous section. Have a look at the following commands:

```
# crudini --set /etc/nova/nova.conf database connection mysql://
nova:nova@controller/nova

# crudini --set /etc/nova/nova.conf DEFAULT auth_strategy keystone

# crudini --set /etc/nova/nova.conf keystone_authtoken auth_host
controller

# crudini --set /etc/nova/nova.conf keystone_authtoken auth_protocol http

# crudini --set /etc/nova/nova.conf keystone_authtoken auth_port 35357

# crudini --set /etc/nova/nova.conf keystone_authtoken admin_user nova

# crudini --set /etc/nova/nova.conf keystone_authtoken admin_tenant_name
service

# crudini --set /etc/nova/nova.conf keystone_authtoken admin_password
nova
```

Next, configure Nova (Compute) to use the Qpid messaging broker configured on the controller node:

```
# crudini --set /etc/nova/nova.conf DEFAULT rpc_backend nova.openstack.
common.rpc.impl_qpid

# crudini --set /etc/nova/nova.conf DEFAULT qpid_hostname controller
```

Then configure Nova (Compute) to provide remote console access to instances through a proxy on the controller node. The remote console is accessible through the Horizon dashboard. The IP configured as follows should be the management IP of the compute node:

```
# crudini --set /etc/nova/nova.conf DEFAULT my_ip 10.254.254.101

# crudini --set /etc/nova/nova.conf DEFAULT vnc_enabled True

# crudini --set /etc/nova/nova.conf DEFAULT vncserver_listen 0.0.0.0

# crudini --set /etc/nova/nova.conf DEFAULT vncserver_proxyclient_address
10.254.254.101

# crudini --set /etc/nova/nova.conf DEFAULT novncproxy_base_url http://
controller:6080/vnc_auto.html
```

Specify the host that runs the Glance image service. In this installation, Glance runs on the controller node:

```
# crudini --set /etc/nova/nova.conf DEFAULT glance_host controller
```

Edit the /etc/nova/api-paste.ini configuration to add credentials to the [filter:authtoken] section:

```
# crudini --set /etc/nova/api-paste.ini filter:authtoken auth_host
controller
# crudini --set /etc/nova/api-paste.ini filter:authtoken auth_port 35357
# crudini --set /etc/nova/api-paste.ini filter:authtoken auth_protocol
http
# crudini --set /etc/nova/api-paste.ini filter:authtoken admin_tenant_
name service
# crudini --set /etc/nova/api-paste.ini filter:authtoken admin_user nova
# crudini --set /etc/nova/api-paste.ini filter:authtoken admin_password
nova
```

Ensure that the api_paste_config=/etc/nova/api-paste.ini option is set in the /etc/nova/nova.conf file:

```
# crudini --set /etc/nova/nova.conf DEFAULT api_paste_config /etc/nova/
api-paste.ini
```

Start the Nova (Compute) service and configure it to start when the system boots:

```
# service libvirtd start
# service messagebus start
# service openstack-nova-compute start
# chkconfig libvirtd on
# chkconfig messagebus on
# chkconfig openstack-nova-compute on
```

Verify communication between services

To check the status of Nova services throughout the environment, use the Nova service-list command on the controller node as follows:

```
# nova service-list
```

The command should return statuses on all Nova services that have checked in:

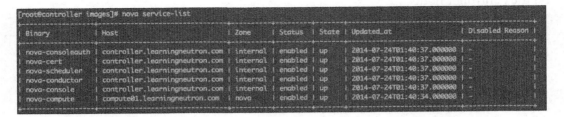

In the above output, the state of the services on both the controller and compute nodes are reflected under the `Status` column. The `nova service-list` command can be run on any node in the environment but will require proper authentication credentials. If there are inconsistencies in the output among multiple nodes, it's worth ensuring that network time (NTP) is synchronized properly on all nodes.

Installing the OpenStack dashboard

The OpenStack Dashboard, also known as Horizon, provides a web-based user interface to OpenStack services, including Compute, Networking, Storage, and Identity, among others.

To install Horizon, install the following packages on the controller node:

```
# yum -y install mod_wsgi openstack-dashboard
```

Allowing connections to the dashboard

A setting called `ALLOWED_HOSTS` exists in the `/etc/openstack-dashboard/local_settings` file with the following defaults:

```
ALLOWED_HOSTS = ['horizon.example.com', 'localhost']
```

The domain and host names in the list represent HTTP hosts for which the Apache web server will respond. The preceding settings would require users who wish to access the Horizon dashboard to do so via `http://horizon.example.com` in their browser. Feel free to add your own domain that references the management/API address of the controller. Otherwise, comment out the line using a pound sign, and save the file to allow any host header to be used:

```
# sed -i 's/ALLOWED_HOSTS/#ALLOWED_HOSTS/' /etc/openstack-dashboard/
local_settings
```

Identifying the Keystone server

Edit the `/etc/openstack-dashboard/local_settings` file to set the hostname of the Identity server. In this installation, the Keystone services are running on the controller node. Change the `OPENSTACK_HOST` and `OPENSTACK_KEYSTONE_URL` values using the following commands:

```
# sed -i "/OPENSTACK_HOST/c\OPENSTACK_HOST = \"controller\"" /etc/
openstack-dashboard/local_settings
```

```
# sed -i -e "\$aOPENSTACK_KEYSTONE_URL = \"http://controller:5000/v2.0\""
/etc/openstack-dashboard/local_settings
```

Changing the listener address

By default, the Apache web server is configured to listen for HTTP requests on port 80 and any IPv6 address. To change this behavior, edit `/etc/httpd/conf/httpd.conf`, and change the `Listen` address to `10.254.254.100`:

```
# sed -i 's/Listen 80/Listen 10.254.254.100:80/' /etc/httpd/conf/httpd.
conf
```

Following this, save the file and start the dashboard services. Use `chkconfig` to enable the services to start at boot:

```
# service httpd start
# chkconfig httpd on
```

Testing connectivity to the dashboard

From a machine that has access to the management network of the controller node, open the following URL in a web browser:

```
http://controller/dashboard/
```

The /etc/hosts file of my client has been updated to include the same hostname-to-IP mappings configured earlier in this chapter. The following screenshot demonstrates a successful connection to the dashboard. The username and password were created in the *Defining users, tenants, and roles in Keystone* section earlier in this chapter. In this installation, the username is admin, and the password is secrete. Have a look at the following screenshot:

Upon successful login, the dashboard defaults to the administrative tab. From here, information about the environment is provided in a graphical format. In the next screenshot, the **System Info** panel provides the user with information about the environment, including **Services**, **Compute Services**, **Availability Zones**, and **Host Aggregates**. The services listed in the following screenshot are services that were installed earlier in this chapter:

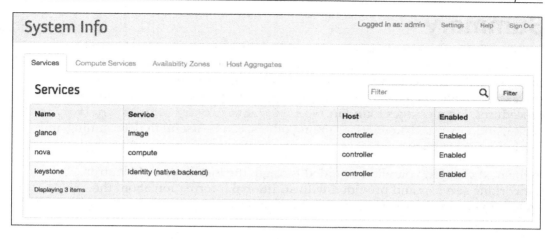

To view the status of Nova (Compute) services, click on the **Compute Services** tab. Doing so will return output similar to that of `nova service-list` in the CLI, as follows:

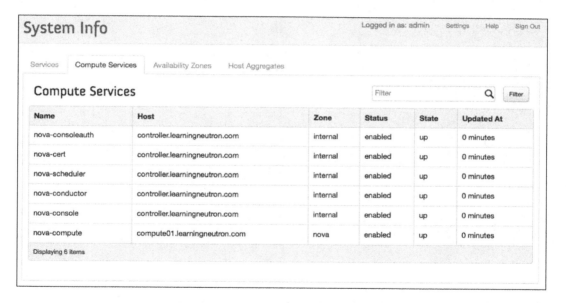

Summary

At this point in the installation, the OpenStack Identity, Image, Dashboard, and Compute services have been deployed across the nodes of the cloud. The environment is not ready to host instances just yet, as OpenStack Networking services have not been installed. If issues arise during the installation and test procedures, log messages found in `/var/log/nova/`, `/var/log/glance`, `/var/log/httpd`, and `/var/log/keystone`, among others, can be useful in determining and resolving the problem.

In the next chapter, you will be guided through the installation of Neutron networking services and provided with additional information about the underlying architecture of OpenStack Networking.

3
Installing Neutron

In a nutshell, OpenStack Networking provides virtual networking services to resources managed by the Nova (Compute) service. In this chapter, I will walk you through the installation of the Neutron networking services in the OpenStack environment installed in the previous chapter.

The services to be installed include:

- Neutron API server
- Switching plugins
- DHCP agent
- Metadata agent

By the end of this chapter, you will have a basic understanding of the functions of various Neutron agents, as well as the foundation on which a virtual switching infrastructure can be built.

Basic Neutron constructs

Network configuration in the Havana release of OpenStack is managed using version 2.0 of the Neutron API. The Neutron API can be used to manage the following resources, among others:

- **Network**: A network is an isolated layer-2 broadcast domain. Typically reserved for the tenants that created them, networks can be shared among tenants if configured appropriately. The network is the core of the Neutron API. Subnets and ports must always be associated with a network.

- **Subnet**: A subnet is an IPv4 or IPv6 address block from which IP addresses can be assigned to virtual machine instances. Each subnet must have a CIDR and must be associated with a network. Multiple subnets can be associated with a single network and can be noncontiguous. DHCP allocation ranges can be set for the subnet which limits the addresses provided to instances.

- **Port**: A port in Neutron represents a virtual switch port on a logical virtual switch. Virtual machine interfaces are mapped to Neutron ports, and the ports define both the MAC and IP addresses to be assigned to the interfaces plugged into them. Neutron port definitions are stored in the Neutron database, which is then used by the respective plugin agent to build and connect the virtual switching infrastructure.

Cloud operators can configure network topologies by creating and configuring networks and subnets and then, instructing services such as Nova (Compute) to attach virtual devices to ports on these networks. The Neutron API provides a consistent experience to the user despite the chosen networking plugin. For more information on interacting with the Neutron API, visit `http://docs.openstack.org/api/openstack-network/2.0/content/`.

Overlapping networks using network namespaces

OpenStack was designed with multitenancy in mind; this means that multiple groups of users can create and manage their own set of compute and network resources. Neutron supports the ability for each tenant to have multiple private networks, routers, firewalls, and load balancers. Neutron is able to isolate these objects through the use of network namespaces.

A network namespace is defined as a logical copy of the network stack, with its own routes, firewall rules, and network interface devices. Every network, router, and load balancer that is created by a tenant is represented by a network namespace. When network namespaces are enabled, Neutron is able to provide isolated DHCP and routing services to each network, allowing tenants to create overlapping networks with other tenants and even other networks in the same tenant.

The following naming convention for network namespaces should be observed:

```
qdhcp-<network UUID>
qrouter-<router UUID>
qlbaas-<load balancer UUID>
```

The `qdhcp` namespace contains a DHCP service that provides IP addresses to instances using the DHCP protocol. The `qdhcp` namespace has an interface plugged into the virtual switch and is able to communicate with other resources in the same network or subnet.

The `qrouter` namespace represents a router and routes traffic for instances in subnets that it is connected to. Like the `qdhcp` namespace, the `qrouter` namespace is connected to one or more virtual switches, depending on the configuration.

The `qlbaas` namespace represents a load balancer and might contain a load-balancing service, such as HAProxy, which load balances traffic to instances. The `qlbaas` namespace is connected to a virtual switch and can communicate with other resources in the same network or subnet.

Often, network namespaces will exist only on the controller or network nodes (if you have them). The `ip netns` command can be used to list the available namespaces, and commands can be executed within the namespace using the following syntax:

```
ip netns exec NAME <command>
```

Commands that can be executed in the namespace include `ip`, `route`, `iptables`, and more. The output of these commands corresponds to information specific to the namespace they are executed in.

For more information on network namespaces, see the man page for `ip netns` at `http://man7.org/linux/man-pages/man8/ip-netns.8.html`.

Extending network functions with plugins

Prior to Neutron, the original OpenStack network implementation (nova-network) provided basic networking through Linux bridges, VLANs, and iptables. Neutron introduces support for third-party plugins that extend network functionality and implementation of the Neutron API.

Plugins that use a variety of software and hardware-based technologies to implement the network built by operators and tenants can be created. In this book, the following networking plugins will be discussed:

- LinuxBridge
- Open vSwitch

The LinuxBridge and Open vSwitch plugins are used to provide layer 2 connectivity to instances and other network resources through the use of VLANs or overlay networking technologies such as GRE or VXLAN. Both provide a layer 2 switching infrastructure, but they do so in unique ways.

Both plugins are considered monolithic plugins; this means that they cannot be used simultaneously with any other networking plugin. The LinuxBridge and Open vSwitch plugins are deprecated in Icehouse in favor of the Modular Layer 2 (ML2) plugin, which allows for the use of multiple Layer 2 plugins simultaneously. ML2 configuration is outside the scope of this chapter, but I have provided an ML2 plugin file and configuration details relevant to this installation in *Appendix B, ML2 Configuration*. For more information on how ML2 works, refer to the presentation titled *OpenStack Neutron Modular Layer 2 Plugin Deep Dive* available at `http://www.openstack.org/`.

Third-party vendors, including Cisco, Brocade, VMWare, and more, have created plugins that allow Neutron to interface with hardware switches, OpenFlow controllers, and other network resources. The configuration and use of these plugins is outside the scope of this book. Visit `http://docs.openstack.org/admin-guide-cloud/content/section_plugin-arch.html` for more information on the available plugins for Neutron.

Installing and configuring Neutron services

In this installation, the various services that make up OpenStack Networking will be installed on the controller node rather than on a dedicated networking node. However, some Neutron configuration files must exist on all nodes, and the configuration files can only be installed via packages.

To install Neutron services, issue the following command on all nodes:

```
# yum -y install openstack-neutron
```

As a result, the following services will be installed in `/etc/init.d/`:

```
neutron-server
neutron-dhcp-agent
neutron-metadata-agent
neutron-l3-agent
neutron-lbaas-agent
```

In this installation, the services mentioned will run only on the controller node despite them being installed across all nodes.

Creating the Neutron database

Due to an unresolved bug, it is not possible to use the `openstack-db` command to properly create the Neutron database and user. Instead, use the `mysql` client on the controller as follows:

```
# mysql -u root -p
```

Enter the MySQL root password when prompted. For this installation, the root password is `openstack`.

In the `mysql>` prompt, enter the following commands:

```
CREATE DATABASE neutron;
GRANT ALL PRIVILEGES ON neutron.* TO 'neutron'@'localhost' IDENTIFIED BY
'neutron';
GRANT ALL PRIVILEGES ON neutron.* TO 'neutron'@'%' IDENTIFIED BY
'neutron';
quit;
```

Configure Neutron on all the nodes to use a MySQL database connection string, based on the preceding values:

```
# crudini --set /etc/neutron/neutron.conf database connection mysql://
neutron:neutron@controller/neutron
```

Configuring the Neutron user, role, and endpoint in Keystone

Neutron requires a user, role, and endpoint to be created in Keystone in order to function properly. When executed from the controller node, the following commands will create a user called `neutron` in Keystone and add the `neutron` user to the `admin` tenant:

```
# keystone user-create --name=neutron --pass=neutron --email=neutron@
learningneutron.com
# keystone user-role-add --user=neutron --tenant=service --role=admin
```

Create a service in Keystone that describes the OpenStack Networking service by executing the following:

```
# keystone service-create --name=neutron --type=network
--description="OpenStack Networking Service"
```

The preceding command will result in the following output:

```
+-------------+--------------------------------+
| Property    |             Value              |
+-------------+--------------------------------+
| description |   OpenStack Networking Service |
|     id      |  42856efa0bcd4fd6a279e8c84b060b90 |
|    name     |            neutron             |
|    type     |            network             |
+-------------+--------------------------------+
```

To create the endpoint, use the `keystone endpoint-create` command:

```
# keystone endpoint-create \
    --service-id `keystone service-get neutron | awk '/ id / { print $4
}'` \
    --publicurl http://controller:9696 \
    --adminurl http://controller:9696 \
    --internalurl http://controller:9696
```

The resulting endpoint is as follows:

```
+-------------+----------------------------------+
| Property    |              Value               |
+-------------+----------------------------------+
|   adminurl  |      http://controller:9696      |
|     id      | 627d19b745b347c0a57b0226221ef161 |
| internalurl |      http://controller:9696      |
|  publicurl  |      http://controller:9696      |
|   region    |            regionOne             |
| service_id  | 42856efa0bcd4fd6a279e8c84b060b90 |
+-------------+----------------------------------+
```

Enabling packet forwarding

Before the nodes can properly forward traffic for virtual machine instances, there are three kernel parameters that must be configured on all nodes:

- `net.ipv4.ip_forward`
- `net.ipv4.conf.all.rp_filter`
- `net.ipv4.conf.default.rp_filter`

The `net.ipv4.ip_forward` kernel parameter allows the nodes to forward traffic from the instances to the network. The default value is 0 (zero) and can be observed with the `sysctl` command:

```
[root@controller ~]# sysctl net.ipv4.ip_forward
net.ipv4.ip_forward = 0
```

The value for `net.ipv4.ip_forward` should be set to `1` to enable IP forwarding. Use the following command to implement this change on all nodes:

```
# sed -i "/net.ipv4.ip_forward/c\net.ipv4.ip_forward = 1" /etc/sysctl.
conf
```

The `net.ipv4.conf.default.rp_filter` and `net.ipv4.conf.all.rp_filter` kernel parameters are related to reverse path filtering, a mechanism intended to prevent denial of service attacks by preventing IP address spoofing at the router level. When enabled, the Linux kernel will examine every packet to ensure that the source address of the packet is routable back through the interface from which it came. Without this validation, a router can be used to forward malicious packets from a sender who has spoofed the source address to prevent the target machine from responding properly.

In OpenStack, antispoofing rules are implemented by Neutron on each compute node within iptables. Therefore, the preferred configuration for these two `rp_filter` values is to disable them by setting them to `0`.

To change the value of the parameters in `/etc/sysctl.conf`, issue the following commands on all nodes:

```
# sed -i "/net.ipv4.conf.default.rp_filter/c\net.ipv4.conf.default.rp_
filter = 0" /etc/sysctl.conf
# sed -i -e "\$anet.ipv4.conf.all.rp_filter = 0" /etc/sysctl.conf
```

Load the changes into memory on all nodes with the `sysctl` command as follows:

```
# sysctl -p
```

Configuring Neutron to use Keystone

The Neutron configuration file found at `/etc/neutron/neutron.conf` has dozens of settings that can be modified to meet the needs of the OpenStack cloud administrator. A handful of these settings must be changed from their defaults as part of this installation.

Using the `crudini` utility, configure the following Neutron settings on all nodes.

To use Keystone as the authentication method for Neutron, execute the following:

```
# crudini --set /etc/neutron/neutron.conf DEFAULT auth_strategy keystone
```

Configure Neutron to use the proper `api_paste_config` middleware configuration file:

```
# crudini --set /etc/neutron/neutron.conf DEFAULT api_paste_config /etc/
neutron/api-paste.ini
```

Configure the proper `keystone_authentication` settings as follows. The username and password for the `neutron` user in Keystone were set earlier in the chapter:

```
# crudini --set /etc/neutron/neutron.conf keystone_authtoken auth_host
controller

# crudini --set /etc/neutron/neutron.conf keystone_authtoken auth_port
35357

# crudini --set /etc/neutron/neutron.conf keystone_authtoken auth_
protocol http

# crudini --set /etc/neutron/neutron.conf keystone_authtoken admin_
tenant_name service

# crudini --set /etc/neutron/neutron.conf keystone_authtoken admin_user
neutron

# crudini --set /etc/neutron/neutron.conf keystone_authtoken admin_
password neutron
```

The `/etc/neutron/api-paste.ini` middleware configuration file must be edited to contain the appropriate authentication settings for the environment. Configure the following settings to allow Neutron to access the Identity Service API:

```
# crudini --set /etc/neutron/api-paste.ini filter:authtoken auth_host
controller

# crudini --set /etc/neutron/api-paste.ini filter:authtoken auth_uri
http://controller:5000

# crudini --set /etc/neutron/api-paste.ini filter:authtoken admin_tenant_
name service

# crudini --set /etc/neutron/api-paste.ini filter:authtoken admin_user
neutron

# crudini --set /etc/neutron/api-paste.ini filter:authtoken admin_
password neutron
```

Configuring Neutron to use a messaging service

Neutron communicates with various OpenStack services on the AMQP messaging bus. Configure Neutron to use Qpid as the messaging broker on all the nodes with the following settings:

```
# crudini --set /etc/neutron/neutron.conf DEFAULT rpc_backend neutron.
openstack.common.rpc.impl_qpid
```

The Qpid authentication settings should match what was previously configured for the other OpenStack services:

```
# crudini --set /etc/neutron/neutron.conf DEFAULT qpid_hostname
controller
```

```
# crudini --set /etc/neutron/neutron.conf DEFAULT qpid_port 5672
```

```
# crudini --set /etc/neutron/neutron.conf DEFAULT qpid_username guest
```

```
# crudini --set /etc/neutron/neutron.conf DEFAULT qpid_password guest
```

Configuring a root helper

The use of a root helper is a security mechanism built into OpenStack that prevents misuse of root privileges on the host that executes an OpenStack-related command. Rather than run commands directly as root, OpenStack calls `sudo neutron-rootwrap /etc/neutron/rootwrap.conf <command>` when Neutron-related commands are executed. A generic `sudoers` entry on the host allows OpenStack to run `neutron-rootwrap` as root. `Neutron-rootwrap` looks for filter definition directories within the configuration file and loads command filters from them. If the command requested matches a command defined by a filter, it executes the command as root. Otherwise, the request is denied.

As your environment grows, you might observe performance degradation when executing OpenStack commands that make calls to the Neutron API. By removing the use of the `neutron-rootwrap` command filter and using `sudo` instead, you can increase the execution of commands on the hosts at the expense of security.

The following statement and configuration option can be found in the `/etc/neutron.conf` file:

```
# Change to "sudo" to skip the filtering and just run the command
directly
```

```
# root_helper = sudo neutron-rootwrap /etc/neutron/rootwrap.conf
```

To disable command filtering, change the `root_helper` value to `sudo` only. To activate the change, uncomment the line and restart the `neutron-server` service.

Configuring Nova to utilize Neutron networking

Before Neutron can be utilized as the network manager for Nova (Compute), the appropriate configuration options must be set in the `/etc/nova/nova.conf` file. Using `crudini`, configure Nova on all nodes to use the Neutron networking setting:

```
# crudini --set /etc/nova/nova.conf DEFAULT network_api_class nova.
network.neutronv2.api.API
```

```
# crudini --set /etc/nova/nova.conf DEFAULT neutron_url http://
controller:9696
```

The following options provide Nova with the proper Neutron credentials for Keystone:

```
# crudini --set /etc/nova/nova.conf DEFAULT neutron_auth_strategy
keystone
```

```
# crudini --set /etc/nova/nova.conf DEFAULT neutron_admin_tenant_name
service
```

```
# crudini --set /etc/nova/nova.conf DEFAULT neutron_admin_username
neutron
```

```
# crudini --set /etc/nova/nova.conf DEFAULT neutron_admin_password
neutron
```

```
# crudini --set /etc/nova/nova.conf DEFAULT neutron_admin_auth_url
http://controller:35357/v2.0
```

Nova uses the `firewall_driver` configuration option to determine how to implement firewalling, and it is meant for use with the `nova-network` service. When Neutron is used, this option should be set to `nova.virt.firewall.NoopFirewallDriver` to instruct Nova to not implement firewalling:

```
# crudini --set /etc/nova/nova.conf DEFAULT firewall_driver nova.virt.
firewall.NoopFirewallDriver
```

The `security_group_api` configuration option specifies which API Nova should use when working with security groups. For installations using Neutron instead of nova-network, this option should be set to `neutron` as follows:

```
# crudini --set /etc/nova/nova.conf DEFAULT security_group_api neutron
```

Nova (Compute) requires additional configuration once a networking plugin has been determined. The LinuxBridge and Open vSwitch networking plugins and their respective Nova configuration changes will be discussed in further detail in *Chapter 4, Building a Virtual Switching Infrastructure*.

Configuring Neutron services

Once installed, the various plugins and agents of Neutron must be configured properly before they can be started and consumed. At this point of the installation, a decision should be made on the Neutron plugin that will be used. The neutron-server service and the neutron-dhcp-agent service at a minimum, cannot be started without specifying a networking plugin as part of their configuration.

Install the LinuxBridge and Open vSwitch plugins with the following commands on all the nodes:

```
# yum -y install openstack-neutron-linuxbridge
# yum -y install openstack-neutron-openvswitch
```

These two switching options will be discussed in further detail in *Chapter 4, Building a Virtual Switching Infrastructure*. However, for the sake of starting Neutron services and demonstrating the Neutron CLI in this chapter, a network configuration based on the LinuxBridge plugin will be used.

Configuring neutron-server

The neutron-server service exposes the Neutron API to users and passes all calls to the appropriate Neutron plugin for processing.

By default, Neutron is configured to listen for API calls on all configured addresses as seen by the default bind_hosts configuration in /etc/neutron/neutron.conf.

```
bind_host = 0.0.0.0
```

To enhance security, it is recommended that the API be exposed only on the management or API network. Using crudini, configure bind_host to use the management address on the controller node as follows:

```
# crudini --set /etc/neutron/neutron.conf DEFAULT bind_host
10.254.254.100
```

Other configuration options that might require tweaking include:

- `core_plugin`
- `dhcp_lease_duration`
- `allow_overlapping_ips`

The `core_plugin` configuration option instructs Neutron to use the specified networking plugin. Both LinuxBridge and Open vSwitch require their own respective plugins, which are as follows:

- **LinuxBridge**: `neutron.plugins.linuxbridge.lb_neutron_plugin.LinuxBridgePluginV2`

- **Open vSwitch**: `neutron.plugins.openvswitch.ovs_neutron_plugin.OVSNeutronPluginV2`

Using `crudini`, set the `core_plugin` option in `/etc/neutron/neutron.conf` to use the LinuxBridge plugin on all nodes:

```
# crudini --set /etc/neutron/neutron.conf DEFAULT core_plugin neutron.
plugins.linuxbridge.lb_neutron_plugin.LinuxBridgePluginV2
```

The `dhcp_lease_duration` configuration option specifies the duration of an IP address lease by an instance. The default value is 86400 seconds, or 24 hours. The DHCP client on the instance itself is responsible for renewing the lease, and this operation varies between operating systems. It is not uncommon for instances to attempt to renew their lease well before exceeding the lease duration.

However, the value set for `dhcp_lease_duration` does not dictate how long an IP address stays associated to an instance. Once an IP address has been allocated to an instance by Neutron, it remains associated with the instance until the instance or the port is deleted, even if the instance is shut off.

The `allow_overlapping_ips` configuration option specifies whether or not Neutron should allow tenant-created subnets to overlap one another. This feature requires the use of network namespaces. Not all distributions and kernels support network namespaces; this might limit how tenant networks are built out. The kernel recommended in *Chapter 2, Installing OpenStack*, does support network namespaces. In this installation, leave the value set to its default (`True`).

Starting neutron-server

Before the `neutron-server` service can be started on RHEL-based distributions (such as CentOS), a symbolic link to the chosen plugin configuration file must exist in the `/etc/neutron/` directory. Each plugin has its own configuration file that can be found in the following directories:

- **LinuxBridge**: `/etc/neutron/plugins/linuxbridge/linuxbridge_conf.ini`

- **Open vSwitch**: `/etc/neutron/plugins/openvswitch/ovs_neutron_plugin.ini`

To create a symbolic link to the LinuxBridge configuration file, execute the following command on all nodes:

```
# ln -s /etc/neutron/plugins/linuxbridge/linuxbridge_conf.ini /etc/
neutron/plugin.ini
```

Once the symbolic link has been created, the Neutron database must be stamped with the version of OpenStack currently installed to allow the proper schema to be laid down.

Use the `neutron-db-manage` command on the controller to stamp the database as Havana.

```
# neutron-db-manage --config-file /etc/neutron/plugin.ini --config-file /
etc/neutron/neutron.conf stamp havana
```

To start the `neutron-server` service on the controller and configure it to start at boot, use the following syntax:

```
# service neutron-server start
# chkconfig neutron-server on
```

Configuring the Neutron DHCP agent

The `neutron-dhcp-agent` service is responsible for spawning and controlling dnsmasq processes for each network that leverages DHCP. This agent also spawns `neutron-ns-metadata-proxy` processes as part of the metadata system and is used across all Neutron plugins.

Out of the box, Neutron utilizes `dnsmasq`, a free, lightweight DNS forwarder and DHCP server that is used to provide DHCP services to networks. The DHCP driver is specified in the `dhcp_agent.ini` configuration file found at `/etc/neutron/dhcp_agent.ini`.

```
# The agent can use other DHCP drivers.  Dnsmasq is the simplest and
requires
# no additional setup of the DHCP server.
# dhcp_driver = neutron.agent.linux.dhcp.Dnsmasq
```

The default `dhcp_driver` is `neutron.agent.linux.dhcp.Dnsmasq` and can be left commented out without any issue.

Other notable configuration options found in the `dhcp_agent.ini` configuration file include:

- `interface_driver`
- `use_namespaces`
- `enable_isolated_metadata`
- `enable_metadata_network`
- `dhcp_domain`

The `interface_driver` configuration option should be configured appropriately, based on the networking plugin chosen for your environment.

- **LinuxBridge**: `neutron.agent.linux.interface.BridgeInterfaceDriver`
- **Open vSwitch**: `neutron.agent.linux.interface.OVSInterfaceDriver`

Only one `interface_driver` can be configured at a single time. In this installation, the configured `interface_driver` should correspond to the LinuxBridge plugin. Using `crudini`, set the DHCP `interface_driver` option to use `neutron.agent.linux.interface.BridgeInterfaceDriver` on the controller node.

```
# crudini --set /etc/neutron/dhcp_agent.ini DEFAULT interface_driver
neutron.agent.linux.interface.BridgeInterfaceDriver
```

The `use_namespaces` configuration option instructs Neutron to disable or enable the use of network namespaces for DHCP. When `True`, every network scheduled to a DHCP agent will have a namespace by the name of `qdhcp-<Network UUID>`, where `<Network UUID>` is a unique UUID associated with every network. By default, `use_namespaces` is set to `True`. When set to `False`, overlapping networks between tenants are not allowed. Not all distributions and kernels support network namespaces; this might limit how tenant networks are built out. The kernel recommended in *Chapter 2, Installing OpenStack*, supports network namespaces. For the installation of OpenStack, leave the value set to `True`.

The `enable_isolated_metadata` configuration option is useful in cases where a physical network device (such as a firewall or router) serves as the default gateway for instances, but Neutron is still required to provide metadata services to instances. When the L3 agent is used, an instance reaches the metadata service through the Neutron router that serves as its default gateway. An isolated network is assumed to be the one in which a Neutron router is not serving as the gateway, but Neutron handles DHCP requests for the instances. Often, this is the case when instances are leveraging flat or VLAN networks and the L3 agent is not used. The default value for `enable_isolated_metadata` is `False`. When set to `True`, Neutron can provide instances with a static route to the metadata service via DHCP in certain cases. More information on the use of metadata and this configuration can be found in *Chapter 5, Creating Networks with Neutron*. For this installation, change the value from `False` to `True` and uncomment the line in the configuration file:

```
# sed -i "/# enable_isolated_metadata/c\enable_isolated_metadata = True"
/etc/neutron/dhcp_agent.ini
```

The `enable_metadata_network` configuration option is useful in cases where the L3 agent might be used, but the metadata agent is not on the same host as the router. By setting `enable_metadata_network` to `True`, Neutron networks whose subnet CIDR is included in 169.254.0.0/16 will be regarded as metadata networks. When connected to a Neutron router, a metadata proxy is spawned on the node that hosts the router, granting metadata access to all the networks connected to the router.

The `dhcp_domain` configuration option specifies the DNS search domain that is provided to instances via DHCP when they obtain a lease. The default value is `openstacklocal`. This can be changed to whatever fits your organization. For the purpose of this installation, change the value from `openstacklocal` to `learningneutron.com` and uncomment the line in the configuration file:

```
# sed -i "/# dhcp_domain/c\dhcp_domain = learningneutron.com" /etc/
neutron/dhcp_agent.ini
```

Configuration options that are not mentioned here have sufficient default values and should not be changed unless your environment requires it.

Starting the Neutron DHCP agent

Use the following commands to start the `neutron-dhcp-agent` service on the controller node and configure it to start automatically at boot time:

```
# service neutron-dhcp-agent start
# chkconfig neutron-dhcp-agent on
```

Confirm the status of the `neutron-dhcp-agent` as shown in the following screenshot:

```
[root@controller ~]# service neutron-dhcp-agent status
neutron-dhcp-agent (pid  7380) is running...
```

The agent should be in a running status.

 At the time of writing this book, the DHCP agent code expects the existence of the Open vSwitch plugin and associated files before it will properly start up. Bug 1019487 at `https://bugzilla.redhat.com` documents this issue. If the agent is dead, install the `openstack-neutron-openvswitch` package as a prerequisite for any chosen plugin (including LinuxBridge).

Configuring the Neutron metadata agent

The Nova (Compute) service uses a special metadata service to enable virtual machine instances to retrieve specific details about themselves. This includes information such as hostname, public keys, and more. Instances access the metadata service over HTTP at `http://169.254.169.254` during boot.

The `neutron-metadata-agent` provides a proxy via the DHCP or router namespaces to the `openstack-nova-metadata-api` (or `openstack-nova-api`) service on the controller node. Each network has a corresponding `neutron-ns-metadata-proxy` process that is spawned by the metadata agent. With Neutron, the process of providing metadata to instances varies and is based on the use of the Neutron routers. More information on the use of metadata and how it works can be found in *Chapter 5, Creating Networks with Neutron*.

The following diagram provides a high-level overview of this process when the controller node hosts Neutron networking services:

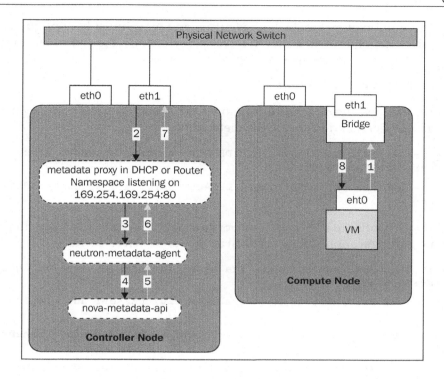

In the preceding diagram, the following actions take place when an instance makes a request to the metadata service:

1. An instance sends metadata request to 169.254.269.254 via HTTP at boot
2. The metadata request hits either the router or DHCP namespace depending on the route
3. The metadata proxy sends request to the Neutron metadata agent via the Unix socket
4. The Neutron metadata agent forwards request to the Nova metadata API
5. The Nova metadata API service responds to the request and forwards it to the Neutron metadata agent
6. The Neutron metadata agent sends the response back through the metadata proxy
7. The metadata proxy forwards the HTTP response to the instance
8. The instance processes metadata and continues the boot process

For proper operation of metadata, both Neutron and Nova must be configured to communicate together with a shared secret password. On the controller node, use the `openssl` utility to create a random shared secret.

```
# METADATA_SECRET=$(openssl rand -hex 10)
```

On the controller, use the `crudini` utility to update the `/etc/nova/nova.conf` file with the shared secret and to enable the metadata proxy.

```
# crudini --set /etc/nova/nova.conf DEFAULT neutron_metadata_proxy_
shared_secret $METADATA_SECRET
# crudini --set /etc/nova/nova.conf DEFAULT service_neutron_metadata_
proxy true
```

Use `crudini` to configure the `/etc/neutron/metadata_agent.ini` file with the appropriate authentication settings as well as the same shared secret.

```
# crudini --set /etc/neutron/metadata_agent.ini DEFAULT auth_url http://
controller:5000/v2.0
# crudini --set /etc/neutron/metadata_agent.ini DEFAULT auth_region
regionOne
# crudini --set /etc/neutron/metadata_agent.ini DEFAULT admin_tenant_name
service
# crudini --set /etc/neutron/metadata_agent.ini DEFAULT admin_user
neutron
# crudini --set /etc/neutron/metadata_agent.ini DEFAULT admin_password
neutron
# crudini --set /etc/neutron/metadata_agent.ini DEFAULT nova_metadata_ip
controller
# crudini --set /etc/neutron/metadata_agent.ini DEFAULT metadata_proxy_
shared_secret $METADATA_SECRET
```

Use the following commands on the controller to start the `neutron-metadata-agent` service and configure it to start automatically at boot time:

```
# service neutron-metadata-agent start
# chkconfig neutron-metadata-agent on
```

Configuring the Neutron L3 agent

OpenStack Networking includes an extension that provides users with the ability to dynamically provision and configure virtual routers using the API. These routers interconnect L2 networks and provide floating IPs to make the ports on private networks publically accessible. The `neutron-l3-agent` uses the Linux IP stack and iptables to perform both L3 forwarding and NAT. In order to support multiple routers with potentially overlapping IP networks, the `neutron-l3-agent` defaults to using network namespaces to provide isolated forwarding contexts. More information on creating and managing routers in Neutron can be found in *Chapter 6, Creating Routers with Neutron*.

Configuring the Neutron LBaaS agent

OpenStack Networking includes an extension that provides users with the ability to dynamically provision and configure virtual load balancers using the API. Both the Havana and Icehouse releases of OpenStack leverage the open-source HAProxy software load balancer in their reference implementations. The `neutron-lbaas-agent` defaults to using network namespaces to provide isolated load-balancing contexts per virtual IP, or VIP. More information on creating and managing load balancers in Neutron can be found in *Chapter 7, Load Balancing Traffic in Neutron*.

Using the Neutron command-line interface

Besides the networking services installed, the `openstack-neutron` package provides a command-line client to interface with the Neutron API. The Neutron shell can be invoked by issuing the `neutron` command from the Linux command line:

```
# neutron
```

The `neutron` shell provides commands that can be used to create, read, update, and delete the networking configuration within the OpenStack cloud. By typing a question mark or `help` within the Neutron shell, a list of commands can be found. Additionally, running `neutron help` from the Linux command line provides a brief description of each command's function.

Many of the commands listed will be covered in subsequent chapters of this book. Commands outside the scope of basic Neutron functionality, such as those relying on third-party plugins, can be found in *Appendix A, Additional Neutron Commands*.

Summary

Neutron maintains the overall network architecture in a database, and the network plugin agent on each node is responsible for configuring the virtual network accordingly. DHCP and metadata services that run on the controller or dedicated network node deliver IP addresses and instance-specific data at boot time.

Now that OpenStack Networking services have been installed across all nodes in the environment, the configuration of a Layer 2 networking plugin is all that remains before instances can be created.

In the next chapter, you will be guided through the configuration of the LinuxBridge and Open vSwitch monolithic networking plugins. You will also be provided with an overview of the differences between the two plugins in terms of how they function and provide layer 2 connectivity to instances. The use of the ML2 plugin is not required in Havana, but for your reference, its configuration has been provided in *Appendix B, ML2 Configuration*.

4
Building a Virtual Switching Infrastructure

One of the core functions of OpenStack Networking is to provide connectivity to and from instances by dynamically configuring the virtual and/or physical network infrastructure in the cloud. Before instances can be utilized in a useful manner, an underlying switching infrastructure must be configured.

In this chapter, you will be introduced to two networking plugins available in the Havana release of OpenStack: LinuxBridge and **Open vSwitch** (**OVS**). Both networking plugins are known as monolithic plugins, which means only one of them can be active at any given time. They are deprecated in future releases in favor of ML2, the modular layer 2 plugin for Neutron first introduced in Havana. ML2 can be configured to use multiple layer 2 technologies simultaneously. The configuration of ML2 is outside the scope of this chapter, but has been included in the appendix.

Each networking plugin has unique requirements and both provide connectivity to instances and other virtual networking resources in their own particular ways. You will be guided through the installation and configuration of both plugins in anticipation of creating networks and instances in later chapters.

Providing layer 2 connectivity to instances

Neutron and Nova work in tandem to configure networking on physical servers in the cloud. The LinuxBridge and Open vSwitch plugins provide both Neutron and Nova with the methods to provide connectivity to instances and other network resources.

Virtual network interfaces

By default, OpenStack leverages KVM, a kernel-based virtual machine, to provide a virtualization infrastructure to the Linux kernel that utilizes the hardware virtualization features of various processors.

When an instance is booted for the first time, a virtual network interface is created on the host that is referred to as a tap interface. The tap interface corresponds directly to a network interface within the guest instance. This action results in the host exposing the guest instance to the physical network.

In OpenStack, the name of the tap interface corresponds to the Neutron port UUID, or unique identifier, that the instance is plugged in to. The correlation of the tap interface name and Neutron port UUID is simply cosmetic, and the naming convention means that tap interface names should persist after a reboot of the host. An example of this behavior can be seen in later chapters.

Bridging

Neutron leverages the concept of network bridges to provide connectivity to and from instances. Network bridging is described as the action of connecting two or more layer 2 networks to create a single aggregate network. A Linux bridge is a virtual interface that connects multiple network interfaces. In Neutron, a bridge will usually include a physical interface and one or more virtual or tap interfaces. A physical interface includes Ethernet interfaces, such as `eth0`, and bonded interfaces consisting of one or more Ethernet interfaces or virtual VLAN interfaces of either type. You can connect multiple physical or virtual network interfaces to a Linux bridge.

In normal operation, a network interface is in non-promiscuous mode, which means that when the interface receives a frame that is not directly addressed to it or is not a broadcast frame, then the interface drops that frame. In order to serve in a bridge, the physical network interface must be placed in promiscuous mode. In the promiscuous mode, the interface allows all frames through, thus allowing the host to see and process frames intended for other machines or network devices.

The following diagram provides a high-level view of a Linux bridge leveraged by Neutron:

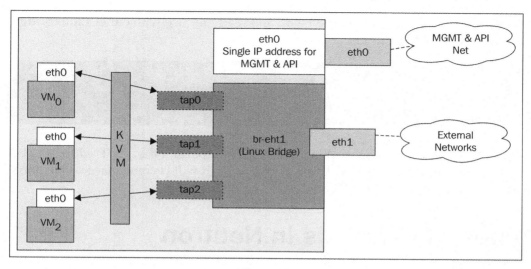

Figure 4.1

In the preceding figure, the Linux bridge `br-eth1` contains a single physical interface (`eth1`) and three virtual interfaces: `tap0`, `tap1`, and `tap2`. The three tap interfaces correspond to a network interface within their respective guest instance. Traffic from `eth0` on an instance can be observed on the respective tap interfaces as well as the bridge interface and the physical interface in the bridge.

Configuring the bridge interface

In this installation, the physical network interface `eth1` will be utilized for bridging purposes. On both the controller and compute nodes, configure the `eth1` interface configuration file at `/etc/sysconfig/network-scripts/ifcfg-eth1` as follows:

```
# nano /etc/sysconfig/network-scripts/ifcfg-eth1
```

```
DEVICE=eth1
TYPE=Ethernet
ONBOOT=yes
NM_CONTROLLED=yes
BOOTPROTO=none
```

Save the file and cycle the interface with the following command:

```
# ifdown eth1; ifup eth1
```

If all goes well, the interface should be up and ready for use with either LinuxBridge or Open vSwitch plugins:

```
3: eth1: <BROADCAST,MULTICAST,UP,LOWER_UP> mtu 1500 qdisc mq state UP qlen 1000
    link/ether 00:1d:09:66:54:b9 brd ff:ff:ff:ff:ff:ff
    inet6 fe80::21d:9ff:fe66:54b9/64 scope link
       valid_lft forever preferred_lft forever
```

Because the interface will be used in a bridge, it is important that an IP address not be directly applied. If there is an IP applied to eth1, it will become inaccessible once the interface is placed in a bridge.

Types of networks in Neutron

In Neutron, there are two categories used to describe networks that provide connectivity to instances:

- Provider networks
- Tenant networks

Provider networks are networks, created by the OpenStack administrator, that map directly to a physical network in the data center. Useful network types in this category include flat (untagged) and VLAN (802.1q tagged). Other network types, such as local and GRE, are configurable options but are rarely implemented as provider networks.

Tenant networks are networks created by users to provide connectivity between instances within a tenant. By default, tenant networks are fully isolated from each other, including other networks within the same tenant.

Neutron supports a range of networking types, including:

- Local
- Flat
- VLAN
- VXLAN and GRE

A local network is one that is isolated from other networks and nodes. Instances connected to a local network may communicate with other instances in the same network on the same compute node, but are unable to communicate with instances in the same network that reside on another host. Because of this designed limitation, local networks are recommended for testing purposes only.

In a flat network, no VLAN tagging or other network segregation takes place. In some configurations, instances can reside in the same network as host machines.

VLAN networks are networks that utilize 802.1q tagging to segregate network traffic. Instances in the same VLAN are considered part of the same network and are in the same layer 2 broadcast domain. Inter-VLAN routing, or routing between VLANs, is only possible through the use of a router.

Using the Open vSwitch plugin, GRE and VXLAN networks can be created that leverage the concept of overlay networks. An overlay network is defined as a computer network that is built on top of another network. Peer-to-peer tunnels are built between all hosts in the cloud. These peer-to-peer tunnels create what is called a **mesh network**, where every host is connected to every other host. A cloud consisting of one controller and three compute nodes would have a fully meshed overlay network that resembles the following diagram:

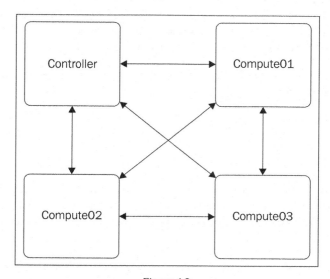

Figure 4.2

In the preceding diagram, a fully meshed GRE or VXLAN overlay network is built between all hosts.

When GRE or VXLAN networks are created, a unique ID is specified that is used to encapsulate the traffic. Network traffic between instances in the same network, but on different hosts, is encapsulated on one host and sent to another through the point-to-point GRE or VXLAN tunnel, where it is decapsulated and forwarded accordingly.

Because GRE and VXLAN network traffic is encapsulated, many physical network devices cannot communicate on these networks. As a result, GRE and VXLAN networks are effectively isolated from other networks in the cloud without the use of a Neutron router. More information on creating Neutron routers can be found in *Chapter 6, Creating Routers with Neutron*.

Choosing a networking plugin

Neutron networking plugins are responsible for implementing features that provide network connectivity to and from instances. The two plugins discussed in this book, LinuxBridge and Open vSwitch, implement those features in different ways.

LinuxBridge

When configured to utilize the LinuxBridge networking plugin, Neutron relies on the `bridge` and `8021q` kernel modules to properly connect instances and other network resources to the virtual switch and forward traffic.

In a LinuxBridge-based network implementation, there are three distinct types of virtual networking devices:

- Tap devices
- VLAN interfaces
- Linux bridges

A tap device is how a hypervisor such as KVM implements a virtual network interface card. These virtual interfaces on the host correspond to an interface inside the guest instance. An Ethernet frame sent to the tap device is received by the guest operating system.

Linux supports 802.1q VLAN tagging through the use of **virtual VLAN interfaces**. The kernel can send and receive VLAN-tagged packets when a VLAN interface named `ethX.<vlan>` has been created and properly configured. The VLAN interface is associated with its physical interface, `ethX`.

A Linux bridge is a virtual interface that connects multiple network interfaces. In Neutron, a bridge will usually include a physical interface and one or more virtual or tap interfaces. A physical interface includes Ethernet interfaces, such as `eth0`, `eth1`, and so on; bonded interfaces consisting of one or more Ethernet interfaces; or VLAN interfaces of either type.

Internal network connections when using LinuxBridge

For an Ethernet frame to travel from the virtual machine instance to a remote physical network, it will pass through three or four devices inside the host:

- Tap interface: `tapXXXX`
- Linux bridge: `brqYYYY`
- VLAN interface: `ethX.ZZZ` (only when VLAN tagging is used)
- Physical interface: `ethX`

To help conceptualize how Neutron uses Linux bridges, a few examples of LinuxBridge architectures have been provided.

VLAN

Imagine a basic OpenStack cloud that consists of a single network, VLAN 100, for use with instances. The network architecture within the compute node would resemble the following diagram:

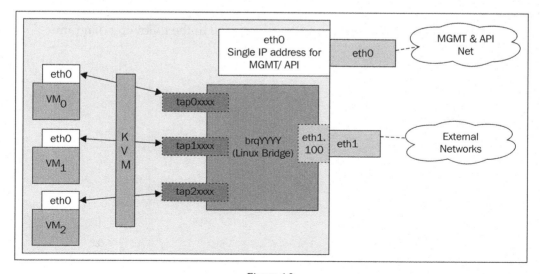

Figure 4.3

In the preceding diagram, three guest instances are connected to a Linux bridge, named brqYYYY, via their tap interfaces. A virtual interface named eth1.100 was automatically created and placed in the bridge by Neutron. Eth1.100 is bound to physical interface eth1. As traffic from instances traverses the Linux bridge and out towards the physical interface, the eth1.100 interface tags that traffic as VLAN 100 and drops it on eth1. Ingress traffic towards the instances through eth1 is inversely untagged by eth1.100 and sent to the appropriate instance through the bridge.

Using the brctl show command, the preceding diagram can be realized in the Linux CLI as the following:

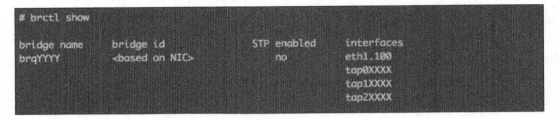

```
# brctl show

bridge name       bridge id              STP enabled       interfaces
brqYYYY           <based on NIC>              no           eth1.100
                                                           tap0XXXX
                                                           tap1XXXX
                                                           tap2XXXX
```

The bridge id in the output is dynamically generated based on the parent NIC of the virtual VLAN interface. In this bridge, the parent interface is eth1.

The bridge name, beginning with the brq prefix, is generated based on the UUID of the corresponding Neutron network it is associated with. Each network uses its own bridge.

In the event that more than one VLAN network is needed, another Linux bridge will be created which contains a separate virtual VLAN interface. The new virtual interface, eth1.101, is placed on a new bridge, brqWWWW, as seen in the following diagram:

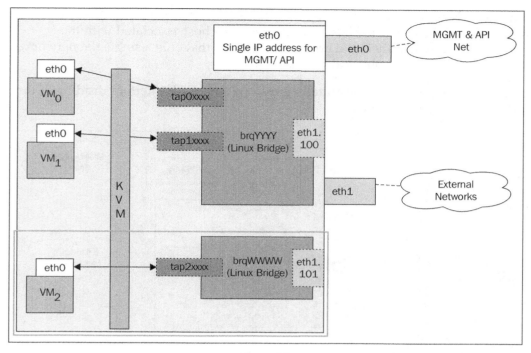

Figure 4.4

On the compute node, the preceding diagram can be realized as follows:

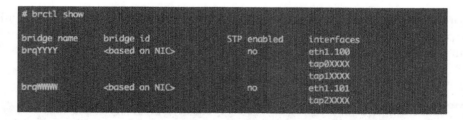

Flat

A flat network in Neutron is meant to describe a network in which vlan tagging does not take place. All instances in a flat network are effectively in the same layer 2 broadcast domain.

Unlike VLAN-tagged networks, flat networks require that virtual VLAN interfaces are not created. Instead, the physical interface of the host associated with the network is placed directly in the bridge. This means that only a single flat network can exist per bridge and physical interface.

The following diagram demonstrates a physical (untagged) interface residing in the bridge in a flat network scenario:

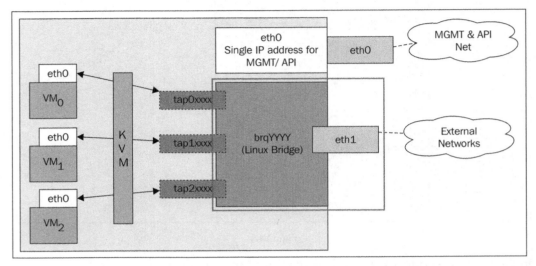

Figure 4.5

In the preceding diagram, `eth1` resides on the bridge named `brqYYYY`, along with three tap interfaces that correspond to guest instances. The Linux kernel does not perform any VLAN tagging on the host.

On the compute node, the preceding diagram can be realized as follows:

When multiple flat networks are created, a separate physical interface must be associated with each flat network. The following diagram demonstrates the use of a second physical interface used for flat networks:

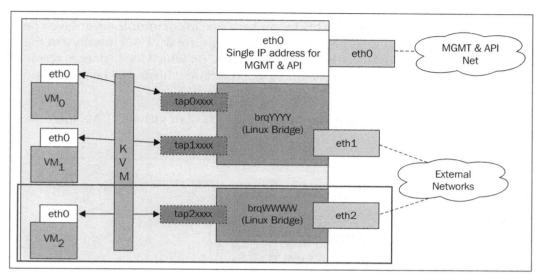

Figure 4.6

On the compute node, the use of two physical interfaces for separate flat networks can be realized as follows:

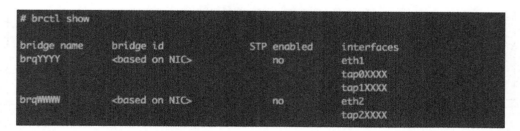

With the two flat networks, the host does not perform any VLAN tagging on the traffic traversing those bridges. Instances connected to the two bridges require a router to communicate with one another.

Local

When creating a local network in Neutron, it is not possible to specify a VLAN ID or physical interface. The LinuxBridge plugin agent will create a bridge and place only the tap interface of the instance in the bridge. Instances in the same local network will be placed in the same bridge and are free to communicate amongst one another. Because the host does not have a physical or virtual VLAN interface in the bridge, traffic between instances is limited to the host on which the instances reside. Instances in the same local network that reside on different hosts will be unable to communicate with one another.

The following diagram demonstrates the lack of physical or virtual VLAN interfaces in the bridge:

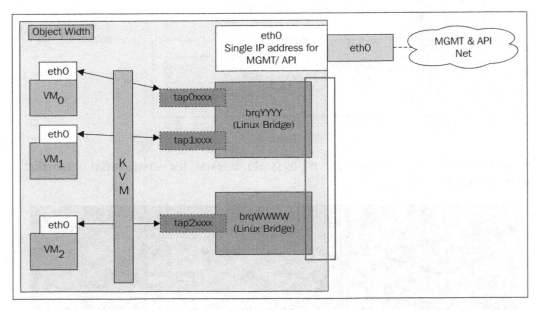

Figure 4.7

In the preceding diagram, two local networks exist that utilize their respective bridges, brqYYYY and brqWWWW. Instances connected to the same bridge can communicate with one another but with nothing else outside of the bridge. There is no mechanism to permit traffic between instances on different bridges or hosts when using local networks.

Open vSwitch

Within OpenStack Networking, Open vSwitch operates as a software-based switch that uses virtual network bridges and flow rules to forward packets between hosts. Although it is capable of supporting many technologies and protocols, only a subset of Open vSwitch features are leveraged by Neutron.

There are three main components of Open vSwitch that you should be aware of:

- **Kernel module**: The Open vSwitch kernel module is the equivalent of ASICs on a hardware switch. It is the data plane of the switch where all packet processing takes place.

- **vSwitch daemon**: The Open vSwitch daemon, `ovs-vswitchd`, is a Linux process that runs in user space on every physical host and dictates how the kernel module will be programmed.

- **Database server**: Open vSwitch uses a local database on every physical host called the **Open vSwitch Database Server (OVSDB)** that maintains the configuration of the virtual switches.

When configured to utilize the Open vSwitch networking plugin, Neutron relies on the `bridge` and `openvswitch` kernel modules, along with user-space utilities, such as `ovs-vsctl` and `ovs-ofctl`, to properly manage the Open vSwitch database and connect instances and other network resources to virtual switches.

In an Open vSwitch-based network implementation, there are five distinct types of virtual networking devices:

- Tap devices
- Linux bridges
- Virtual Ethernet cables
- OVS bridges
- OVS patch ports

Tap devices and Linux bridges were described briefly in the previous section, and their use in an Open vSwitch-based network remains the same. **Virtual Ethernet (veth)** cables are virtual interfaces that mimic network patch cables. An Ethernet frame sent to one end of the veth cable is received by the other end, much like a real network patch cable. Neutron makes use of veth cables to make connections between various network resources, including namespaces and bridges.

An OVS bridge behaves like a physical switch, only virtualized. Network interface devices, including interfaces used by DHCP or router namespaces and instance tap interfaces, connect to OVS bridge ports. The ports themselves can be configured much like a physical switch port. Open vSwitch maintains information about connected devices, including MAC addresses and interface statistics.

Open vSwitch has a built-in port type that mimics the behavior of a Linux veth cable but is optimized for use with OVS bridges. When connecting two Open vSwitch bridges, a port on each switch is reserved as a **patch port**. Patch ports are configured with a peer name that corresponds to the patch port on the other switch. Graphically, it looks something like the following diagram:

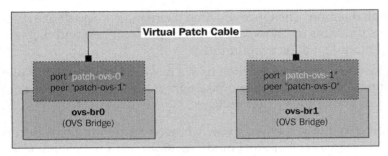

Figure 4.8

In the preceding diagram, two OVS bridges are cross-connected via a patch port on each switch.

Open vSwitch patch ports are used to connect Open vSwitch bridges to each other, while Linux veth cables are used to connect Open vSwitch bridges to Linux bridges, or Linux bridges to other Linux bridges.

Internal network connections when using Open vSwitch

For an Ethernet frame to travel from the virtual machine instance out through the physical server interface, it will pass through nine devices inside the host:

- Tap interface: tapXXXX
- Linux bridge: qbrYYYY
- Veth pair: qvbYYYY, qvoYYYY
- OVS integration bridge: br-int
- OVS patch ports: int-br-ethX, phy-br-ethX
- OVS provider bridge: br-ethX
- Physical interface: ethX

The Open vSwitch bridge `br-int` is known as the **integration bridge**. The integration bridge is the central virtual switch that many network resources are connected to, including instances, DHCP servers, routers, and more. When Neutron security groups are enabled, however, instances are *not* directly connected to the integration bridge. Instead, instances are connected to a Linux bridge that is cross-connected to the integration bridge. The reliance on Linux bridges in an Open vSwitch-based network implementation stems from the current inability to place iptables rules on tap interfaces connected to Open vSwitch bridge ports, a core function of Neutron security groups. To work around this limitation, tap interfaces are placed on Linux bridges, which, in turn, are connected to the integration bridge. More information on security group rules and how they are applied to interfaces can be found in *Chapter 8, Protecting Instances on the Network*.

The Open vSwitch bridge `br-ethX` is known as the **provider bridge**. The provider bridge provides connectivity to the physical network interface ethX, where X represents the enumerated physical NIC, and is connected to the integration bridge by a virtual patch cable provided by patch ports `int-br-ethX` and `phy-br-ethX`.

A visual representation of the architecture described can be seen in the following diagram:

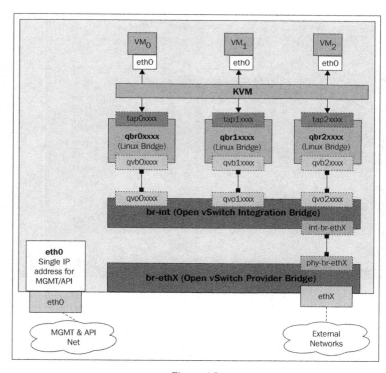

Figure 4.9

In the preceding diagram, instances are connected to a Linux bridge via their respective tap interfaces. The Linux bridges are connected to the OVS integration bridge via a veth cable. OpenFlow rules on the integration bridge dictate how traffic is forwarded through the virtual switch. The integration bridge is connected to the provider bridge via an OVS patch cable. Lastly, the provider bridge contains the physical network interface, which allows traffic to enter and exit the host onto the physical network infrastructure.

When using the Open vSwitch plugin, each controller, network, or compute node in the environment has its own integration bridge and provider bridge. The virtual switches across nodes are effectively cross-connected to one another through the physical network. More than one provider bridge can be configured on a host, but it requires the use of a dedicated physical interface, or virtual VLAN interface in some cases, per provider bridge.

Identifying ports on the virtual switch

Using the `ovs-ofctl show <bridge>` command, you can see a logical representation of the specified virtual switch. The following screenshot demonstrates the use of this command to show the switch ports of the integration bridge on `compute01`:

```
[root@compute01 ~]# ovs-ofctl show br-int
OFPT_FEATURES_REPLY (xid=0x2): dpid:0000f6606ec02545
n_tables:254, n_buffers:256
capabilities: FLOW_STATS TABLE_STATS PORT_STATS QUEUE_STATS ARP_MATCH_IP
actions: OUTPUT SET_VLAN_VID SET_VLAN_PCP STRIP_VLAN SET_DL_SRC SET_DL_DST SET_NW_SRC SET_NW_DST SET_NW_TOS SET_TP_SRC SET_TP_DST ENQUEUE
 1(patch-tun): addr:aa:93:5d:8b:bc:68
     config:     0
     state:      0
     speed: 0 Mbps now, 0 Mbps max
 2(int-br-eth1): addr:02:7e:02:f9:9b:5e
     config:     0
     state:      0
     current:    10GB-FD COPPER
     speed: 10000 Mbps now, 0 Mbps max
 5(qvo04c49e4a-a6): addr:3a:39:e2:e2:df:ca
     config:     0
     state:      0
     current:    10GB-FD COPPER
     speed: 10000 Mbps now, 0 Mbps max
 6(qvofe2d048e-bc): addr:e6:98:c5:04:c7:85
     config:     0
     state:      0
     current:    10GB-FD COPPER
     speed: 10000 Mbps now, 0 Mbps max
 LOCAL(br-int): addr:f6:60:6e:c0:25:45
     config:     0
     state:      0
     speed: 0 Mbps now, 0 Mbps max
OFPT_GET_CONFIG_REPLY (xid=0x4): frags=normal miss_send_len=0
```

The following are the components demonstrated in the preceding screenshot:

- Port number 1 is named `patch-tun`, and is one end of an OVS patch cable. The other end connects to the tunnel bridge (not pictured).

- Port number 2 is named `int-br-eth1` and is one end of a Linux veth cable. The other end connects to the provider bridge, `br-eth1` (not pictured).

- Port number 5 is named `qvo04c49e4a-a6` and corresponds to a Neutron port UUID starting with `04c49e4a-a6`.

- Port number 6 is named `qvofe2d048e-bc` and corresponds to a Neutron port UUID starting with `qvofe2d048e-bc`.

- The LOCAL port is named `br-int`, and is used for management traffic to and from the virtual switch.

The following screenshot demonstrates the switch configuration in a graphical manner:

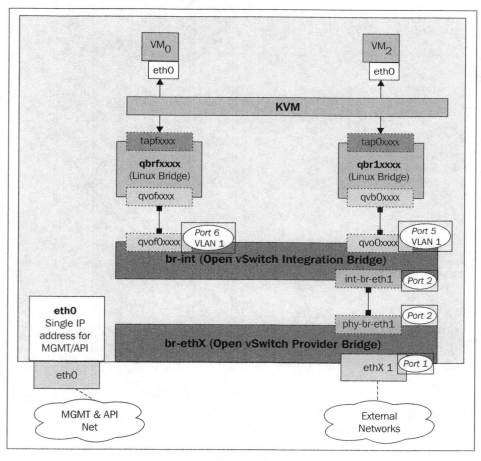

Figure 4.10

Identifying the local VLANs associated with ports

Every port on the integration bridge connected to an instance or other network resource is placed in a VLAN that is local to that host. Every Open vSwitch database is independent of another and manages its own VLAN database that is not related to the physical network infrastructure. Instances in the same Neutron network on a particular host are placed in the same VLAN on the integration bridge.

Using the `ovs-vsctl show` command, you can identify the internal VLAN tag of all ports on all virtual switches on the host. The following screenshot demonstrates this command in action on `compute01`:

```
[root@compute01 ~]# ovs-vsctl show
f3b5fa36-6459-40a0-b823-468e7d6fed7f
    Bridge "br-eth1"
        Port "br-eth1"
            Interface "br-eth1"
                type: internal
        Port "eth1"
            Interface "eth1"
        Port "phy-br-eth1"
            Interface "phy-br-eth1"
    Bridge br-tun
        Port "gre-1"
            Interface "gre-1"
                type: gre
                options: {in_key=flow, local_ip="172.18.0.101", out_key=flow, remote_ip="172.18.0.100"}
        Port patch-int
            Interface patch-int
                type: patch
                options: {peer=patch-tun}
        Port br-tun
            Interface br-tun
                type: internal
    Bridge br-int
        Port "int-br-eth1"
            Interface "int-br-eth1"
        Port patch-tun
            Interface patch-tun
                type: patch
                options: {peer=patch-int}
        Port "qvofe2d048e-bc"
            tag: 1
            Interface "qvofe2d048e-bc"
        Port br-int
            Interface br-int
                type: internal
        Port "qvo04c49e4a-a6"
            tag: 2
            Interface "qvo04c49e4a-a6"
    ovs_version: "1.11.0"
```

Inside the integration bridge sit two ports, `qvo04c49e4a-a6` and `qvofe2d048e-bc`, each assigned their own VLAN tag. These ports correspond to two instances in two different Neutron networks as evidenced by their difference in VLAN IDs. The VLAN IDs are arbitrarily assigned by Open vSwitch and may change upon restart of the `openvswitch` service or after a reboot.

Programming flow rules

Unlike the LinuxBridge plugin architecture, the Open vSwitch plugin does not use virtual VLAN interfaces on the host to tag traffic. Instead, the Open vSwitch plugin agent programs flow rules on the virtual switches that dictate how traffic traversing the switch should be manipulated before forwarding. When traffic traverses a virtual switch, flow rules on the switch can transform, add, or strip the VLAN tags before forwarding the traffic. In addition, flow rules can be added that drop traffic if it matches certain characteristics. Open vSwitch is capable of performing other types of actions on traffic, but those are outside the scope of this book.

By using the `ovs-ofctl dump-flows <bridge>` command, you can observe the flows currently programmed on the specified bridge. The Open vSwitch plugin agent is responsible for converting information about the network in the Neutron database to Open vSwitch flows, and it constantly maintains the flows as changes are being made to the network.

Flow rules for VLAN networks

In the following example, VLAN 30 represents a network in the data center and is trunked down to both the controller and compute nodes. Traffic that enters physical interface `eth1` in the provider bridge is processed by the flow rules on that bridge. Have a look at the following screenshot:

```
[root@compute01 ~]# ovs-ofctl dump-flows br-eth1
NXST_FLOW reply (xid=0x4):
 cookie=0x0, duration=6114.377s, table=0, n_packets=101, n_bytes=5984, idle_age=723, priority=4,in_port=2,dl_vlan=1 actions=mod_vlan_vid:30,NORMAL
 cookie=0x0, duration=6120.067s, table=0, n_packets=31, n_bytes=2300, idle_age=830, priority=2,in_port=2 actions=drop
 cookie=0x0, duration=6121.345s, table=0, n_packets=27866, n_bytes=1816978, idle_age=1, priority=1 actions=NORMAL
```

Flow rules are processed in order from top to bottom. The first two rules specify a particular inbound port:

```
in_port=2
```

According to the diagram in Figure 4.10, traffic entering the bridge `br-eth1` from physical interface `eth1` does so through port 1, not port 2, so the first two rules do not apply. The traffic is forwarded to the integration bridge via the third rule:

```
cookie=0x0, duration=6121.345s, table=0, n_packets=27866, n_
bytes=1816978, idle_age=1, priority=1 actions=NORMAL
```

Flows with an action of NORMAL instruct Open vSwitch to act as a learning switch, which means traffic will be forwarded out all ports until the switch learns and updates its FDB table, or forwarding database. The FDB table is the equivalent of a CAM or MAC address table. This behavior is similar to that of a hardware switch that floods traffic out to all ports until it learns the proper path.

As the traffic exits port 2 on the provider bridge and enters port 2 on the integration bridge, it is evaluated, in order, by the flow rules as follows:

```
[root@compute01 ~]# ovs-ofctl dump-flows br-int
NXST_FLOW reply (xid=0x4):
 cookie=0x0, duration=6100.376s, table=0, n_packets=15, n_bytes=1904, idle_age=709, priority=3,in_port=2,dl_vlan=30 actions=mod_vlan_vid:1,NORMAL
 cookie=0x0, duration=6106.342s, table=0, n_packets=7, n_bytes=532, idle_age=6079, priority=2,in_port=2 actions=drop
 cookie=0x0, duration=6107.76s, table=0, n_packets=126, n_bytes=7680, idle_age=709, priority=1 actions=NORMAL
```

The first rule performs the action of modifying the VLAN ID from the original VLAN to a VLAN that is local to the integration bridge on the compute node when the original VLAN ID is 30:

```
cookie=0x0, duration=6100.376s, table=0, n_packets=15, n_bytes=1904,
idle_age=709, priority=3,in_port=2,dl_vlan=30 actions=mod_vlan_
vid:1,NORMAL
```

When traffic tagged as VLAN 30 is sent to an instance and forwarded through the provider bridge to the integration bridge, the VLAN tag is stripped and replaced with local VLAN 1. It is then forwarded to a port that corresponds to the appropriate instance based on the MAC address. The second rule states that if traffic entering port number 2 from the provider bridge is anything but VLAN 30, it is dropped:

```
cookie=0x0, duration=6106.342s, table=0, n_packets=7, n_bytes=532, idle_
age=6079, priority=2,in_port=2 actions=drop
```

Return traffic from the instance through the integration bridge is tagged as VLAN 1 and is forwarded to the provider bridge by the third rule, as follows:

```
cookie=0x0, duration=6107.76s, table=0, n_packets=126, n_bytes=7680,
idle_age=709, priority=1 actions=NORMAL
```

Once traffic hits the provider bridge, it is processed by the flow rules, as follows:

```
[root@compute01 ~]# ovs-ofctl dump-flows br-eth1
NXST_FLOW reply (xid=0x4):
 cookie=0x0, duration=6114.377s, table=0, n_packets=101, n_bytes=5984, idle_age=723, priority=4,in_port=2,dl_vlan=1 actions=mod_vlan_vid:30,NORMAL
 cookie=0x0, duration=6120.067s, table=0, n_packets=31, n_bytes=2300, idle_age=830, priority=2,in_port=2 actions=drop
 cookie=0x0, duration=6121.345s, table=0, n_packets=27866, n_bytes=1816978, idle_age=1, priority=1 actions=NORMAL
```

These rules should look familiar as they are the same flow rules on the provider bridge shown earlier. This time, however, traffic from the integration bridge connected to port 2 is processed by the first two rules:

```
cookie=0x0, duration=6114.377s, table=0, n_packets=101, n_bytes=5984,
idle_age=723, priority=4,in_port=2,dl_vlan=1 actions=mod_vlan_
vid:30,NORMAL

cookie=0x0, duration=6120.067s, table=0, n_packets=31, n_bytes=2300,
idle_age=830, priority=2,in_port=2 actions=drop
```

The first flow rule on the provider bridge checks the VLAN ID in the Ethernet header, and if it is 1, modifies it to 30 before forwarding the traffic to the physical interface. All other traffic from the integration bridge on port 2 that is not tagged as VLAN 1 is dropped.

Flow rules for a particular network will not exist on a bridge if there are no instances or resources scheduled to that node in that network. The neutron-openvswitch-agent service on each node is responsible for creating the appropriate flow rules for virtual switches on that node.

Flow rules for flat networks

Flat networks in Neutron are untagged networks, which means that there is no 802.1q VLAN tag associated with the network when it is created. Internally, however, Neutron treats flat networks like it does VLAN networks when programming the virtual switches. Flat networks are assigned a local VLAN ID in the Open vSwitch database just like a VLAN network, and instances in the same flat network connected to the same integration bridge are placed in the same local VLAN. However, there is a difference between VLAN and flat networks that can be observed in the flow rules that are created on the integration and provider bridges. Instead of mapping the local VLAN ID to a physical VLAN ID, and vice-versa, as traffic traverses the bridges, the local VLAN ID is added to or stripped from the Ethernet header by flow rules.

In another example, a flat network has been added in Neutron that has no VLAN tag, as follows:

```
Created a new network:
+------------------------------+--------------------------------------+
| Field                        | Value                                |
+------------------------------+--------------------------------------+
| admin_state_up               | True                                 |
| id                           | 0eec5d14-4d67-448d-abbd-01d7e9931217 |
| name                         | FLAT1                                |
| provider:network_type        | flat                                 |
| provider:physical_network    | physnet1                             |
| provider:segmentation_id     |                                      |
| shared                       | False                                |
| status                       | ACTIVE                               |
| subnets                      |                                      |
| tenant_id                    | b1e5de8d1cfc45d6a15d9c0cb442a8ab     |
+------------------------------+--------------------------------------+
```

On the physical switch, this network is configured as the native VLAN (untagged) on the switch port connected to eth1 of compute01. An instance has been spun up on the FLAT1 network that results in the following virtual switch configuration:

```
Bridge br-int
    Port "int-br-eth1"
        Interface "int-br-eth1"
    Port "qvofe2d048e-bc"
        tag: 1
        Interface "qvofe2d048e-bc"
    Port br-int
        Interface br-int
            type: internal
    Port "qvo04c49e4a-a6"
        tag: 3
        Interface "qvo04c49e4a-a6"
    Port patch-tun
        Interface patch-tun
            type: patch
            options: {peer=patch-int}
    Port "qvob7f563c0-c0"
        tag: 2
        Interface "qvob7f563c0-c0"
```

Notice that the port associated with the instance has been assigned a local VLAN ID of 2 even though it is a flat network. On the integration bridge exists a flow rule that modifies the VLAN header of an incoming Ethernet frame when it has no VLAN ID set. Have a look at the following screenshot:

```
[root@compute01 ~]# ovs-ofctl dump-flows br-int
NXST_FLOW reply (xid=0x4):
 cookie=0x0, duration=558.978s, table=0, n_packets=1, n_bytes=70, idle_age=555, priority=3,in_port=2,vlan_tci=0x0000 actions=mod_vlan_vid:2,NORMAL
 cookie=0x0, duration=559.677s, table=0, n_packets=0, n_bytes=0, idle_age=559, priority=3,in_port=2,dl_vlan=30 actions=mod_vlan_vid:1,NORMAL
 cookie=0x0, duration=565.53s, table=0, n_packets=5, n_bytes=398, idle_age=559, priority=2,in_port=2 actions=drop
 cookie=0x0, duration=566.935s, table=0, n_packets=31, n_bytes=2252, idle_age=342, priority=1 actions=NORMAL
```

The result is that incoming traffic is tagged as VLAN 2 and forwarded to instances connected to the integration bridge that reside in VLAN 2.

As return traffic from the instance is processed by flow rules on the provider bridge, the local VLAN ID is stripped and the traffic becomes untagged:

```
[root@compute01 ~]# ovs-ofctl dump-flows br-eth1
NXST_FLOW reply (xid=0x4):
 cookie=0x0, duration=647.829s, table=0, n_packets=4, n_bytes=288, idle_age=641, priority=4,in_port=2,dl_vlan=1 actions=mod_vlan_vid:30,NORMAL
 cookie=0x0, duration=647.129s, table=0, n_packets=10, n_bytes=686, idle_age=430, priority=4,in_port=2,dl_vlan=2 actions=strip_vlan,NORMAL
 cookie=0x0, duration=653.425s, table=0, n_packets=26, n_bytes=1564, idle_age=643, priority=2,in_port=2 actions=drop
 cookie=0x0, duration=654.687s, table=0, n_packets=2983, n_bytes=196849, idle_age=1, priority=1 actions=NORMAL
```

The untagged traffic is then forwarded out physical interface eth1 and processed by the physical switch.

Flow rules for local networks

Local networks in an Open vSwitch implementation behave like those of a LinuxBridge implementation: instances are connected to the integration bridge and can communicate with other instances in the same network or local VLAN. There are no flow rules created for local networks. Traffic between instances in the same network remains local to the virtual switch, and by definition, local to the compute node on which they reside. This means that DHCP and metadata services will be unavailable to any instances not on the same host as those services.

Configuring a layer 2 networking plugin

Before you can start the neutron-server service and consume the Neutron API, a networking plugin must be defined. The remainder of this chapter is dedicated to providing instructions on installing and configuring the monolithic LinuxBridge and Open vSwitch networking plugins.

Switching between the plugins is not a trivial operation and can result in a complete loss of Neutron network configurations. For simplicity, I recommend sticking with the LinuxBridge plugin.

Configuring the LinuxBridge plugin

Neutron was configured to use the LinuxBridge plugin at the end of the preceding chapter to allow you to access the Neutron command-line interface. Other services, such as Nova (Compute) and the DHCP agent, require that a plugin be specified before they can be started as well.

Configuring Nova to use LinuxBridge

In order to properly connect instances to the network, Nova (Compute) must be aware that LinuxBridge is the networking plugin. The `linuxnet_interface_driver` and `libvirt_vif_driver` configuration options in `/etc/nova/nova.conf` instruct Nova (Compute) how to properly connect instances to the network.

Using `crudini`, update the values in `nova.conf`, and use the appropriate LinuxBridge drivers on all nodes, as follows:

```
# crudini --set /etc/nova/nova.conf DEFAULT linuxnet_interface_
driver linuxnet_interface_driver=nova.network.linux_net.
LinuxBridgeInterfaceDriver
```

```
# crudini --set /etc/nova/nova.conf DEFAULT libvirt_vif_driver nova.virt.
libvirt.vif.NeutronLinuxBridgeVIFDriver
```

Configuring the DHCP agent to use LinuxBridge

For Neutron to properly connect DHCP namespace interfaces to the appropriate network bridge, the DHCP agent must be configured to use the LinuxBridge interface driver.

Using `crudini`, set the Neutron DHCP agent `interface_driver` configuration option to use the LinuxBridge driver on the controller node:

```
# crudini --set /etc/neutron/dhcp_agent.ini DEFAULT interface_driver
neutron.agent.linux.interface.BridgeInterfaceDriver
```

Additional DHCP agent configuration options can be found in the preceding chapter.

LinuxBridge plugin configuration options

Once installed, the configuration file for the LinuxBridge plugin can be found at
`/etc/neutron/plugins/linuxbridge/linuxbridge_conf.ini`.

The `linuxbridge_conf.ini` file contains the following configuration options:

- `tenant_network_type`
- `physical_interface_mappings`
- `network_vlan_ranges`
- `firewall_driver`

Tenant network type

The `tenant_network_type` configuration option describes the type of network that
a tenant can create. When using the monolithic LinuxBridge plugin, the supported
tenant network types are `flat`, `vlan`, and `local`.

 The ML2 plugin with LinuxBridge introduced support for VXLAN
overlay networking and the use of a `vxlan` tenant network. At the time of
writing, however, VXLAN is not supported by the CentOS 6.5 kernel.

The `crudini` utility can be used to update the plugin configuration file. Use the
following command to set `tenant_network_type` to `vlan` on all nodes:

```
# crudini --set /etc/neutron/plugins/linuxbridge/linuxbridge_conf.ini
vlans tenant_network_type vlan
```

If, at any time, you wish to change `tenant_network_type`, edit the plugin
configuration file appropriately on all nodes, and restart the LinuxBridge
plugin agent.

Physical interface mappings

The `physical_interface_mappings` configuration option describes the mapping
of an artificial interface name or label to a physical interface in the server. When
networks are created, they are associated with an interface label, such as `physnet1`.
The label `physnet1` is then mapped to a physical interface, such as `eth1`, by the
`physical_interface_mappings` option. This mapping can be observed as follows:

```
physical_interface_mappings = physnet1:eth1
```

The chosen label must be consistent between all nodes in the environment. However, the physical interface mapped to the label may be different. A difference in mappings is often observed when one node maps `physnet1` to a 1 Gbit interface, and another maps `physnet1` to a 10 Gbit interface.

More than one interface mapping is allowed, and can be added to the list using a comma as the separator:

```
physical_interface_mappings = physnet1:eth1,physnet2:eth2
```

In this installation, the `eth1` interface will be utilized as the physical network interface, which means that any VLANs provided for use by tenants must traverse `eth1`. The physical switch port connected to `eth1` must support 802.1q VLAN tagging if VLAN networks are to be created by tenants.

Using `crudini`, configure the LinuxBridge plugin to use `physnet1` as the physical interface label and `eth1` as the physical network interface on all hosts:

```
# crudini --set /etc/neutron/plugins/linuxbridge/linuxbridge_conf.ini
linux_bridge physical_interface_mappings physnet1:eth1
```

Network VLAN ranges

The `network_vlan_ranges` configuration option defines a range of VLANs that tenant networks will be associated with upon their creation. When the number of available VLANs reaches zero, tenants will no longer be able to create networks. This configuration option is only useful when `tenant_network_type` is set to `vlan`. If left blank, only local networks can be created, as the virtual VLAN interfaces will not be created on the host.

Using `crudini`, associate a range of VLANs with physnet1 for use with tenant networks on all hosts:

```
# crudini --set /etc/neutron/plugins/linuxbridge/linuxbridge_conf.ini
vlans network_vlan_ranges physnet1:30:33
```

Firewall driver

The `firewall_driver` configuration option instructs Neutron to use a particular firewall driver for security group functionality. The two available options are:

- `neutron.agent.firewall.NoopFirewallDriver`
- `neutron.agent.linux.iptables_firewall.IptablesFirewallDriver`

If you do not want to use a firewall and want to disable the application of security group rules, set `firewall_driver` to `neutron.agent.firewall.NoopFirewallDriver`. If you do want to use an iptables-based firewall for security groups, set `firewall_driver` to `neutron.agent.linux.iptables_firewall.IptablesFirewallDriver`. By default, the LinuxBridge plugin is configured to use `NoopFirewallDriver`.

In this installation, the iptables-based firewall will be used, and Neutron will handle the configuration of the rules on the hosts. Using `crudini`, set the `firewall_driver` option on all hosts as follows:

```
# crudini --set /etc/neutron/plugins/linuxbridge/linuxbridge_conf.ini
securitygroup firewall_driver neutron.agent.linux.iptables_firewall.
IptablesFirewallDriver
```

Restarting services

Now that the OpenStack configuration files have been modified to use LinuxBridge as the networking plugin, certain services must be started or restarted for the changes to take effect.

The following services should be started on all hosts in the environment and configured to start at boot:

```
# service neutron-linuxbridge-agent start
```

```
# chkconfig neutron-linuxbridge-agent on
```

The following services should be restarted on the controller node:

```
# service openstack-nova-api restart
```

```
# service neutron-server restart
```

```
# service neutron-dhcp-agent restart
```

The following service should be restarted on the compute node:

```
# service openstack-nova-compute restart
```

Configuring the Open vSwitch plugin

The LinuxBridge and Open vSwitch monolithic plugins use different database schemas, making sharing the database between them impossible. The use of ML2 solves this issue by creating a common schema for use by all plugins, not just LinuxBridge and Open vSwitch:

1. On the controller node, create a new database specifically for use with the Open vSwitch plugin using the MySQL client:

   ```
   # mysql -u root -p
   ```

2. Use the password set earlier in the OpenStack installation. In this guide, the password was set to openstack.

3. At the mysql> prompt, execute the following commands to create a database named ovs_neutron and to grant permissions to the neutron user:

   ```
   CREATE DATABASE ovs_neutron;
   GRANT ALL PRIVILEGES ON ovs_neutron.* TO 'neutron'@'localhost'
   IDENTIFIED BY 'neutron';
   GRANT ALL PRIVILEGES ON ovs_neutron.* TO 'neutron'@'%';
   QUIT;
   ```

Configuring Neutron to use Open vSwitch

Before the Open vSwitch plugin can be used, changes must be made to the Neutron configuration on all hosts that include specifying the core plugin and database options.

Configure Neutron to use the following MySQL database connection string using values previously configured earlier in the chapter:

```
# crudini --set /etc/neutron/neutron.conf database connection mysql://
neutron:neutron@controller/ovs_neutron
```

The core_plugin configuration must be set to use the Open vSwitch plugin neutron.plugins.openvswitch.ovs_neutron_plugin.OVSNeutronPluginV2 as follows:

```
# crudini --set /etc/neutron/neutron.conf DEFAULT core_plugin neutron.
plugins.openvswitch.ovs_neutron_plugin.OVSNeutronPluginV2
```

In addition to configuration file changes, a symbolic link named `plugin.ini` must be created in the `/etc/neutron/` directory that points to the appropriate plugin configuration file before `neutron-server` will start. For Open vSwitch, the link can be created with the following command:

```
# ln -s /etc/neutron/plugins/openvswitch/ovs_neutron_plugin.ini /etc/
neutron/plugin.ini
```

The Neutron database must be stamped as the `havana` release before `neutron-server` will start. Use the `neutron-db-manage` command to accomplish this task on the controller only using the following command:

```
# neutron-db-manage --config-file /etc/neutron/plugin.ini --config-file /
etc/neutron/neutron.conf stamp havana
```

If you previously used LinuxBridge and are switching to Open vSwitch, be sure to remove the symbolic link pointing to the LinuxBridge plugin configuration file prior to creating a new one for Open vSwitch.

Configuring Nova to use Open vSwitch

Nova must be aware that Open vSwitch is the networking plugin for instances to be properly connected to the network. The `linuxnet_interface_driver` and `libvirt_vif_driver` configuration options in `/etc/nova/nova.conf` are two settings that must be modified.

Using `crudini`, set the `linuxnet_interface_driver` and `libvirt_vif_driver` options to their proper values on all hosts as follows:

```
# crudini --set /etc/nova/nova.conf DEFAULT linuxnet_interface_driver
nova.network.linux_net.LinuxOVSInterfaceDriver
```

```
# crudini --set /etc/nova/nova.conf DEFAULT libvirt_vif_driver nova.virt.
libvirt.vif.LibvirtHybridOVSBridgeDriver
```

Configuring the DHCP agent to use Open vSwitch

To properly connect DHCP namespace tap interfaces to the integration bridge, the DHCP agent must be configured to use the Open vSwitch interface driver.

Using `crudini`, set the DHCP `interface_driver` configuration option on the controller to use the proper driver:

```
# crudini --set /etc/neutron/dhcp_agent.ini DEFAULT interface_driver
neutron.agent.linux.interface.OVSInterfaceDriver
```

Additional DHCP agent configuration options can be found in the preceding chapter.

Open vSwitch plugin configuration options

Once installed, the configuration file for the Open vSwitch plugin can be found at `/etc/neutron/plugins/openvswitch/ovs_neutron_plugin.ini`.

The `ovs_neutron_plugin.ini` file contains the following commonly used configuration options:

- `tenant_network_type`
- `network_vlan_ranges`
- `enable_tunneling`
- `tunnel_type`
- `tunnel_id_ranges`
- `integration_bridge`
- `tunnel_bridge`
- `local_ip`
- `bridge_mappings`
- `firewall_driver`
- `database`

Bridge mappings

The `bridge_mappings` configuration option describes the mapping of an artificial interface name or label to a network bridge configured on the server. Unlike the LinuxBridge plugin that configures multiple bridges containing individual virtual VLAN interfaces, the Open vSwitch plugin uses a single-bridge interface containing a single physical interface and uses flow rules to add or remove VLAN tags if necessary.

When networks are created they are associated with an interface label, such as `physnet1`. The label `physnet1` is then mapped to a bridge, such as `br-eth1`, that contains a physical interface, such as `eth1`. The mapping of the label to the bridge interface is handled by the `bridge_mappings` option. This mapping can be observed as follows:

```
bridge_mappings = physnet1:br-eth1
```

The label itself must be consistent between all nodes in the environment. However, the bridge interface mapped to the label may be different. A difference in mappings is often observed when one node maps `physnet1` to a 1 Gbit bridge interface, and another maps `physnet1` to a 10 Gbit bridge interface.

More than one interface mapping is allowed and can be added to the list using a comma as the separator as seen in the following example:

```
bridge_mappings = physnet1:br-eth1,physnet2:br-eth2
```

In this installation, `physnet1` will map to `br-eth1`. Use `crudini` to add the bridge mapping to the Open vSwitch plugin configuration file on all hosts as follows:

```
# crudini --set /etc/neutron/plugins/openvswitch/ovs_neutron_plugin.ini
OVS bridge_mappings physnet1:br-eth1
```

Configuring the bridges

Before the Open vSwitch plugin agent can be started, any bridge referenced in the `bridge_mappings` configuration must exist on the host. Start the `openvswitch` service on all hosts to proceed with the bridge configuration and configure it to start at boot:

```
# service openvswitch start
```

```
# chkconfig openvswitch on
```

On all hosts, use the Open vSwitch utility `ovs-vsctl` to create bridge `br-eth1` as follows:

```
# ovs-vsctl add-br br-eth1
```

Use the same command to add the physical interface `eth1` to the bridge:

```
# ovs-vsctl add-port br-eth1 eth1
```

The physical switch port connected to `eth1` must support 802.1q VLAN tagging if VLAN networks of any type are to be created.

Tenant network type

As with the LinuxBridge plugin, the `tenant_network_type` configuration option describes the type of network that a tenant can create. When using the Open vSwitch plugin, the supported tenant network types are `flat`, `vlan`, `local`, `gre`, `vxlan`, and `none`. Administrators are free to create any or all of the five networks at any time as long as the proper configuration and architecture is in place.

Using `crudini`, set the `tenant_network_type` option to `vlan` on all hosts:

```
# crudini --set /etc/neutron/plugins/openvswitch/ovs_neutron_plugin.ini
OVS tenant_network_type vlan
```

If at any time you wish to change `tenant_network_type` to something other than `vlan`, edit the plugin configuration file appropriately on all nodes, and restart the Open vSwitch plugin agent.

Network VLAN ranges

The `network_vlan_ranges` configuration option defines a range of VLANs that tenant networks will be associated with upon their creation when `tenant_network_type` is set to `vlan`. When the number of available VLANs reaches zero, tenants will no longer be able to create networks. If left blank, only GRE, VXLAN, and local networks can be created.

In the following example, VLANs 30 through 33 are available for tenant network allocation:

```
network_vlan_ranges = physnet1:30:33
```

Non-contiguous VLANs can be allocated by using a comma-separated list as follows:

```
network_vlan_ranges = physnet1:30:33,physnet1:50:55,physnet1:66:70
```

The `network_vlan_ranges` configuration option must be configured for the Neutron plugin agent to load properly. At a minimum, you must specify an interface label. In this installation, `physnet1` will be used with VLANs 30 through 33 available for tenant allocation. Use `crudini` to set a value for `network_vlan_ranges` on all hosts as follows:

```
# crudini --set /etc/neutron/plugins/openvswitch/ovs_neutron_plugin.ini
OVS network_vlan_ranges physnet1:30:33
```

If at any time this configuration option is updated, you must restart the `neutron-server` service for the changes to take effect.

Enable tunneling

To enable support for GRE or VXLAN, the `enable_tunneling` configuration option must be set to `true`. Open vSwitch releases newer than Version 1.10 should support both technologies. To determine the version of Open vSwitch you have installed, run `ovs-vsctl -V` as follows:

```
[root@controller ~]# ovs-vsctl -V
ovs-vsctl (Open vSwitch) 1.11.0
Compiled Jul 30 2013 18:14:53
```

To enable GRE or VXLAN tunneling, set the configuration option manually, or use `crudini` to set the option to `true` on all hosts:

```
# crudini --set /etc/neutron/plugins/openvswitch/ovs_neutron_plugin.ini
OVS enable_tunneling true
```

Tunnel type

The `tunnel_type` configuration option specifies the type of tunnel supported by the plugin. The two available options are `gre` and `vxlan`. If left unconfigured, the default value is `gre` when `enable_tunneling` is set to `true`. If using `vxlan`, set this option to `vxlan`.

> As of this writing, both the Havana and Icehouse releases of OpenStack have a bug that does not allow Neutron to properly determine the version of the installed Open vSwitch module in the CentOS and RHEL operating systems. As a result, Neutron is unable to enable VXLAN support using the Open vSwitch kernel module. For more information, please refer to the following bug report:
>
> https://bugs.launchpad.net/neutron/+bug/1322139

Tunnel ID ranges

When GRE- or VXLAN-based networks are created, each network is assigned a unique ID, or segmentation ID, that is used to encapsulate traffic. As traffic traverses the Open vSwitch tunnel bridge, the segmentation ID is used to populate a field in the encapsulation header of the packet. For VXLAN encapsulation, the VXLAN ID header field is used. For GRE packets, the KEY header field is used.

The `tunnel_id_ranges` configuration option is a comma-separated list of ID ranges that are available for tenant network allocation when `tunnel_type` is set to `gre` or `vxlan`.

In the following example, segmentation IDs 1 through 1,000 are to be allocated to tenant networks upon creation:

```
tunnel_id_ranges = 1:1000
```

This `tunnel_id_ranges` option supports non-contiguous IDs as well using a comma separated list as follows:

```
tunnel_id_ranges = 1:1000,2000:2500
```

When all segmentation IDs have been exhausted, tenants will be unable to create new networks. The OpenStack administrator is not bound to the ranges specified in `tunnel_id_ranges` and is free to create networks using any ID.

For this installation, set the value to `1:1000` using `crudini` on all hosts:

```
# crudini --set /etc/neutron/plugins/openvswitch/ovs_neutron_plugin.ini
OVS tunnel_id_ranges 1:1000
```

Integration bridge

The `integration_bridge` configuration option specifies the name of the integration bridge used on each node. There is a single integration bridge per node. As mentioned earlier, the integration bridge is the virtual switch where all virtual machine VIFs, otherwise known as **virtual network interfaces**, are connected. The default name of the integration bridge is `br-int` and should not be modified.

Before the Open vSwitch plugin agent can be started, the integration bridge must exist on the host. On all hosts, use the Open vSwitch utility `ovs-vsctl` to create bridge `br-int` as follows:

```
# ovs-vsctl add-br br-int
```

You do not need to add an interface to the integration bridge, as Neutron is responsible for connecting network resources to this virtual switch.

Tunnel bridge

The tunnel bridge is a virtual switch, similar to the integration and provider bridge, and is used to connect GRE and VXLAN tunnel endpoints. Flow rules exist on this bridge that are responsible for properly encapsulating and decapsulating tenant traffic as it traverses the bridge.

The `tunnel_bridge` configuration option specifies the name of the tunnel bridge. The default value is `br-tun` and should not be modified. It is not necessary to create this bridge, as Neutron does it automatically.

Local IP

The `local_ip` configuration option specifies the local IP address on the node that will be used to build the GRE or VXLAN overlay network between hosts when `enable_tunneling` is set to `true`. Refer to *Chapter 1, Preparing the Network for OpenStack*, for ideas on how the overlay network should be architected. In this installation, all guest traffic through overlay networks will traverse VLAN 20 using a virtual VLAN interface off `eth1`.

The following table provides the IP address and virtual interface name to be created on each host:

Hostname	Interface	IP Address
Controller	`eth1.20`	172.18.0.100
Compute01	`eth1.20`	172.18.0.101

Using `crudini`, set the `local_ip` configuration option accordingly.

On the controller node, run the following command:

```
# crudini --set /etc/neutron/plugins/openvswitch/ovs_neutron_plugin.ini
OVS local_ip 172.18.0.100
```

On the compute node, run the following command:

```
# crudini --set /etc/neutron/plugins/openvswitch/ovs_neutron_plugin.ini
OVS local_ip 172.18.0.101
```

Configuring a virtual VLAN interface for overlay traffic

In CentOS, virtual VLAN interfaces (often called subinterfaces) are configured like physical interfaces are. An interface file should be created in `/etc/sysconfig/network-scripts/` for both the physical interface and the subinterface you are attempting to create.

Using a text editor, create the file `/etc/sysconfig/network-scripts/ifcfg-eth1.20` on each host. The following is the recommended configuration for `eth1.20` on the controller node:

```
DEVICE=eth1.20
BOOTPROTO=none
ONBOOT=yes
IPADDR=172.18.0.100
NETMASK=255.255.255.0
VLAN=yes
```

The following is the recommended configuration for `eth1.20` on the compute node:

```
DEVICE=eth1.20
BOOTPROTO=none
ONBOOT=yes
IPADDR=172.18.0.101
NETMASK=255.255.255.0
VLAN=yes
```

To activate the changes, cycle the interfaces using the `ifdown` and `ifup` commands on each node:

```
# ifdown eth1; ifdown eth1.20; ifup eth1; ifup eth1.20
```

Issue a ping from the controller to the compute node using the 172.18.0.x IP address to confirm connectivity:

```
[root@controller ~]# ping 172.18.0.101
PING 172.18.0.101 (172.18.0.101) 56(84) bytes of data.
64 bytes from 172.18.0.101: icmp_seq=1 ttl=64 time=1.13 ms
64 bytes from 172.18.0.101: icmp_seq=2 ttl=64 time=0.168 ms
^C
--- 172.18.0.101 ping statistics ---
2 packets transmitted, 2 received, 0% packet loss, time 1408ms
rtt min/avg/max/mdev = 0.168/0.650/1.133/0.483 ms
```

Troubleshoot any issues before proceeding with the creation of overlay networks.

Firewall driver

The `firewall_driver` configuration option instructs Neutron to use a particular firewall driver for the security group functionality. The two available options when using OpenvSwitch are:

- `neutron.agent.firewall.NoopFirewallDriver`
- `neutron.agent.linux.iptables_firewall.OVSHybridIptablesFirewallDriver`

If you do not want to use a firewall and want to disable the application of security group rules, set `firewall_driver` to use `neutron.agent.firewall.NoopFirewallDriver`. If you do want to use an iptables-based firewall for security groups, set `firewall_driver` to `neutron.agent.linux.iptables_firewall.OVSHybridIptablesFirewallDriver`.

In this installation, the iptables-based firewall will be used, and Neutron will handle the configuration of the rules on the hosts. You can set the configuration option manually or use `crudini` to set the `firewall_driver` option on all hosts as follows:

```
# crudini --set /etc/neutron/plugins/openvswitch/ovs_neutron_
plugin.ini securitygroup neutron.agent.linux.iptables_firewall.
OVSHybridIptablesFirewallDriver
```

Database

The Open vSwitch plugin configuration file must also be configured to use the proper database before the plugin will operate.

On all hosts, configure the plugin to use the following MySQL database connection string using the new database and values previously configured earlier in the chapter:

```
# crudini --set /etc/neutron/plugins/openvswitch/ovs_neutron_plugin.ini
database connection mysql://neutron:neutron@controller/ovs_neutron
```

Restarting services to enable the Open vSwitch plugin

Now that the OpenStack configuration files have been modified to use Open vSwitch as the networking plugin, certain services must be started or restarted for the changes to take effect.

If you previously configured the LinuxBridge plugin and are switching to the Open vSwitch plugin, be sure to stop the LinuxBridge plugin agent, and disable it from starting at boot:

```
# service neutron-linuxbridge-agent stop
# chkconfig neutron-linuxbridge-agent off
```

The Open vSwitch plugin agent should be started on all nodes and configured to start at boot:

```
# service neutron-openvswitch-agent start
# chkconfig neutron-openvswitch-agent on
```

The following services should be restarted on the controller node:

```
# service neutron-server restart
# service neutron-dhcp-agent restart
```

The following services should be restarted on the compute node:

```
# service openstack-nova-compute restart
```

Summary

Both the LinuxBridge and Open vSwitch networking plugins for Neutron provide unique solutions to the same problem of connecting virtual machine instances to the network. While Open vSwitch provides features not available with the monolithic LinuxBridge plugin, including the use of overlay networks, its configuration, administration, and troubleshooting methods are more complex. Open vSwitch relies on flow rules to determine how traffic in and out of the environment should be processed and requires both user-space utilities and kernel modules to perform such actions. The LinuxBridge plugin requires the 8021q and bridge kernel modules, and relies on the use of virtual VLAN interfaces on the host to provide VLAN tagging of traffic. The advent of the ML2 plugin pairs VXLAN overlay networking technology with the simplicity of Linux bridges. For most environments, I recommend the LinuxBridge approach unless integration with OpenFlow controllers or the use of a third-party solution or plugin is required.

In the next chapter, you will be guided through the process of creating different types of networks to provide connectivity to instances. The process of creating networks is agnostic across plugins, but the underlying network implementation may vary based on the plugin in use.

5
Creating Networks with Neutron

In the previous chapter, you laid down the virtual switching infrastructure that will support cloud networking features moving forward. In this chapter, you will build OpenStack resources on top of this foundation. I will guide you through the following tasks:

- Creating networks and subnets
- Attaching instances to networks
- Demonstrating DHCP and metadata services

Three major Neutron resources, networks, subnets, and ports were introduced in *Chapter 3, Installing Neutron*. The relationship between these resources and instances, DHCP, and metadata services can be seen in the following sections.

Network management

Neutron provides users with the ability to execute commands from the CLI that interface with the Neutron API. To enter the Neutron client, type neutron in the command prompt on the controller node:

```
[root@controller ~]# neutron
(neutron)
```

From the prompt, a number of commands that deal with the creation, modification, and deletion of networks, subnets, and ports in the cloud can be executed.

The primary commands associated with network management are:

- `net-create`
- `net-delete`
- `net-list`
- `net-update`
- `subnet-create`
- `subnet-delete`
- `subnet-list`
- `subnet-show`
- `subnet-update`
- `port-list`
- `port-show`
- `port-update`

Whether you've chosen the LinuxBridge or Open vSwitch networking plugin, the process to create, modify, and delete networks and subnets is the same. Behind the scenes, however, the process of connecting instances and other resources to the network differs between the two plugins.

In the previous chapter, I introduced two categories of networks that provide connectivity to instances:

- Provider networks
- Tenant networks

While there are no real technical differences between a provider and a tenant network, there are differences in how they are utilised by users of the cloud. Provider networks are created by the OpenStack administrator and have attributes that allow them to be connected to the external interfaces of routers, thereby providing external network access to the instances behind them. When provider networks are used as the gateway to the Internet and other external networks, they will often be configured as flat networks or VLANs and utilize an external router to properly route traffic in and out of the cloud. Tenants are prevented from attaching instances directly to external provider networks.

Tenant networks, on the other hand, are created by users and are isolated from other networks in the cloud by default. The inability to configure the physical infrastructure means that tenants should connect their networks to Neutron routers when external connectivity is required. More information on the configuration and use of Neutron routers can be found in *Chapter 6, Creating Routers with Neutron*.

Managing networks in the CLI

To view the syntax necessary to create a network using the Neutron client, type net-create -h at the (neutron) prompt:

```
(neutron) net-create -h

usage: net-create [-h] [-f {shell,table}] [-c COLUMN]
          [--variable VARIABLE] [--prefix PREFIX]
          [--request-format {json,xml}]
          [--tenant-id TENANT_ID]
          [--admin-state-down] [--shared]
          NAME
```

The usage syntax here fails to list all of the configurable properties of a provider network. For reference, the following are the three provider attributes that can be defined:

- provider:network_type
- provider:physical_network
- provider:segmentation_id

Other attributes that can be set for provider networks include:

- router:external
- shared

Options that can be set for both provider and tenant networks include:

- admin-state-down
- tenant-id

The network_type provider attribute defines the type of network being created. Available options include flat, vlan, local, gre, and vxlan, depending on the networking plugin in use. As a provider network, an overlay network type such as GRE or VXLAN would be a rare choice. However, the OpenStack administrator can create GRE or VXLAN networks on behalf of tenants by specifying a tenant ID.

The physical_network provider attribute defines the physical interface that will be used to forward traffic through the host. The value specified here corresponds to the bridge_mappings or physical_interface_mappings option set in the LinuxBridge or Open vSwitch plugin configuration file.

The `segmentation_id` provider attribute specifies the unique ID for the network. If you are creating a VLAN, the value used for `segmentation_id` should be the 802.1q VLAN ID trunked to the host. If you are creating a GRE or VXLAN network, the `segmentation_id` value should be an arbitrary, but unique, integer not used by any other network of the same type. This ID is used to provide network isolation via the GRE key or VXLAN VNI header field, depending on the network. When `segmentation_id` is not specified, one is automatically allocated from the tenant range specified in the plugin configuration file. Users have no visibility or option to specify an ID when creating networks. When all available IDs in the range available to tenants are exhausted, users will no longer be able to create networks of this type.

The `router:external` attribute is a Boolean value that, when set to `true`, allows the network to be utilized as a gateway network for Neutron routers. For more information on Neutron routers, refer to *Chapter 6, Creating Routers with Neutron*.

The `shared` switch is a Boolean value that, when set to `true`, allows the network to be utilized amongst all tenants. This attribute is available *only* for networks created by administrators and is *not* available for networks created by users.

The `admin-state-down` switch is a Boolean value that, when set to `true`, means that the network is not available upon creation.

Finally, the `tenant-id` option allows the administrator to create networks on behalf of the tenants.

Creating a flat network in the CLI

If you recall from *Chapter 4, Building a Virtual Switching Infrastructure*, a flat network is a network in which no 802.1q VLAN tagging takes place.

The syntax to create a flat network can be seen here:

```
Syntax: net-create --provider:network_type=flat
        --provider:physical_network=<provider_bridge_label>
        [--router:external=true] [--tenant-id TENANT_ID]
        [--admin-state-down] [--shared]
        NAME
```

 Attributes in the `[]` brackets are considered optional and are not required to create the network.

The following is an example of using the Neutron `net-create` command to create a flat network with the name `MyFlatNetwork`. The network will utilize a bridge labeled `physnet1` and can be shared by all tenants. The command is as follows:

```
(neutron) net-create --provider:network_type=flat --provider:physical_
network=physnet1 --shared MyFlatNetwork
```

The output from the `net-create` command is as follows:

```
(neutron) net-create --provider:network_type=flat --provider:physical_network=physnet1 --shared MyFlatNetwork
Created a new network:
+---------------------------+--------------------------------------+
| Field                     | Value                                |
+---------------------------+--------------------------------------+
| admin_state_up            | True                                 |
| id                        | 3b56346d-9f9a-4447-98f1-4eb470cdad6d |
| name                      | MyFlatNetwork                        |
| provider:network_type     | flat                                 |
| provider:physical_network | physnet1                             |
| provider:segmentation_id  |                                      |
| shared                    | True                                 |
| status                    | ACTIVE                               |
| subnets                   |                                      |
| tenant_id                 | b1e5de8d1cfc45d6a15d9c0cb442a8ab     |
+---------------------------+--------------------------------------+
```

In the preceding output, the tenant ID corresponds to the `admin` tenant where the `net-create` command was executed. As the network is shared, all tenants can create instances and network resources that utilize the `MyFlatNetwork` network.

 You can only create one flat network per provider bridge, as there is no mechanism to segment traffic.

Creating a VLAN in the CLI

A VLAN is one in which Neutron will tag traffic based on an 802.1q VLAN ID. The syntax used to create a VLAN is provided in the `net-create` command:

```
Syntax: net-create --provider:network_type=vlan
        --provider:physical_network=<provider_bridge_label>
        --provider:segmentation_id=<vlan_id>
        [--router:external=true] [--tenant-id TENANT_ID]
        [--admin-state-down] [--shared]
        NAME
```

> Attributes in the [] brackets are considered optional and are
> not required to create the network.

The following is an example of using the Neutron `net-create` command to create
a VLAN by the name of MyVLANNetwork. The network will utilize the same bridge
labeled `physnet1`, and the traffic will be tagged as VLAN ID 200. By specifying the
`--shared` flag, the network can be shared by all tenants:

```
(neutron) net-create --provider:network_type=vlan --provider:physical_
network=physnet1 --provider:segmentation_id=200 --shared MyVLANNetwork
```

The resulting output is as follows:

> You can create more than one VLAN per provider bridge.
> Additional networks on the same bridge must have a unique
> segmentation ID.

To create an additional network on the same `physnet1` bridge, simply specify
another segmentation ID. In the following example, VLAN 201 is used for the new
network, MyVLANNetwork2:

```
(neutron) net-create --provider:network_type=vlan --provider:physical_
network=physnet1 --provider:segmentation_id=201 --shared MyVLANNetwork2
```

The resulting output is as follows:

```
(neutron) net-create --provider:network_type=vlan --provider:physical_network=physnet1 --provider:segmentation_id=201 --shared MyVLANNetwork2
Created a new network:
+----------------------------+--------------------------------------+
| Field                      | Value                                |
+----------------------------+--------------------------------------+
| admin_state_up             | True                                 |
| id                         | cb88384c-ebd1-4277-b01e-6f707170004f |
| name                       | MyVLANNetwork2                       |
| provider:network_type      | vlan                                 |
| provider:physical_network  | physnet1                             |
| provider:segmentation_id   | 201                                  |
| shared                     | True                                 |
| status                     | ACTIVE                               |
| subnets                    |                                      |
| tenant_id                  | b1e5de8d1cfc45d6a15d9c0cb442a8ab     |
+----------------------------+--------------------------------------+
```

Creating a local network in the CLI

When an instance sends traffic on a local network, the traffic remains local to the
network bridge connected to the instance. Services such as DHCP and metadata
might not be available to instances on local networks, especially if they are located
on a different node.

To create a local network, use the following syntax:

```
Syntax: net-create --provider:network_type=local
[--tenant-id TENANT_ID] [--admin-state-down] [--shared]
NAME
```

When using the LinuxBridge plugin, a bridge is created for the local network, but no
physical or virtual VLAN interface is added. Traffic is kept local to this bridge. Using
the Open vSwitch plugin, instances are attached to the integration bridge, and can
only communicate with other instances in the same local VLAN.

Listing networks in the CLI

To list the existing networks in Neutron, use the net-list command as follows:

```
(neutron) net-list
+--------------------------------------+----------------+---------+
| id                                   | name           | subnets |
+--------------------------------------+----------------+---------+
| 3b56346d-9f9a-4447-98f1-4eb470cdad6d | MyFlatNetwork  |         |
| c4272c0b-4430-427a-a537-81bd733c2266 | MyVLANNetwork  |         |
| cb88384c-ebd1-4277-b01e-6f707170004f | MyVLANNetwork2 |         |
+--------------------------------------+----------------+---------+
```

The list output provides the network ID, network name, and any associated subnets.
The OpenStack administrator can see all networks, while tenants can see shared
networks or networks that they have created.

Showing network properties in the CLI

To list the properties of a network, use the Neutron net-show command as follows:

`Syntax: net-show <network uuid or name>`

The output of the command can be seen in the following screenshot:

```
(neutron) net-show c4272c0b-4430-427a-a537-81bd733c2266
+---------------------------+--------------------------------------+
| Field                     | Value                                |
+---------------------------+--------------------------------------+
| admin_state_up            | True                                 |
| id                        | c4272c0b-4430-427a-a537-81bd733c2266 |
| name                      | MyVLANNetwork                        |
| provider:network_type     | vlan                                 |
| provider:physical_network | physnet1                             |
| provider:segmentation_id  | 200                                  |
| router:external           | False                                |
| shared                    | True                                 |
| status                    | ACTIVE                               |
| subnets                   |                                      |
| tenant_id                 | b1e5de8d1cfc45d6a15d9c0cb442a8ab     |
+---------------------------+--------------------------------------+
```

Information about the specified network, including the network type, provider bridge, segmentation ID, and more, can be observed in the net-show output.

Updating networks in the CLI

At times, it might be necessary to update the attributes of a network after it has been created. To update a network, use the Neutron net-update command as follows:

`Syntax: net-update <network uuid or name>`

`[--router:external] [--shared] [--admin-state-up]`

Provider attributes are among those that cannot be changed once a network has been created. The following attributes, however, can be modified:

- `router:external`
- `shared`
- `admin-state-up`

The `router:external` attribute is a Boolean value that, when set to `true`, allows the network to be utilized as a gateway network for Neutron routers. For more information on Neutron routers, refer to *Chapter 6, Creating Routers with Neutron.*

The `shared` switch is a Boolean value that, when set to `true`, allows the network to be used by all tenants.

The `admin-state-up` switch is a Boolean value. When this is set to `false`, DHCP and metadata services are no longer available in the network. The network interfaces within the DHCP namespace are destroyed, and any instance that attempts to obtain or renew a lease will fail. When set to `true`, DHCP and metadata services are restored.

Deleting networks in the CLI

To delete a network, use the Neutron `net-delete` command and specify the UUID or name of the network:

`Syntax: net-delete <network uuid or name>`

To delete a network named `MyFlatNetwork`, you can enter the following command:

`(neutron) net-delete MyFlatNetwork`

Alternatively, you can use the network's UUID:

`(neutron) net-delete 3b56346d-9f9a-4447-98f1-4eb470cdad6d`

Neutron will successfully delete the network as long as there are no instances or other network resources, including floating IPs or load balancer VIPs, utilizing it.

Creating networks in the dashboard

Networks can be created in the dashboard either as an administrator or user. Both have their own methods, which are described in the upcoming sections.

Using the Admin tab as an administrator

In order to create a network in the dashboard as the cloud administrator, perform the following steps:

1.   Navigate to **Admin** | **System Panel** | **Networks**:

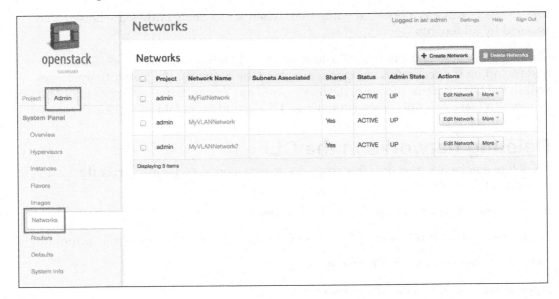

2.   Click on **Create Network** in the upper right-hand corner of the screen. A window that lets us create a network will pop up:

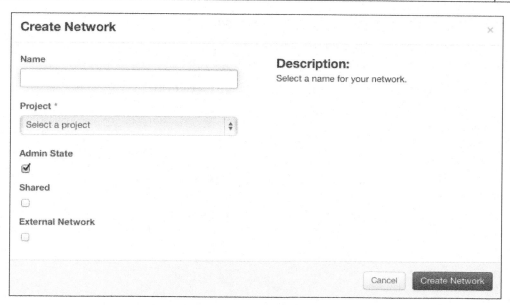

The available options include associating the network with a project (or tenant), setting the admin state on or off, enabling sharing, and enabling the network to be used as an external network for Neutron routers.

Notice that there is no option to specify either the *type* of network to be created or a segmentation ID. Networks created via the dashboard are limited to network types specified by the `tenant_network_type` configuration option defined in the Neutron plugin configuration file. This limitation means most provider networks will need to be created within the CLI.

Using the Project tab as a user

As a normal user, networks are created under the **Project** tab in the dashboard. To create a network as a user, perform the following steps:

1. Navigate to **Project** | **Manage Network** | **Networks**:

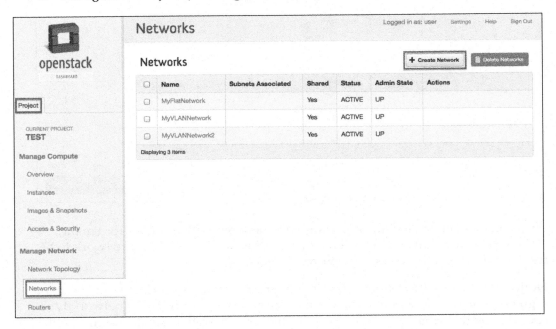

   From here, notice that there are no actions available next to the networks currently defined. Even though the networks are shared, they are not editable by users and must be edited by an administrator.

2. Click on **Create Network** in the upper right-hand corner of the screen. A window that lets us create a network will pop up:

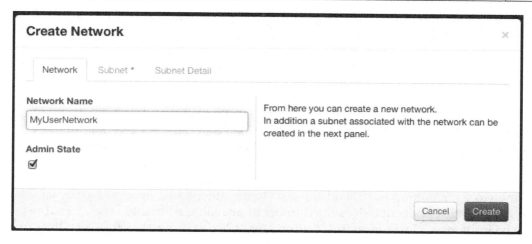

From the **Network** tab, you can define **Network Name** and **Admin State** (on or off). Marking a network as **Shared** or **External**, as seen in the admin panel earlier, is only available to networks created by an administrator.

Users creating networks within the dashboard are required to create a subnet at the time the network is created. The process to create subnets will be explained later in this chapter.

Subnets in Neutron

Once a network has been created, the next step is to create a subnet within the network. A subnet in Neutron is a layer 3 resource, and can be an IPv4 or IPv6 network defined by the **classless inter-domain routing (CIDR)** notation. CIDR is a method of allocating IP addresses and routing IP packets, and it is based on **variable-length subnet masking (VLSM)**. VLSM allows a network to be divided into various sized subnets, providing the opportunity to size a network more appropriately for local needs. More information on CIDR and VLSM can be found on Wikipedia at http://en.wikipedia.org/wiki/Classless_Inter-Domain_Routing.

A few examples of subnets in the CIDR notation are described as follows:

- 192.168.100.50/24 represents the IP address 192.168.100.50, its associated routing prefix 192.168.100.0, and the subnet mask 255.255.255.0 (that is, 24 "1" bits)

- 172.16.1.200/23 represents the IP address 172.16.0.200, its associated routing prefix 172.16.0.0, and the subnet mask 255.255.254.0 (that is, 23 "1" bits)

- 10.0.10.4/22 represents the IP address 10.0.10.4, its associated routing prefix 10.0.8.0, and the subnet mask 255.255.252.0 (that is, 22 "1" bits)

The CIDR notation can be used to quickly identify the total number of IP addresses in a subnet. For example, the subnet mask 255.255.255.0 in the CIDR notation is /24. To determine the number of host IP addresses available in /24, subtract 24 from 32 or from the total number of bits in an IPv4 address. Take the remainder, which is 8, and use it as x in the following formula:

```
2ˣ = number of addresses in a subnet
```

Using the following formula, it can be determined that there are 256 IP addresses in /24 (2^8 = 256). One great thing about dealing with powers of two is that every incremental increase of the exponent doubles the number of available host addresses. The /23 subnet can be written as 2^9, resulting in 512 addresses, and /22 can be written as 2^{10}, resulting in 1024 addresses. On the other hand, every incremental decrease of the exponent halves the number of available addresses. The /25 subnet can be written as 2^7, resulting in 128 addresses, /26 can be written as 2^6, resulting in 64 host addresses, and so on.

Not every address in the subnet might be useable, however, as the first and last addresses are usually reserved as the network and broadcast addresses, respectively. Neutron will *not* assign the first or last address of a subnet to resources, including instances. Use the following formula to determine the total number of useable addresses in a subnet when sizing your network. The x variable represents the number of host bits available in the subnet mask:

```
2ˣ-2 = number of useable addresses in a subnet
```

When creating a subnet, it is important to plan ahead, as neither the CIDR nor the DHCP allocation pool is a currently updateable attribute. When instances and other resources consume all of the available IP addresses in a subnet, devices can no longer be added to the network. A new subnet will need to be created and added to the network. Depending on your network infrastructure, this might not be an easy change to implement.

Creating subnets in the CLI

To view the syntax necessary to create a subnet using the Neutron client, type `subnet-create -h` in the (neutron) prompt:

```
(neutron) subnet-create -h

usage: subnet-create [-h] [-f {shell,table}] [-c COLUMN]
       [--variable VARIABLE][--prefix PREFIX]
       [--request-format {json,xml}][--tenant-id TENANT_ID]
       [--name NAME][--ip-version {4,6}] [--gateway GATEWAY_IP]
       [--no-gateway][--allocation-pool start=IP_ADDR,end=IP_ADDR]
       [--host-route destination=CIDR,nexthop=IP_ADDR]
       [--dns-nameserver DNS_NAMESERVER] [--disable-dhcp]
       NETWORK CIDR
```

The `prefix` attribute is not defined in the v2 API and can be safely ignored.

The `tenant-id` attribute specifies the tenant ID the subnet should be associated with. This should be the same tenant associated with the parent network.

The `name` attribute specifies the name of the subnet. While you can create multiple subnets with the same name, it is recommended that subnet names remain unique for easy identification.

The `ip-version` attribute defines the version of the Internet protocol in use by the subnet. Possible options include 4 for IPv4 and 6 for IPv6. IPv4 is the default when the version is not specified.

The `gateway` attribute defines the gateway address for the subnet. When the subnet is attached to the instance side of a Neutron router, the router's interface will be configured with the address specified here. The address is then used as the default gateway for instances in the subnet. If the subnet is attached to the external side of a Neutron router, the address is used as the default gateway for the router itself. To see this behavior in action, refer to *Chapter 6, Creating Routers with Neutron.*

The `no-gateway` attribute is a Boolean value that, when set to `true`, instructs Neutron not to automatically reserve an IP for use as the gateway for the subnet. It also triggers the injection of a metadata route via DHCP when `enable_isolated_metadata` is set to `true` in the DHCP configuration file.

The `allocation-pool` attribute defines the range of IP addresses within the subnet that can be assigned to instances. Depending on the type of network in use, it is possible for devices outside of OpenStack to utilize the same subnet. Instances can be limited to a subset of addresses in the subnet so that they can coexist with devices outside of the OpenStack cloud.

The `host-route` attribute defines one or more static routes to be injected via DHCP. Multiple routes listed as `destination` and `nexthop` pairs can be separated by a space. The default maximum number of routes per subnet is 20 and can be modified in the `/etc/neutron/neutron.conf` file.

The `dns-nameserver` attribute sets the nameservers for the subnet. The default maximum number of nameservers is five per subnet; this can be modified in the `/etc/neutron/neutron.conf` file.

The `disable-dhcp` attribute is a Boolean value that, when set to `true`, disables DHCP services for the subnet. Instances that rely on DHCP to procure or renew a lease might lose IP connectivity when DHCP is disabled.

The `NETWORK` argument defines the network the subnet should be associated with. Multiple subnets can be associated with a single network as long as the subnet does not overlap with another in the same network. `NETWORK` can be the UUID or the name of a network.

The `CIDR` argument defines the CIDR notation of the subnet being created.

> Despite the syntax output here, both the `NETWORK` and `CIDR` arguments are positional arguments and should be placed at the beginning of the `subnet-create` command, before any other options.

Creating a subnet in the CLI

A subnet can be created from within the Neutron client using the `subnet-create` command, as follows:

```
Syntax: subnet-create NETWORK CIDR --name <name> --ip-version=4
--gateway=<gateway ip> --allocation-pool start=<start addr>,end=<end
addr> --dns-nameservers <dns server1> <dns server2>
```

To demonstrate this command in action, a request has been made to create a subnet within the `MyFlatNetwork` network with the following characteristics:

- **Internet Protocol**: IPv4
- **Subnet**: 192.168.100.0/24
- **Subnet mask**: 255.255.255.0
- **External gateway**: 192.168.100.1
- **DNS servers**: 8.8.8.8, 8.8.4.4

To create the subnet and associate it with `MyFlatNetwork`, the following syntax can be used:

```
(neutron) subnet-create MyFlatNetwork 192.168.100.0/24 --name
MyFlatSubnet --ip-version=4 --gateway=192.168.100.1 --allocation-pool sta
rt=192.168.100.2,end=192.168.100.254 --dns-nameservers 8.8.8.8 8.8.4.4
```

Using --dns-nameservers rather than --dns-nameserver allows you to specify more than one nameserver address using a space-separated list.

The output of the preceding command is seen in the following screenshot:

```
(neutron) subnet-create MyFlatNetwork 192.168.100.0/24 --name MyFlatSubnet --ip-version=4 --gateway=192.168.100.1
--allocation-pool start=192.168.100.2,end=192.168.100.254 --dns-nameservers 8.8.8.8 8.8.4.4
Created a new subnet:
+------------------+--------------------------------------------------+
| Field            | Value                                            |
+------------------+--------------------------------------------------+
| allocation_pools | {"start": "192.168.100.2", "end": "192.168.100.254"} |
| cidr             | 192.168.100.0/24                                 |
| dns_nameservers  | 8.8.4.4                                          |
|                  | 8.8.8.8                                          |
| enable_dhcp      | True                                             |
| gateway_ip       | 192.168.100.1                                    |
| host_routes      |                                                  |
| id               | 739b5bfd-d224-45bc-89b3-b29147be075d             |
| ip_version       | 4                                                |
| name             | MyFlatSubnet                                     |
| network_id       | 3b56346d-9f9a-4447-98f1-4eb470cdad6d             |
| tenant_id        | b1e5de8d1cfc45d6a15d9c0cb442a8ab                 |
+------------------+--------------------------------------------------+
```

Listing subnets in the CLI

To list existing subnets in Neutron, use the subnet-list command, as shown in the following screenshot:

```
(neutron) subnet-list
+--------------------------------------+--------------+------------------+-------------------------------------------------------+
| id                                   | name         | cidr             | allocation_pools                                      |
+--------------------------------------+--------------+------------------+-------------------------------------------------------+
| 739b5bfd-d224-45bc-89b3-b29147be075d | MyFlatSubnet | 192.168.100.0/24 | {"start": "192.168.100.2", "end": "192.168.100.254"}  |
+--------------------------------------+--------------+------------------+-------------------------------------------------------+
```

The list output provides the subnet ID, subnet name, CIDR notation, and the DHCP allocation range of all subnets when executed as an administrator. As a user, the command returns subnets within the tenant or subnets associated with shared networks.

Showing subnet properties in the CLI

To list the properties of a subnet, use the Neutron `subnet-show` command, as shown in the following screenshot:

```
(neutron) subnet-show 739b5bfd-d224-45bc-89b3-b29147be075d
+------------------+--------------------------------------------------------+
| Field            | Value                                                  |
+------------------+--------------------------------------------------------+
| allocation_pools | {"start": "192.168.100.2", "end": "192.168.100.254"}   |
| cidr             | 192.168.100.0/24                                       |
| dns_nameservers  | 8.8.4.4                                                |
|                  | 8.8.8.8                                                |
| enable_dhcp      | True                                                   |
| gateway_ip       | 192.168.100.1                                          |
| host_routes      |                                                        |
| id               | 739b5bfd-d224-45bc-89b3-b29147be075d                   |
| ip_version       | 4                                                      |
| name             | MyFlatSubnet                                           |
| network_id       | 3b56346d-9f9a-4447-98f1-4eb470cdad6d                   |
| tenant_id        | b1e5de8d1cfc45d6a15d9c0cb442a8ab                       |
+------------------+--------------------------------------------------------+
```

Updating a subnet in the CLI

To update a subnet in the CLI, use the Neutron `subnet-update` command:

```
(neutron) subnet-update -h
usage: subnet-update [-h] [--request-format {json,xml}] SUBNET
```

Not all the attributes of a subnet can be updated after it has been created. The following attributes can be updated:

- `dns_nameservers`
- `enable_dhcp`
- `gateway_ip`
- `host_routes`

 Attempting to update an attribute not listed here might result in a **400 Bad Request** error being returned.

The `dns-nameservers` attribute sets the nameservers for the subnet. To update the nameservers in a subnet, use the Neutron `subnet-update` command and specify the new nameservers in a space-separated list with the `dns_nameservers` option, as seen in the following command:

```
(neutron) subnet-update <subnet uuid or name> --dns-nameservers <dns
server1> <dns server2>
```

The `enable-dhcp` attribute is a Boolean value that, when set to `true`, enables DHCP services in the subnet. To enable or disable DHCP in a subnet, use the Neutron `subnet-update` command and specify `true` or `false` as follows:

```
(neutron) subnet-update <subnet uuid or name> --enable-dhcp=<true|false>
```

The `gateway_ip` attribute sets the default gateway for the subnet. To overwrite an existing gateway address, use the Neutron `subnet-update` command and specify a new value for `gateway_ip`, as shown in the following command:

```
(neutron) subnet-update <subnet uuid or name> --gateway_ip=<gateway
address>
```

To completely remove a gateway address from the subnet, use the `action=clear` directive as follows:

```
(neutron) subnet-update <subnet uuid or name> --gateway_ip action=clear
```

 Not all commands support the `action=clear` directive to destroy option values.

The `host-routes` attribute defines one or more routes to be injected via DHCP. To update a subnet to provide additional routes, use the Neutron `subnet-update` command with the `host-routes` option, as demonstrated in the following command:

```
(neutron) subnet-update <subnet uuid or name> --host-routes type=dict
list=true destination=10.0.0.0/24,nexthop=192.168.100.5 destination=172.1
6.0.0/24,nexthop=192.168.100.10
```

 The `type=dict` and `list=true` attributes are required to help Python interpret the data being passed in the form of `destination` and `nexthop` key/value pairs.

Using `subnet-update` to update the existing `dns_nameservers` or `host_routes` value will result in the overwriting of existing values. To avoid possible network-related downtime, care should be taken to ensure that workloads are not affected by changes made to subnet attributes such as `enable_dhcp`, `gateway_ip`, and others. Changes made to these options can affect the running instances.

Creating subnets in the dashboard

Subnets can be created in the dashboard either as an administrator or user. Both have their own methods, which are described in the upcoming sections.

Using the Admin tab as an administrator

To create a subnet as the cloud administrator, perform the following steps:

1. Navigate to **Admin | System Panel | Networks**, and click on the name of the network you wish to add a subnet to, as in the following screenshot:

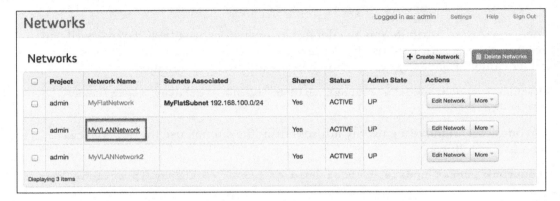

2. Clicking on **MyVLANNetwork** provides a list of details of the network, including the associated subnets and ports:

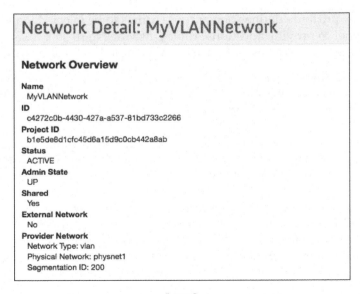

3. To add a subnet to the network, click on the **Create Subnet** button on the right-hand side:

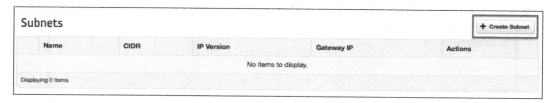

4. A window will appear that will allow you to define the properties of the subnet:

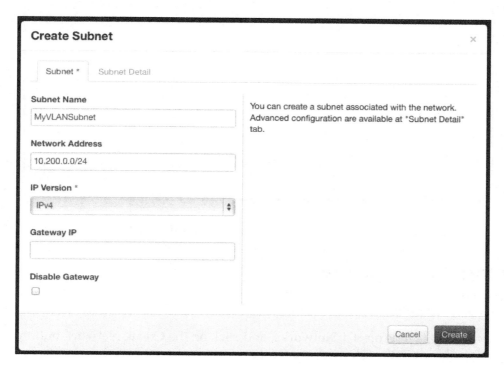

5. Each option pictured here corresponds to an option available with the Neutron `subnet-create` command. Clicking on **Subnet Detail** reveals additional configuration options:

6. To complete the creation of the subnet, click on the blue **Create** button.

Using the Project tab as a user

In the dashboard, users are required to create networks and subnets at the same time. To create a network and subnet as a user, perform the following steps:

1. Navigate to **Project | Networks**, and click on the **Create Network** button, as shown in the following screenshot:

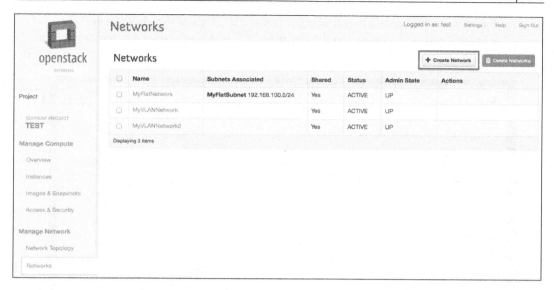

2. Clicking on **Create Network** will open a window where you can specify the network and subnet details:

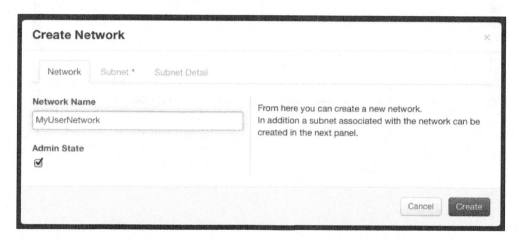

3. As a user, you cannot create shared networks. This ability is reserved for administrators. Clicking on the **Subnet** tab allows you to specify information on the subnet, including the network address, CIDR, and gateway information:

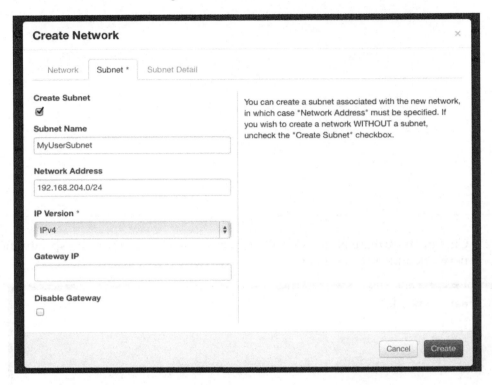

4. Finally, clicking on **Subnet Detail** allows you to specify details such as the DHCP allocation pool, DNS nameservers, and static routes. Click on the blue **Create** button to complete the creation of the network and subnet:

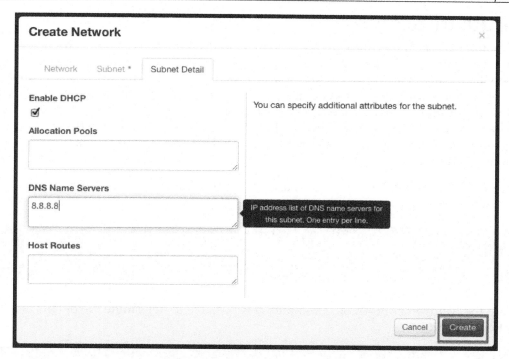

The ability to add additional subnets or delete the network entirely is provided within the **More** menu, pictured in the following screenshot:

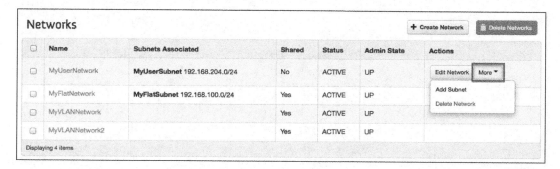

Neutron ports

As mentioned earlier in this chapter, a port in Neutron is a logical connection of a cloud resource to a subnet. By storing the state of cloud networks in a database, OpenStack is aware of every cloud resource or device connected to a Neutron subnet. The information in the Neutron database is used to build the switching connections at the physical or virtual switch layer through the networking plugin and agent. Resources that utilize Neutron ports include virtual interfaces associated with instances and interfaces associated with DHCP, router, and vip namespaces, among others.

To retrieve a list of all Neutron ports, use the Neutron `port-list` command, as shown in the following screenshot:

Using the Neutron `port-show` command, it is possible to determine the details of a particular port:

The port here is owned by an interface used by a DHCP namespace. The `network_id` field reveals the network to be 3b56346d-9f9a-4447-98f1-4eb470cdad6d, otherwise known as `MyFlatNetwork`. The interface's MAC address corresponds to the mentioned `mac_address` field, while the name of the interface corresponds to the Neutron port UUID.

```
[root@controller ~]# ip netns exec qdhcp-3b56346d-9f9a-4447-98f1-4eb470cdad6d ip a
15: tap8e955573-bd  <BROADCAST,UP,LOWER_UP> mtu 1500 qdisc noqueue state UNKNOWN
    link/ether fa:16:3e:ea:69:72 brd ff:ff:ff:ff:ff:ff
    inet 192.168.100.2/24 brd 192.168.100.255 scope global tap8e955573-bd
    inet 169.254.169.254/16 brd 169.254.255.255 scope global tap8e955573-bd
    inet6 fe80::f816:3eff:feea:6972/64 scope link
       valid_lft forever preferred_lft forever
17: lo: <LOOPBACK,UP,LOWER_UP> mtu 16436 qdisc noqueue state UNKNOWN
    link/loopback 00:00:00:00:00:00 brd 00:00:00:00:00:00
    inet 127.0.0.1/8 scope host lo
    inet6 ::1/128 scope host
       valid_lft forever preferred_lft forever
```

Attaching instances to networks

Instances can be attached to networks in a variety of ways. At the first boot, an instance can be attached to a network using the nova boot command. Running instances can be attached to networks using the nova interface-attach command. Both methods are explained in the upcoming sections.

Attaching instances to networks using Nova boot

Instances are attached to networks at the first boot through the nova boot command, the dashboard, or the Nova API. The following nova boot flag provides a network interface to an instance:

```
--nic net-id=<UUID of Neutron network>
```

By passing the --nic flag multiple times, it is possible to attach an instance to more than one Neutron network. The following nova boot command demonstrates the procedure of connecting an instance to multiple networks at the first boot:

```
nova boot --flavor <flavor-id> --image <image-id> --nic net-id=<network-uuid1> --nic net-id=<network-uuid2> --nic net-id=<network-uuid3> InstanceName
```

Nova attaches instances to networks with a virtual interface or VIF. Each VIF has a corresponding Neutron port in the database. In the preceding example, the InstanceName instance was connected to three different Neutron networks. When using Open vSwitch, each VIF will have its own corresponding veth pair (qvo, qva) and Linux bridge (qbr). When using the LinuxBridge plugin, each VIF resides in the Linux bridge associated with the attached network. Attaching multiple network interfaces to an instance is referred to as **multihoming**.

When multihoming an instance, neither Neutron nor the instance itself is aware of which network takes precedence over another. When attached networks and subnets have their own respective gateway address set, an instance's routing table can be populated with multiple default routes. This scenario can wreak havoc on the connectivity and routing behavior of an instance.

Attaching and detaching network interfaces

When an instance is first booted, Neutron creates a port that maps the MAC address of the VIF and the allocated IP address to the instance.

There are times when it might be necessary to add an additional NIC to a running instance and have it connected to a network. Using the `nova interface-attach` command, you can specify an existing port or create a new port based on specific network or IP requirements.

The `nova interface-attach` command syntax is as follows:

```
nova interface-attach [--port-id <port_id>] [--net-id <net_id>]
                      [--fixed-ip <fixed_ip>]
                      <server>
```

The `--port-id` option allows users to attach an existing Neutron port to an instance. The port must be one that is not currently associated with any other instance or resource.

The `--net-id` option allows users to attach a new interface to an instance from the specified network. A new port that has a unique MAC address and an IP from the specified network is created in Neutron. It is possible to attach an instance to the same network multiple times using multiple `nova interface-attach` commands.

The `--fixed-ip` option can be used in conjunction with the `--net-id` options and allows users to specify a particular IP address for use rather than the next available address in the subnet.

To detach an interface from an instance, use the `nova interface-detach` command as follows:

```
nova interface-detach <server> <port_id>
```

Interfaces detached from instances are removed completely from the Neutron port database.

Adding secondary addresses to interfaces

The default behavior of Neutron is to associate a single IP address with a port. Iptables rules are programmed by Neutron on the compute node that hosts the instance that permits traffic from the instance matching the IP and MAC address of the associated Neutron port. The purpose of this feature is to prevent IP and MAC address spoofing. For more information on source address filtering and security groups, see *Chapter 8, Protecting Instances on the Network*.

There are cases, however, when multiple IP addresses must exist on a single interface in the guest OS. Common scenarios include web hosting with SSL certificates and database clustering. A not-so-common scenario will be one in which an instance is used to route traffic between multiple networks. In this case, additional IP addresses will not be necessary, but the instance will be expected to route traffic from addresses it does not own.

A feature was added to the Havana release of Neutron that addresses the need to have multiple IP or MAC addresses on a single interface within an instance. A Neutron extension called **allowed-address-pairs** provides the ability to update a Neutron port with a set of allowed IP addresses and MAC addresses, other than the IP address initially assigned to the port. When addresses are allowed through the port via the allowed-address-pairs extension, iptables rules on the compute node that hosts the instance are updated appropriately.

 The allowed-address-pairs Neutron extension is currently only supported by the ML2, Open vSwitch, and VMware NSX plugins.

To get a better understanding of how this feature works, observe the standard iptables rules on a compute node that disallows traffic from a particular instance if it is not sourced appropriately. The following example is based on an instance whose interface corresponds to the `b67c75e5-4f9f-4770-ae72-dd6a144ddd26` Neutron port:

```
-A neutron-openvswi-sb67c75e5-4 -s 192.168.100.3/32 -m mac --mac-source
fa:16:3e:02:55:34 -j RETURN

-A neutron-openvswi-sb67c75e5-4 -j DROP
```

Based on the preceding example, traffic from the instance must be sourced from `192.168.100.3` and the source MAC address of `fa:16:3e:02:55:34`. Otherwise, the traffic will be dropped.

To allow traffic to source from an additional IP or MAC address, use the Neutron `port-update` as follows:

`Syntax: port-update <port uuid> --allowed-address-pairs`

`type=dict list=true ip_address=<ip addr w/ CIDR>, mac_address=<source mac addr>`

In the following example, I allowed traffic to be sourced from 192.168.100.253 in addition to the instance's interface IP:

```
[root@controller ~]# neutron port-update 9369da6e-bbea-4317-9ffb-587a10f6eddb \
> --allowed-address-pairs type=dict list=true ip_address=192.168.100.253/32
Updated port: 9369da6e-bbea-4317-9ffb-587a10f6eddb
```

 The `type=dict` and `list=true` options are required to help Python interpret the data being passed in the form of `ip_address` and `mac_address` key/value pairs.

The changes to iptables on the compute host can be seen as follows:

```
-A neutron-openvswi-s9369da6e-b -s 192.168.100.253/32 -m mac --mac-source FA:16:3E:70:95:FB -j RETURN
-A neutron-openvswi-s9369da6e-b -s 192.168.100.3/32 -m mac --mac-source FA:16:3E:70:95:FB -j RETURN
-A neutron-openvswi-s9369da6e-b -j DROP
```

 When a MAC address is not defined in the `port-update` command, the existing MAC address of the port is automatically used.

By defining the appropriate CIDR notation, it is possible to permit entire subnets rather than an individual host IP. The iptables rules on the compute node will be updated accordingly.

Exploring how instances get their addresses

When DHCP is enabled on a subnet, a `dnsmasq` process is spawned in a network namespace whose name corresponds to the network UUID. In the event that a process already exists, the `dnsmasq` process is updated to support the additional subnet in the network.

Most instances rely on DHCP to obtain their associated IP address. DHCP goes through the following stages:

- A DHCP client sends a DHCPDISCOVERY packet using a broadcast address. This is usually 255.255.255.255.

- A DHCP server responds to the request with a DHCPOFFER packet. The packet contains the MAC address of the instance that makes the request, the IP address, the subnet mask, lease duration, and the IP address of the DHCP server.

- In response to the offer, the DHCP client sends a DHCPREQUEST packet back to the DHCP server, requesting the offered address. Clients can receive multiple offers but will only accept one offer.

- In response to the request, the DHCP server will issue a DHCPACK packet or acknowledgement packet to the instance. At this point, the IP configuration is complete. The DHCP server sends other DHCP options such as nameservers, routes, and so on to the instance.

Network namespaces associated with DHCP servers begin with qdhcp in their names, followed by the network UUID. To view a list of namespaces on a controller, type ip netns in the host prompt:

```
[root@controller ~]# ip netns
qdhcp-3b56346d-9f9a-4447-98f1-4eb470cdad6d
qdhcp-e123e990-88af-4267-8c9b-4a37f5dd4a9c
```

The two namespaces correspond to two networks for which DHCP is enabled:

```
[root@controller ~]# neutron net-list
+--------------------------------------+---------------+----------------------------------------------------+
| id                                   | name          | subnets                                            |
+--------------------------------------+---------------+----------------------------------------------------+
| 3b56346d-9f9a-4447-98f1-4eb470cdad6d | MyFlatNetwork | 739b5bfd-d224-45bc-89b3-b29147be075d 192.168.100.0/24 |
| c4272c0b-4430-427a-a537-81bd733c2266 | MyVLANNetwork |                                                    |
| cb88384c-ebd1-4277-b01e-6f707170004f | MyVLANNetwork2 |                                                   |
| e123e990-88af-4267-8c9b-4a37f5dd4a9c | MyUserNetwork | ceac2b42-942b-41d6-9e47-d11fcad8512e 192.168.204.0/24 |
+--------------------------------------+---------------+----------------------------------------------------+
```

Within the qdhcp namespace, there exists a tap device that is used to connect the namespace to the network. The following example demonstrates a network namespace connected to the integration bridge when using the Open vSwitch plugin:

```
[root@controller ~]# ip netns exec qdhcp-3b56346d-9f9a-4447-98f1-4eb470cdad6d ip a
15: tap8e955573-bd: <BROADCAST,UP,LOWER_UP> mtu 1500 qdisc noqueue state UNKNOWN
    link/ether fa:16:3e:ea:69:72 brd ff:ff:ff:ff:ff:ff
    inet 192.168.100.2/24 brd 192.168.100.255 scope global tap8e955573-bd
    inet 169.254.169.254/16 brd 169.254.255.255 scope global tap8e955573-bd
    inet6 fe80::f816:3eff:feea:6972/64 scope link
       valid_lft forever preferred_lft forever
```

The interface can be found in the integration bridge, as shown in the following screenshot:

```
[root@controller ~]# ovs-vsctl show
6f2f8f4e-86ec-4e7f-ac4c-9128fca23b4a
    Bridge br-int
        Port "int-br-eth1"
            Interface "int-br-eth1"
        Port "tap8e955573-bd"
            tag: 2
            Interface "tap8e955573-bd"
                type: internal
```

When DHCP is not enabled on a subnet, an IP address is still associated with the Neutron port of the instance, but a `dnsmasq` process is not spawned. It is then up to the user to manually configure the IP address of the instance within the guest OS.

Exploring how instances retrieve their metadata

In *Chapter 3, Installing Neutron*, I briefly discussed the process of how metadata is provided to instances through the Neutron metadata proxy. There are two ways in which an instance can get its metadata over the network: through the router namespace or through the DHCP namespace. Both methods are described in the upcoming sections.

Router namespace

Although routers will be described and configured in the next chapter, it is important to know their function with regard to metadata. Neutron assumes that when a gateway IP is set on a subnet, one of the following two things is true:

- The gateway IP belongs to a Neutron router
- The specified gateway will handle all the routing requests from instances, including those to the metadata server

When a subnet is connected to a Neutron router that is serving as the gateway for that subnet, the router is responsible for routing all traffic from the subnet, including traffic to the metadata service. When instances make an HTTP request to the metadata service at `http://169.254.169.254`, the Neutron router makes a routing decision that involves examining iptables' chains and rules.

Within the `qrouter` namespace, there exists a `PREROUTING` rule that redirects the HTTP request to a local listener at port 9697:

```
[root@controller ~]# ip netns exec qrouter-c2b8c093-0f9b-43b9-b993-72d04b886738 \
> iptables-save | grep 169.254.169.254
-A neutron-l3-agent-PREROUTING -d 169.254.169.254/32 -p tcp -m tcp --dport 80 -j REDIRECT --to-ports 9697
```

Using `netstat` within the namespace, you can see that there is a process that listens on port 9697:

```
[root@controller ~]# ip netns exec qrouter-c2b8c093-0f9b-43b9-b993-72d04b886738 \
> netstat -tlp
Active Internet connections (only servers)
Proto Recv-Q Send-Q Local Address          Foreign Address         State       PID/Program name
tcp        0      0 *:9697                  *:*                     LISTEN      17550/python
```

The listener in the preceding example is the Neutron metadata proxy service that, in turn, proxies the metadata request to the Nova metadata service:

```
[root@controller ~]# ip netns exec qrouter-c2b8c093-0f9b-43b9-b993-72d04b886738 ps 17550
PID TTY      STAT   TIME COMMAND
17550 ?        S      0:00 /usr/bin/python /usr/bin/neutron-ns-metadata-proxy --pid_file=/var/lib/neutron/external/pids/c2b8c093-0f9b-43b9-b993-72d04b886738.pid --metadata_proxy_socket=/var/lib/neutron/metadata_proxy --router_id=c2b8c093-0f9b-43b9-b993-72d04b886738 --state_path=/var/lib/neutron --metadata_port=9697 --verbose --log-file=neutron-ns-metadata-proxy-c2b8c093-0f9b-43b9-b993-72d04b886738.log --log-dir=/var/log/neutron
```

The DHCP namespace

When instances are connected to a network that is not connected to a Neutron router, the instance must learn how to reach the metadata service. This can be done in a few different ways, including:

- Setting a route manually on the instance
- Allowing DHCP to provide a route

When `enable_isolated_metadata` is set to `True` in the `/etc/neutron/dhcp_agent.ini` configuration file, each DHCP namespace provides a proxy to the metadata service, much like the router namespace did earlier. Rather than use a `PREROUTING` iptables rule to redirect the request to another port, the proxy service listens directly on port 80, as shown in the following screenshot:

```
[root@controller ~]# ip netns exec qdhcp-e123e990-88af-4267-8c9b-4a37f5dd4a9c \
> netstat -tlnp
Active Internet connections (only servers)
Proto Recv-Q Send-Q Local Address          Foreign Address         State       PID/Program name
tcp        0      0 192.168.204.2:53        0.0.0.0:*               LISTEN      11425/dnsmasq
tcp        0      0 169.254.169.254:53      0.0.0.0:*               LISTEN      11425/dnsmasq
tcp        0      0 0.0.0.0:80              0.0.0.0:*               LISTEN      9335/python
tcp        0      0 fe80::f816:3eff:fe98:450:53 :::*                LISTEN      11425/dnsmasq
```

The process associated with this listener is the Neutron metadata proxy:

```
[root@controller ~]# ip netns exec qdhcp-e123e990-88af-4267-8c9b-4a37f5dd4a9c ps 9335
  PID TTY      STAT   TIME COMMAND
 9335 ?        S      0:00 /usr/bin/python /usr/bin/neutron-ns-metadata-proxy --pid_file=/var/lib/neutron/external/pids/e123e990-88af-4267-8c9b-4a37f5dd4a9c.pid
--metadata_proxy_socket=/var/lib/neutron/metadata_proxy --network_id=e123e990-88af-4267-8c9b-4a37f5dd4a9c --state_path=/var/lib/neutron --metadata_port=80 --verb
ose --log-file=neutron-ns-metadata-proxy-e123e990-88af-4267-8c9b-4a37f5dd4a9c.log --log-dir=/var/log/neutron
```

Adding a manual route to 169.254.169.254

Before an instance can reach the metadata service in the DHCP namespace at 169.254.169.254, a route must be configured to use the DHCP namespace interface as the next hop rather than default gateway of the instance.

Observe the IP addresses within the following DHCP namespace:

```
[root@controller ~]# ip netns exec qdhcp-e123e990-88af-4267-8c9b-4a37f5dd4a9c ip a
16: tapdc5145c1-0c: <BROADCAST,UP,LOWER_UP> mtu 1500 qdisc noqueue state UNKNOWN
    link/ether fa:16:3e:98:45:05 brd ff:ff:ff:ff:ff:ff
    inet 192.168.204.2/24 brd 192.168.204.255 scope global tapdc5145c1-0c
    inet 169.254.169.254/16 brd 169.254.255.255 scope global tapdc5145c1-0c
    inet6 fe80::f816:3eff:fe98:4505/64 scope link
       valid_lft forever preferred_lft forever
18: lo: <LOOPBACK,UP,LOWER_UP> mtu 16436 qdisc noqueue state UNKNOWN
    link/loopback 00:00:00:00:00:00 brd 00:00:00:00:00:00
    inet 127.0.0.1/8 scope host lo
    inet6 ::1/128 scope host
       valid_lft forever preferred_lft forever
```

To reach 169.254.169.254 from an instance in the 192.168.204.0/24 network, the following `ip route` command could be issued that uses 192.168.204.2 as the next hop:

```
ip route add 169.254.169.254/32 via 192.168.204.2
```

The process of adding a route to each instance does not scale well, especially when multiple DHCP agents exist in the environment. A single network can be scheduled to multiple agents that, in turn, have their own namespaces and IP addresses in the same subnet. Users will need prior knowledge of the IP to use in their route statement, and the address is subject to change. Allowing DHCP to inject the route automatically is the recommended method; this will be discussed in the following section.

Using DHCP to inject the route

When `enable_isolated_metadata` is set to `true` and a gateway is not set in the subnet, the DHCP service is capable of injecting a route to the metadata service via the classless-static-route DHCP option, otherwise known as option 121.

Once an instance connected to a subnet with the mentioned characteristics has been created, observe the following routes passed to the instance via DHCP:

```
user@instance:~$ ip r
10.200.0.0/24 dev eth0 proto kernel scope link src 10.200.0.5
169.254.169.254 via 10.200.0.3 dev eth0
```

The next hop address for the highlighted metadata route is the IP address of the DHCP server that responded to the DHCP request from the client. If there were multiple DHCP agents in the environment and the same network was scheduled to all of them, it is possible that the next hop address would vary between instances, as any of the DHCP servers could respond to the request.

> As --no-gateway was specified as a way to force DHCP to pass the metadata route, the instance has no default gateway. To work around this, a 0.0.0.0/0 host route can either be added to the subnet at creation or the subnet can be updated after it has been created.

Summary

This chapter laid the foundation for creating networks and subnets that can be leveraged by routers, instances, and other cloud resources. The Neutron command-line client can be used to manage networks, subnets, and ports and is highly recommended over the limited Horizon dashboard for most administrative tasks.

For more information on network, subnet, and port attributes, as well as for guidance on how to use the Neutron API, refer to the OpenStack wiki at https://wiki. openstack.org/wiki/Neutron/APIv2-specification. In addition, OpenStack operations guides can be found at http://docs.openstack.org/openstack-ops/ content/.

In the next chapter, I will expand on the concept of Neutron routers and their involvement in the network, including the configuration and use of floating IPs to provide external connectivity to instances.

6
Creating Routers with Neutron

The Neutron L3 agent enables IP routing and NAT support for instances within the cloud by utilizing network namespaces to provide isolated routing instances. By creating networks and attaching them to routers, tenants can expose connected instances and their applications to the Internet.

In the previous chapter, I explained the difference between provider and tenant networks and demonstrated the process of booting and providing connectivity to instances. In this chapter, I will guide you through the following:

- Creating an external provider network
- Creating a router in the CLI and Horizon dashboard
- Attaching a router to both external and tenant networks
- Booting instances
- Demonstrating instance and namespace connectivity using LinuxBridge
- Demonstrating SNAT and NAT functionality provided by floating IPs

The neutron-l3-agent service was installed on the controller node as part of the overall Neutron installation process documented in *Chapter 3, Installing Neutron*.

Configuring the Neutron L3 agent

Before the neutron-l3-agent service can be started, it must be configured. Neutron stores the L3 agent configuration in the /etc/neutron/l3_agent.ini file. The most common configuration options will be covered here.

Defining an interface driver

Like previously installed agents, the Neutron L3 agent must be configured to use an interface driver that corresponds to the chosen networking plugin.

Using `crudini`, configure the Neutron L3 agent to use one of the following drivers:

- For LinuxBridge:

```
# crudini --set /etc/neutron/l3_agent.ini DEFAULT interface_driver
neutron.agent.linux.interface.BridgeInterfaceDriver
```

- For Open vSwitch:

```
# crudini --set /etc/neutron/l3_agent.ini DEFAULT interface_driver
neutron.agent.linux.interface.OVSInterfaceDriver
```

Setting the external network

The external network connected to a router is one that not only provides external connectivity to the router and the instances behind it, but also serves as the network from which floating IPs are derived. In Havana, each L3 agent in the cloud can be associated with only one external network. In Icehouse, L3 agents are capable of supporting multiple external networks.

To be eligible to serve as an external network, a provider network must have been configured with its `router:external` attribute set to `true`. In Havana, if more than one provider network has the attribute set to `true`, then the `gateway_external_network_id` configuration option must be used to associate an external network to the agent.

To define a specific external network, configure the `gateway_external_network_id` option as follows:

```
gateway_external_network_id = <UUID of eligible provider network>
```

In Havana, if this option is left empty, the agent will enforce that only a single external networks exists. The agent will automatically use the network for which the `router:external` attribute is set to `true`. The default configuration contains an empty or unset value and is sufficient for now.

Setting the external bridge

The L3 agent must be aware of how to connect the external interface of a router to the network. The `external_network_bridge` configuration option defines a bridge on the host in which the external interface will be connected.

In earlier releases of Havana, the default value of `external_network_bridge` was `br-ex`, a bridge expected to be configured manually outside of OpenStack and intended to be dedicated to the external network. As a result of the bridge not being fully managed by OpenStack, provider attributes of the network created within Neutron, including the segmentation ID, network type, and the provider bridge itself, are ignored.

To fully utilize a provider network and its attributes, the `external_network_bridge` configuration option should be set to an empty, or blank, value. By doing so, Neutron will adhere to the attributes of the network and place the external interface of routers into a bridge that it creates, along with a physical or virtual VLAN interface used to provide external connectivity. When using Open vSwitch, the external interface of the router is placed in the integration bridge and assigned to the appropriate local VLAN. With the LinuxBridge plugin, the external interface of routers is placed into a Linux bridge that corresponds to the external network.

Using `crudini`, set the `external_network_bridge` configuration option to an empty value as follows:

```
# crudini --set /etc/neutron/l3_agent.ini DEFAULT external_network_bridge
```

Enabling the metadata proxy

When Neutron routers are used as the gateway for instances, requests for metadata are proxied by the router and forwarded to the Nova metadata service. This feature is enabled by default and can be disabled by setting the `enable_metadata_proxy` value to `false` in the `l3_agent.ini` configuration file.

Starting the Neutron L3 agent

To start the `neutron-l3-agent` service and configure it to start at boot, issue the following commands on the controller node:

```
# service neutron-l3-agent start
# chkconfig neutron-l3-agent on
```

Verify the agent is running:

```
# service neutron-l3-agent status
```

The service should return an output similar to the following:

```
[root@controller neutron]# service neutron-l3-agent status
neutron-l3-agent (pid  13501) is running...
```

If the service remains stopped, troubleshoot any issues that may be found in the /var/log/neutron/l3-agent.log log file.

Router management in the CLI

Neutron offers a number of commands that can be used to create and manage routers. The primary commands associated with router management include:

- router-create
- router-delete
- router-gateway-clear
- router-gateway-set
- router-interface-add
- router-interface-delete
- router-list
- router-list-on-l3-agent
- router-port-list
- router-show
- router-update

Creating routers in the CLI

Routers in Neutron are associated with tenants and are available for use only by users within the tenant that created them. As an administrator, you can create routers on behalf of tenants during the creation process.

To create a router, use the router-create command as follows:

```
Syntax: router-create [--tenant-id TENANT_ID]
[--admin-state-down] NAME
```

Working with router interfaces in the CLI

Neutron routers have two types of interfaces: gateway and internal. The gateway interface of a Neutron router is analogous to the WAN interface of a hardware router. It is the interface connected to an upstream device that provides connectivity to external resources. The internal interfaces of Neutron routers are analogous to the LAN interfaces of hardware routers. Internal interfaces are connected to tenant networks and often serve as the gateway for connected instances.

Attaching internal interfaces to routers

To create an interface in the router and attach it to a subnet, use the `router-interface-add` command as follows:

`Syntax: router-interface-add <router-id> <INTERFACE>`

In this case, `INTERFACE` is the ID of the subnet to be attached to the router.

 In Neutron, a network may contain multiple subnets. It is important to attach the router to each subnet so that it properly serves as the gateway for those subnets.

Once the command is executed, Neutron creates a port in the database that is associated with the router interface. The L3 agent is responsible for connecting interfaces within the router namespace to the proper bridge.

Attaching a gateway interface to a router

The external interface of a Neutron router is referred to as the gateway interface. A router is limited to a single gateway interface. To be eligible for use as an external network that can be used for gateway interfaces, a provider network must have its `router:external` attribute set to `true`.

To attach a gateway interface to a router, use the `router-gateway-set` command as follows:

`Syntax: router-gateway-set <router-id> <external-network-id> [--disable-snat]`

The default behavior of a Neutron router is to source NAT all outbound traffic from instances that do not have a corresponding floating IP. To disable this functionality, append `--disable-snat` to the `router-gateway-set` command.

Listing interfaces attached to routers

To list the interfaces attached to routers, use the `router-port-list` command as follows:

`Syntax: router-port-list <router-id>`

The returned output includes the Neutron port ID, MAC address, IP address, and associated subnet of attached interfaces.

Deleting internal interfaces

To delete an internal interface from a router, use the `router-interface-delete` command as follows:

`Syntax: router-interface-delete <router-id> <INTERFACE>`

Here, `INTERFACE` is the ID of the subnet to be removed from the router. Deleting an interface from a router results in the associated Neutron port being removed from the database.

Clearing the gateway interface

Gateway interfaces cannot be removed from a router using the `router-interface-delete` command. Instead, the `router-gateway-clear` command must be used.

To clear the gateway of a router, use the `router-gateway-clear` command as follows:

`Syntax: router-gateway-clear <router-id>`

Neutron includes checks that will prohibit the clearing of a gateway interface in the event that floating IPs or other resources from the network are associated with the router.

Listing routers in the CLI

To display a list of existing routers, use the Neutron `router-list` command as follows:

`Syntax: router-list [--tenant-id TENANT_ID]`

The returned output includes the router ID, name, external gateway network, and the SNAT state.

Users will only see routers that exist in their tenant or project. When executed by an administrator, Neutron will return a listing of all routers across all tenants unless, the tenant ID is specified.

Displaying router attributes in the CLI

To display the attributes of a router, use the Neutron `router-show` command as follows:

```
Syntax: router-show <router id>
```

Among the output returned is the admin state, the external network, the SNAT state, and the tenant ID associated with the router.

Updating router attributes in the CLI

To update the attributes of a router, use the Neutron `router-update` command as follows:

```
Syntax: router-update <router id> [--admin-state-up]
[--routes destination=<network/cidr>,nexthop=<gateway_ip>]
```

The `admin-state-up` attribute is a Boolean, which when set to `false`, does not allow Neutron to update interfaces within the router. This includes not adding floating IPs or additional internal interfaces to the router. Setting the value to `true` will allow queued changes to be applied.

The `routes` option allows you to add static routes to the routing table of a Neutron router. To add static routes, use the following syntax:

```
Syntax: neutron router-update <router id> --routes type=dict list=true
destination=<network/cidr>,nexthop=<gateway_ip>
```

Adding static routes to a router is an undocumented and broken feature in Havana. In Havana, the command results in the route being added to the database and `router show` output, while not being added to the routing table. To resolve this, add the following line to the `[DEFAULT]` block of the `/etc/neutron/l3_agent.ini` configuration file:

```
root_helper = sudo neutron-rootwrap /etc/neutron/rootwrap.conf
```

Restart the `neutron-l3-agent` service for changes to take effect.

Deleting routers in the CLI

To delete a router, use the Neutron `router-delete` command as follows:

`Syntax: router-delete <router id>`

Before a router can be deleted, all floating IPs and internal interfaces associated with the router must be unassociated or deleted. This may require deleting instances or detaching connected interfaces from instances.

Network Address Translation

Network Address Translation (NAT) is a networking concept that was developed in the early 1990s in response to the rapid depletion of IP addresses throughout the world. Prior to NAT, every host connected to the Internet had a unique IP address.

OpenStack routers support two types of NAT:

- one-to-one
- many-to-one

A **one-to-one** NAT is a method in which one IP address is directly mapped to another. Commonly referred to as a static NAT, a one-to-one NAT is often used to map a unique public address to a privately addressed host. Floating IPs utilize one-to-one NAT concepts.

A **many-to-one** NAT is a method in which multiple addresses are mapped to a single address. A many-to-one NAT employs the use of port address translation (PAT). Neutron uses PAT to provide external access to instances behind the router when floating IPs are not assigned.

For more information on network address translation, please visit Wikipedia at `http://en.wikipedia.org/wiki/Network_address_translation`.

Floating IP addresses

Tenant networks, when attached to a Neutron router, are meant to utilize the router as their default gateway. By default, when a router receives traffic from an instance and routes it upstream, the router performs a port address translation and modifies the source address of the packet to appear as its own external interface address. This ensures that the packet can be routed upstream and returned to the router, where it will modify the destination address to be that of the instance that initiated the connection. Neutron refers to this type of behavior as **Source NAT**.

When users require direct inbound access to instances, a floating IP address can be utilized. A floating IP address in OpenStack is a static NAT that maps an external address to an internal address. This method of NAT allows instances to be reachable from external networks, such as the Internet. Floating IP addresses are configured on the external interface of the router that serves as the gateway for the instance, which is then responsible for modifying the source and/or destination address of packets depending on their direction.

Floating IP Management

Neutron offers a number of commands that can be used to create and manage floating IPs. The primary commands associated with floating IPs include:

- `floatingip-associate`
- `floatingip-create`
- `floatingip-delete`
- `floatingip-disassociate`
- `floatingip-list`
- `floatingip-show`

Creating floating IPs in the CLI

If you recall from previous chapters, IP addresses are not assigned directly to instances. Instead, an IP address is associated with a Neutron port, and that port is logically mapped to the virtual tap interface that connects instances to the network.

A floating IP, when used, is associated with a Neutron port. To create a floating IP from within the CLI, use the Neutron `floatingip-create` command as follows:

```
Syntax: floatingip-create [--tenant-id TENANT_ID]

[--port-id PORT_ID] [--fixed-ip-address FIXED_IP_ADDRESS] FLOATING_
NETWORK
```

Floating IP addresses are usable only within the tenant that created them. An administrator is able to create floating IPs on behalf of tenants. Use the `--tenant-id` option to specify the tenant associated with the floating IP.

By specifying a port ID with the `--port-id` option, it is possible to immediately associate a floating IP with a Neutron port upon creation.

Because a port might have multiple IP addresses associated with it, it may be necessary to define a specific fixed IP to associate the floating IP with. Use the `--fixed-ip-address` option to specify the IP address you wish to associate the floating IP with.

Associating floating IPs to ports in the CLI

Once a floating IP has been created, it is available for use by any user within the tenant that created it. To associate a floating IP with an instance, it is necessary to determine the Neutron port that is associated with the instance.

Use the `neutron port-list` command to determine the port ID associated with the MAC or IP.

For example, the port ID of an instance whose IP address is 192.168.200.2 can be determined in the following way:

```
# neutron port-list | grep 192.168.200.2 | awk '{print $2}'

b8e3a646-9c25-4957-a299-dd05e56d309d
```

Once the port ID has been determined, use the Neutron `floatingip-associate` command to associate the floating IP with the port:

```
Syntax: neutron floatingip-associate [--fixed-ip-address
FIXED_IP_ADDRESS] FLOATINGIP_ID PORT
```

Using the mentioned port ID and a floating IP whose ID is `0995863d-577d-46e2-bc29-1d5ad9a29b4d`, the `floatingip-associate` command can be used to associate the floating IP with the port:

```
(neutron) floatingip-associate 0995863d-577d-46e2-bc29-1d5ad9a29b4d
b8e3a646-9c25-4957-a299-dd05e56d309d
```

 Floating IPs are automatically created on the router connected to the subnet that is associated with the port.

Listing floating IPs in the CLI

To determine the association of floating IPs to Neutron ports and addresses, use the Neutron `floatingip-list` command as follows:

```
Syntax: floatingip-list
```

The output returned includes the floating IP ID, fixed IP address, floating IP address, and associated port ID.

Displaying floating IP attributes in the CLI

To display the attributes of a floating IP in the CLI, use the Neutron `floatingip-show` command as follows:

Syntax: `floatingip-show <floating-ip-id>`

The output returned includes the floating IP address, the external network, and the associated fixed IP address, port, and tenant and router IDs.

Disassociating floating IPs in the CLI

To disassociate a floating IP from a port, use the Neutron `floatingip-disassociate` command as follows:

Syntax: `floatingip-disassociate <floating-ip-id>`

Disassociating a floating IP from a port makes the floating IP available for use by other users within the tenant.

Deleting floating IPs in the CLI

To delete a floating IP, use the Neutron `floatingip-delete` command as follows:

Syntax: `floatingip-delete <floating-ip-id>`

Deleting a floating IP returns the IP address to the allocation pool, where it can be allocated to other network resources including routers, instances, or floating IPs.

Demonstrating traffic flow from instance to Internet

To fully drive home the concept of Neutron routers, floating IPs, and connectivity through the bridges, this section of the chapter is dedicated to a walkthrough that leverages the network foundation that has been laid so far. A VLAN provider network will be used as the external gateway network and a VLAN tenant network will be used for instances. A Neutron router will be used to route traffic from the tenant network to the Internet, and floating IPs will be used to provide direct connectivity to instances.

Setting the foundation

In this example, a Cisco ASA serves as the upstream network gateway and is connected to the Internet. The inside interface of the Cisco ASA has a configured IP address of 10.50.0.1/24 and will serve as the gateway for an external VLAN provider network created here.

The following diagram is the logical diagram of the network to be built as part of this demonstration:

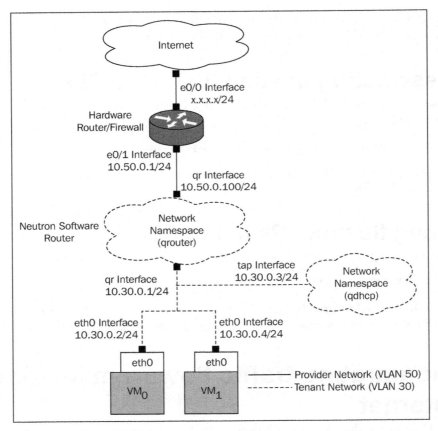

Figure 6.1

In the preceding diagram, a Cisco ASA serves as the lead network device in front of the OpenStack cloud.

Creating an external provider network

In order to provide instances with external connectivity, a Neutron router must be connected to a provider network eligible for use as an external network.

Using the Neutron `net-create` command, create a provider network with the following attributes:

- Name: GATEWAY_NET
- Type: VLAN
- Segmentation ID: 50
- Bridge: physnet1
- External: True
- Shared: True

The following screenshot displays the resulting output of the `net-create` command:

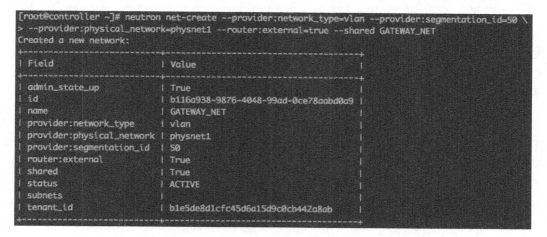

Using the Neutron `subnet-create` command, create a subnet with the following attributes:

- Name: GATEWAY_SUBNET
- Network: 10.50.0.0
- Subnet mask: 255.255.255.0
- Gateway: 10.50.0.1
- DHCP range: 10.50.0.100 - 10.50.0.254

The following screenshot displays the resulting output of the `subnet-create` command:

```
[root@controller ~]# neutron subnet-create GATEWAY_NET 10.50.0.0/24 --name GATEWAY_SUBNET \
> --allocation-pool start=10.50.0.100,end=10.50.0.254 --gateway 10.50.0.1
Created a new subnet:
+------------------+----------------------------------------------------+
| Field            | Value                                              |
+------------------+----------------------------------------------------+
| allocation_pools | {"start": "10.50.0.100", "end": "10.50.0.254"}     |
| cidr             | 10.50.0.0/24                                        |
| dns_nameservers  |                                                    |
| enable_dhcp      | True                                               |
| gateway_ip       | 10.50.0.1                                          |
| host_routes      |                                                    |
| id               | 436ecec3-32b3-4629-97a6-82a3c9fb33d2               |
| ip_version       | 4                                                  |
| name             | GATEWAY_SUBNET                                      |
| network_id       | b116a938-9876-4048-99ad-0ce78aabd0a9               |
| tenant_id        | b1e5de8d1cfc45d6a15d9c0cb442a8ab                   |
+------------------+----------------------------------------------------+
```

Creating a Neutron router

Create a router using the Neutron `router-create` command with the following attribute:

- Name: `MyRouter`

The following screenshot displays the resulting output of the `router-create` command:

```
[root@controller ~]# neutron router-create MyRouter
Created a new router:
+-----------------------+--------------------------------------+
| Field                 | Value                                |
+-----------------------+--------------------------------------+
| admin_state_up        | True                                 |
| external_gateway_info |                                      |
| id                    | 1267aae4-6568-48cf-acef-5dbcf7ecb5db |
| name                  | MyRouter                             |
| status                | ACTIVE                               |
| tenant_id             | b1e5de8d1cfc45d6a15d9c0cb442a8ab     |
+-----------------------+--------------------------------------+
```

Attaching the router to the external network

When attaching a Neutron router to a provider network, the network must have the
`router:external` attribute set to `True` to be eligible for use as an external network.

Using the Neutron `router-gateway-set` command, attach the router `MyRouter` to
the `GATEWAY_NET` network as shown in the following screenshot:

```
[root@controller ~]# neutron router-gateway-set MyRouter GATEWAY_NET
Set gateway for router MyRouter
```

Using the Neutron `router-port-list` command, determine the external IP of the
router as shown in the following screenshot:

The IP address assigned to the router is procured from the DHCP
allocation range of the subnet. In Havana, there is no way to specify
the external address of the router.

Once the gateway interface has been added, the router will be scheduled to an
eligible L3 agent. Using the Neutron `l3-agent-list-hosting-router` command,
you can determine which L3 agent the router was scheduled to, as shown in the
following screenshot:

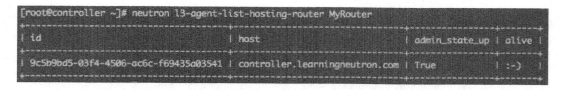

On the node hosting the L3 agent, a network namespace is created that corresponds
to the router. Observe that the name of the namespace incorporates the router's
UUID. Have a look at the following screenshot:

```
[root@controller ~]# ip netns
qrouter-1267aae4-6568-48cf-acef-5dbcf7ecb5db
```

Inside the namespace, an interface exists with a preface, qg. The qg interface is the gateway, or external, interface of the router. Neutron automatically provisions an IP address to the qg interface from the DHCP allocation pool of the external network's subnet. Have a look at the following screenshot:

```
[root@controller ~]# ip netns exec qrouter-1267aae4-6568-48cf-acef-5dbcf7ecb5db ip a
8: lo: <LOOPBACK,UP,LOWER_UP> mtu 16436 qdisc noqueue state UNKNOWN
    link/loopback 00:00:00:00:00:00 brd 00:00:00:00:00:00
    inet 127.0.0.1/8 scope host lo
    inet6 ::1/128 scope host
       valid_lft forever preferred_lft forever
9: qg-9ee818ab-1c: <BROADCAST,MULTICAST,UP,LOWER_UP> mtu 1500 qdisc pfifo_fast state UP qlen 1000
    link/ether fa:16:3e:b3:c5:aa brd ff:ff:ff:ff:ff:ff
    inet 10.50.0.100/24 brd 10.50.0.255 scope global qg-9ee818ab-1c
    inet6 fe80::f816:3eff:feb3:c5aa/64 scope link
       valid_lft forever preferred_lft forever
```

The qg interface is one end of a veth pair whose other end is connected to a bridge on the host. When using the LinuxBridge plugin, the interface is placed into a bridge that corresponds to the external network. Have a look at the following screenshot:

```
[root@controller ~]# brctl show
bridge name      bridge id             STP enabled      interfaces
brqb116a938-98       8000.001d096654b9       no              eth1.50
                 Network UUID                             tap9ee818ab-1c  Veth End (Port UUID)
```

The namespace is able to communicate with other devices in the same subnet through the bridge. The other interface in the bridge, eth1.50, tags traffic as VLAN 50 as it exits the bridge and out of the physical interface eth1.

Observe the route table within the namespace. The default gateway address corresponds to the address defined in the subnet's gateway_ip attribute. In this case, 10.50.0.1, as shown in the following screenshot:

```
[root@controller ~]# ip netns exec qrouter-1267aae4-6568-48cf-acef-5dbcf7ecb5db ip r
10.50.0.0/24 dev qg-9ee818ab-1c  proto kernel  scope link  src 10.50.0.100
default via 10.50.0.1 dev qg-9ee818ab-1c
```

Testing gateway connectivity

To test external connectivity from the Neutron router, ping the edge gateway device from within the router namespace:

```
[root@controller ~]# ip netns exec qrouter-1267aae4-6568-48cf-acef-5dbcf7ecb5db ping 10.50.0.1
PING 10.50.0.1 (10.50.0.1) 56(84) bytes of data.
64 bytes from 10.50.0.1: icmp_seq=1 ttl=255 time=0.683 ms
64 bytes from 10.50.0.1: icmp_seq=2 ttl=255 time=0.619 ms
64 bytes from 10.50.0.1: icmp_seq=3 ttl=255 time=0.614 ms
64 bytes from 10.50.0.1: icmp_seq=4 ttl=255 time=0.589 ms
^C
--- 10.50.0.1 ping statistics ---
4 packets transmitted, 4 received, 0% packet loss, time 3397ms
rtt min/avg/max/mdev = 0.589/0.626/0.683/0.038 ms
```

Successful ping attempts from the router namespace demonstrate proper external VLAN configuration of both hardware- and software-based networking components.

Creating an internal network

Within the `admin` tenant, create an internal network for instances. In this demonstration, a VLAN-based network will be created with the following attributes:

- Name: TENANT_NET1
- Type: VLAN
- VLAN ID: (Auto assigned)

The following screenshot displays the resulting output of the `net-create` command:

```
[root@controller ~]# neutron net-create TENANT_NET1
Created a new network:
+---------------------------+--------------------------------------+
| Field                     | Value                                |
+---------------------------+--------------------------------------+
| admin_state_up            | True                                 |
| id                        | 21b04852-d4c1-48f4-a83a-b46ad7f7b07e |
| name                      | TENANT_NET1                          |
| provider:network_type     | vlan                                 |
| provider:physical_network | physnet1                             |
| provider:segmentation_id  | 30                                   |
| shared                    | False                                |
| status                    | ACTIVE                               |
| subnets                   |                                      |
| tenant_id                 | b1e5de8d1cfc45d6a15d9c0cb442a8ab     |
+---------------------------+--------------------------------------+
```

In the preceding example, Neutron has automatically assigned a segmentation ID (VLAN) from the range specified in the plugin configuration file that was set in *Chapter 4, Building a Virtual Switching Infrastructure*. Have a look at the following code:

```
network_vlan_ranges = physnet1:30:33
```

Using the Neutron `subnet-create` command, create a subnet with the following attributes:

- Name: `TENANT_SUBNET1`
- Network: `10.30.0.0`
- Subnet mask: `255.255.255.0`
- Gateway: `<auto>`
- DHCP range: `<auto>`
- DNS nameserver: `8.8.8.8`

The following screenshot displays the resulting output of the `subnet-create` command:

```
[root@controller ~]# neutron subnet-create TENANT_NET1 10.30.0.0/24 \
> --name TENANT_SUBNET1 --dns-nameserver 8.8.8.8
Created a new subnet:
+-------------------+---------------------------------------------------+
| Field             | Value                                             |
+-------------------+---------------------------------------------------+
| allocation_pools  | {"start": "10.30.0.2", "end": "10.30.0.254"}      |
| cidr              | 10.30.0.0/24                                      |
| dns_nameservers   | 8.8.8.8                                           |
| enable_dhcp       | True                                              |
| gateway_ip        | 10.30.0.1                                         |
| host_routes       |                                                   |
| id                | e47dece9-a9e4-4486-9443-509e76e30f9d              |
| ip_version        | 4                                                 |
| name              | TENANT_SUBNET1                                    |
| network_id        | 21b04852-d4c1-48f4-a83a-b46ad7f7b07e              |
| tenant_id         | b1e5de8d1cfc45d6a15d9c0cb442a8ab                  |
+-------------------+---------------------------------------------------+
```

Attaching the router to the internal network

Using the Neutron `router-interface-add` command, attach the `TENANT_SUBNET1` subnet to `MyRouter`, as shown in the following screenshot:

```
[root@controller ~]# neutron router-interface-add MyRouter TENANT_SUBNET1
Added interface 5ea2d15f-8a5b-46f5-9c6b-f89179bd9f8a to router MyRouter.
```

Using the Neutron `router-port-list` command, determine the internal IP of the router, as shown in the following screenshot:

The IP address assigned to the internal router interface corresponds to the address set in the `gateway_ip` attribute of the subnet. Neutron will not allow you to attach a subnet to a router as an internal interface without the `gateway_ip` attribute set.

 It is not possible to connect a subnet to more than one router at a time. In addition, it is not possible to attach multiple interfaces to a single subnet.

Inside the router namespace, a new interface has been added with a preface of `qr`. The `qr` interface is the internal interface of the router that corresponds to the connected subnet as shown in the following screenshot:

```
[root@controller ~]# ip netns exec qrouter-1267aae4-6568-48cf-acef-5dbcf7ecb5db ip a
8: lo: <LOOPBACK,UP,LOWER_UP> mtu 16436 qdisc noqueue state UNKNOWN
    link/loopback 00:00:00:00:00:00 brd 00:00:00:00:00:00
    inet 127.0.0.1/8 scope host lo
    inet6 ::1/128 scope host
       valid_lft forever preferred_lft forever
9: qg-9ee818ab-1c: <BROADCAST,MULTICAST,UP,LOWER_UP> mtu 1500 qdisc pfifo_fast state UP qlen 1000
    link/ether fa:16:3e:b3:c5:aa brd ff:ff:ff:ff:ff:ff
    inet 10.50.0.100/24 brd 10.50.0.255 scope global qg-9ee818ab-1c
    inet6 fe80::f816:3eff:feb3:c5aa/64 scope link
       valid_lft forever preferred_lft forever
13: qr-5ea2d15f-8a: <BROADCAST,MULTICAST,UP,LOWER_UP> mtu 1500 qdisc pfifo_fast state UP qlen 1000
    link/ether fa:16:3e:fd:d8:90 brd ff:ff:ff:ff:ff:ff
    inet 10.30.0.1/24 brd 10.30.0.255 scope global qr-5ea2d15f-8a
    inet6 fe80::f816:3eff:fefd:d890/64 scope link
       valid_lft forever preferred_lft forever
```

The `qr` interface is one end of a veth pair whose other end is connected to a bridge on the host. When using the LinuxBridge plugin, the interface is placed in a bridge that corresponds to the internal network as shown in the following screenshot:

```
[root@controller ~]# brctl show
bridge name       bridge id            STP enabled      interfaces
brq21b04852-d4          8000.001d096654b9       no            eth1.30
   Internal Network UUID                                 tap5ea2d15f-8a   Veth End (Port UUID)
brqb116a938-98          8000.001d096654b9       no            eth1.50
                                                          tap9ee818ab-1c
```

The namespace is able to communicate with other devices in the same subnet through the bridge. The other interface in the bridge, `eth1.30`, tags traffic as VLAN 30 as it exits the bridge and out of the physical interface `eth1`.

Creating instances

Using the `nova boot` command, create two instances with the following characteristics:

- Name: `MyInstance1, MyInstance2`
- Network: `TENANT_NET1`
- Image: `CirrOS`
- Flavor: `m1.tiny`

The `nova image-list` command can be used to determine the images available for use, as shown in the following screenshot:

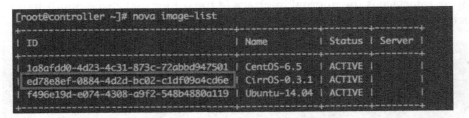

Using the UUID of the CirrOS image, boot the instances on the `TENANT_NET1` network as shown in the following screenshot:

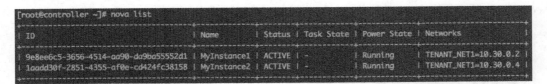

The `nova list` command can be used to return a list of instances and their IP addresses as follows:

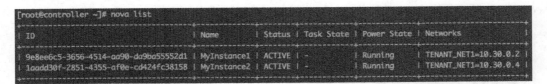

On the compute node, a Linux bridge has been created that corresponds to the
TENANT_NET1 network. Inside the bridge is a VLAN interface and two tap interfaces
that correspond to the instances. Have a look at the following screenshot:

```
[root@compute01 init.d]# brctl show
bridge name         bridge id               STP enabled     interfaces
brq21b04852-d4          8000.001d0929c89c       no              eth1.30
                                                                tap0337299a-38
                                                                tap3547dbf0-58
```

Verifying instance connectivity

Upon spinning up the first instance, a DHCP namespace was created by Neutron
that services DHCP requests from the instance in the TENANT_NET1 network, as
shown in the following screenshot:

```
[root@controller ~]# ip netns
qrouter-1267aae4-6568-48cf-acef-5dbcf7ecb5db
qdhcp-21b04852-d4c1-48f4-a83a-b46ad7f7b07e
```

The name of the DHCP namespace corresponds to the UUID of the TENANT_NET1
network. An IP listing within the namespace reveals that 10.30.0.3 has been assigned
to an interface as shown in the following screenshot:

```
[root@controller ~]# ip netns exec qdhcp-21b04852-d4c1-48f4-a83a-b46ad7f7b07e ip a
17: lo: <LOOPBACK,UP,LOWER_UP> mtu 16436 qdisc noqueue state UNKNOWN
    link/loopback 00:00:00:00:00:00 brd 00:00:00:00:00:00
    inet 127.0.0.1/8 scope host lo
    inet6 ::1/128 scope host
       valid_lft forever preferred_lft forever
18: ns-4dd99827-91: <BROADCAST,MULTICAST,UP,LOWER_UP> mtu 1500 qdisc pfifo_fast state UP qlen 1000
    link/ether fa:16:3e:c7:ec:81 brd ff:ff:ff:ff:ff:ff
    inet 10.30.0.3/24 brd 10.30.0.255 scope global ns-4dd99827-91
    inet 169.254.169.254/16 brd 169.254.255.255 scope global ns-4dd99827-91
    inet6 fe80::f816:3eff:fec7:ec81/64 scope link
       valid_lft forever preferred_lft forever
```

The `ns` interface is one end of a veth pair whose other end is connected to a bridge on the host. The namespace is able to communicate with other devices in the same subnet through the bridge. When using the LinuxBridge plugin, the interface is placed into a bridge that corresponds to the TENANT_NET1 network:

```
[root@controller ~]# brctl show
bridge name        bridge id              STP enabled    interfaces
brq21b04852-d4         8000.001d096654b9         no            eth1.30
    TENANT_NET1 UUID                                       tap4dd99827-91  Veth End
                                                           tap5ea2d15f-8a
brqb116a938-98         8000.001d096654b9         no            eth1.50
                                                           tap9ee818ab-1c
```

As the instances came online, they sent a DHCP request that was served by the `dnsmasq` process in the DHCP namespace. A populated ARP table within the namespace confirms instances are functioning at layer 2 as shown in the following screenshot:

```
[root@controller ~]# ip netns exec qrouter-1267aae4-6568-48cf-acef-5dbcf7ecb5db arp -an
? (10.30.0.2) at fa:16:3e:d7:6d:9e [ether] on qr-5ea2d15f-8a  ←──── MyInstance1
? (10.30.0.4) at fa:16:3e:de:fb:3d [ether] on qr-5ea2d15f-8a  ←──── MyInstance2
? (10.50.0.1) at 00:18:b9:08:bc:f1 [ether] on qg-9ee818ab-1c
```

Before you can connect to the instances, however, security group rules must be updated to allow ICMP and SSH. *Chapter 8, Protecting Instances on the Network*, focuses on the implementation and administration of security group rules in more detail. For now, add ICMP and SSH access to the default security group rules with the following command:

```
for SECID in $(neutron security-group-list | grep default | awk '{print $2}'); \

do neutron security-group-rule-create --protocol icmp $SECID; \

neutron security-group-rule-create --protocol tcp --port-range-min 22 --port-range-max 22 $SECID; \

done;
```

Using an SSH client, connect to the instances from either the router or DHCP namespace. The CirrOS image has a built-in user named `cirros` with a password, `cubswin:)`:

```
[root@controller ~]# ip netns exec qrouter-1267aae4-6568-48cf-acef-5dbcf7ecb5db ssh cirros@10.30.0.2
The authenticity of host '10.30.0.2 (10.30.0.2)' can't be established.
RSA key fingerprint is de:4b:62:58:f0:d7:73:41:8a:65:70:5a:48:e5:89:11.
Are you sure you want to continue connecting (yes/no)? yes
Warning: Permanently added '10.30.0.2' (RSA) to the list of known hosts.
cirros@10.30.0.2's password:
$ ip r
default via 10.30.0.1 dev eth0
10.30.0.0/24 dev eth0  src 10.30.0.2
$ exit
Connection to 10.30.0.2 closed.
[root@controller ~]# ip netns exec qrouter-1267aae4-6568-48cf-acef-5dbcf7ecb5db ssh cirros@10.30.0.4
The authenticity of host '10.30.0.4 (10.30.0.4)' can't be established.
RSA key fingerprint is 2a:83:06:34:6c:9d:87:dc:7c:dc:9d:a4:3f:6a:5d:7d.
Are you sure you want to continue connecting (yes/no)? yes
Warning: Permanently added '10.30.0.4' (RSA) to the list of known hosts.
cirros@10.30.0.4's password:
$ ip r
default via 10.30.0.1 dev eth0
10.30.0.0/24 dev eth0  src 10.30.0.4
$ exit
Connection to 10.30.0.4 closed.
```

Observe the routing table of each instance. The default gateway of each instance is the Neutron router interface created earlier. Pinging an external resource from an instance should be successful, provided external connectivity from the Neutron router exists. Have a look at the following screenshot:

```
[root@controller ~]# ip netns exec qrouter-1267aae4-6568-48cf-acef-5dbcf7ecb5db ssh cirros@10.30.0.2
cirros@10.30.0.2's password:
$ ping 8.8.8.8
PING 8.8.8.8 (8.8.8.8): 56 data bytes
64 bytes from 8.8.8.8: seq=0 ttl=46 time=38.457 ms
64 bytes from 8.8.8.8: seq=1 ttl=46 time=39.243 ms
64 bytes from 8.8.8.8: seq=2 ttl=46 time=38.735 ms
^C
--- 8.8.8.8 ping statistics ---
3 packets transmitted, 3 packets received, 0% packet loss
round-trip min/avg/max = 38.457/38.811/39.243 ms
```

Observing default NAT behavior

The default behavior of the Neutron router is to source NAT traffic from instances without floating IPs when traffic egresses the gateway interface. From the external network gateway device, in this case a Cisco ASA, observe ICMP traffic from the instances appearing as the external gateway address of the router. Have a look at the following screenshot:

```
pixfirewall# debug icmp trace
debug icmp trace enabled at level 1
pixfirewall# ICMP echo request from GATEWAY_NET:10.50.0.100 to outside:8.8.8.8 ID=38429 seq=10 len=56
ICMP echo request from GATEWAY_NET:10.50.0.100 to outside:8.8.8.8 ID=38429 seq=11 len=56
ICMP echo request from GATEWAY_NET:10.50.0.100 to outside:8.8.8.8 ID=38429 seq=12 len=56
ICMP echo request from GATEWAY_NET:10.50.0.100 to outside:8.8.8.8 ID=38429 seq=13 len=56
```

In the following screenshot, a look at the iptables rules within the router namespace reveals the NAT rules responsible for this behavior:

```
[root@controller ~]# ip netns exec qrouter-1267aae4-6568-48cf-acef-5dbcf7ecb5db iptables-save
# Generated by iptables-save v1.4.7 on Wed Aug 13 23:36:21 2014
*nat
:PREROUTING ACCEPT [19:2630]
:POSTROUTING ACCEPT [31:2252]
:OUTPUT ACCEPT [44:3152]
:neutron-l3-agent-OUTPUT - [0:0]
:neutron-l3-agent-POSTROUTING - [0:0]
:neutron-l3-agent-PREROUTING - [0:0]
:neutron-l3-agent-float-snat - [0:0]
:neutron-l3-agent-snat - [0:0]
:neutron-postrouting-bottom - [0:0]
-A PREROUTING -j neutron-l3-agent-PREROUTING
-A POSTROUTING -j neutron-l3-agent-POSTROUTING
-A POSTROUTING -j neutron-postrouting-bottom
-A OUTPUT -j neutron-l3-agent-OUTPUT
-A neutron-l3-agent-POSTROUTING ! -i qg-9ee818ab-1c ! -o qg-9ee818ab-1c -m conntrack ! --ctstate DNAT -j ACCEPT
-A neutron-l3-agent-PREROUTING -d 169.254.169.254/32 -p tcp -m tcp --dport 80 -j REDIRECT --to-ports 9697
-A neutron-l3-agent-snat -j neutron-l3-agent-float-snat
-A neutron-l3-agent-snat -s 10.30.0.0/24 -j SNAT --to-source 10.50.0.100
-A neutron-postrouting-bottom -j neutron-l3-agent-snat
COMMIT
# Completed on Wed Aug 13 23:36:21 2014
# Generated by iptables-save v1.4.7 on Wed Aug 13 23:36:21 2014
```

In this configuration, instances can communicate with outside resources as long as the instances initiate the traffic. Outside resources cannot communicate with instances directly without the use of floating IPs.

> While it is possible to disable SNAT on the Neutron router and add routes to tenant networks on upstream devices, this type of configuration is not recommended as it cannot be fully managed by OpenStack.

Assigning floating IPs

To reach instances directly from outside networks, you must configure a floating IP address and associate it with the instance's port.

Using the Neutron `port-list` command, determine the port ID of each instance recently booted, as shown in the following screenshot:

Using the Neutron `floatingip-create` command, create a single floating IP address and associate it with the port of `MyInstance1`:

```
[root@controller ~]# neutron floatingip-create --port-id=3547dbf0-58e8-4645-b0ed-6f61747b77ba GATEWAY_NET
Created a new floatingip:
+---------------------+--------------------------------------+
| Field               | Value                                |
+---------------------+--------------------------------------+
| fixed_ip_address    | 10.30.0.2                            |
| floating_ip_address | 10.50.0.101                          |
| floating_network_id | b116a938-9876-4048-99ad-0ce78aabd0a9 |
| id                  | ab0d44fd-ddcf-4804-a24f-c59bd94d5c20 |
| port_id             | 3547dbf0-58e8-4645-b0ed-6f61747b77ba |
| router_id           | 1267aae4-6568-48cf-acef-5dbcf7ecb5db |
| tenant_id           | b1e5de8d1cfc45d6a15d9c0cb442a8ab     |
+---------------------+--------------------------------------+
```

Verify that the instance can still communicate with outside resources, as shown in the following screenshot:

```
$ ping 8.8.8.8
PING 8.8.8.8 (8.8.8.8): 56 data bytes
64 bytes from 8.8.8.8: seq=0 ttl=46 time=41.843 ms
64 bytes from 8.8.8.8: seq=1 ttl=46 time=39.590 ms
64 bytes from 8.8.8.8: seq=2 ttl=46 time=38.306 ms
```

From the external gateway device, the ICMP requests should now appear as the floating IP, as shown in the following screenshot:

```
pixfirewall# debug icmp trace
debug icmp trace enabled at level 1
pixfirewall# ICMP echo request from GATEWAY_NET:10.50.0.101 to outside:8.8.8.8 ID=16641 seq=0 len=56
```

A look at the `qg` interface within the router namespace reveals the floating IP address configured as a secondary network address as shown in the following screenshot:

```
[root@controller ~]# ip netns exec qrouter-1267aae4-6568-48cf-acef-5dbcf7ecb5db ip a
8: lo: <LOOPBACK,UP,LOWER_UP> mtu 16436 qdisc noqueue state UNKNOWN
    link/loopback 00:00:00:00:00:00 brd 00:00:00:00:00:00
    inet 127.0.0.1/8 scope host lo
    inet6 ::1/128 scope host
       valid_lft forever preferred_lft forever
9: qg-9ee818ab-1c: <BROADCAST,MULTICAST,UP,LOWER_UP> mtu 1500 qdisc pfifo_fast state UP qlen 1000
    link/ether fa:16:3e:b3:c5:aa brd ff:ff:ff:ff:ff:ff
    inet 10.50.0.100/24 brd 10.50.0.255 scope global qg-9ee818ab-1c
    inet 10.50.0.101/32 brd 10.50.0.101 scope global qg-9ee818ab-1c Floating IP as secondary address
    inet6 fe80::f816:3eff:feb3:c5aa/64 scope link
       valid_lft forever preferred_lft forever
13: qr-5ea2d15f-8a: <BROADCAST,MULTICAST,UP,LOWER_UP> mtu 1500 qdisc pfifo_fast state UP qlen 1000
    link/ether fa:16:3e:fd:d8:90 brd ff:ff:ff:ff:ff:ff
    inet 10.30.0.1/24 brd 10.30.0.255 scope global qr-5ea2d15f-8a
    inet6 fe80::f816:3eff:fefd:d890/64 scope link
       valid_lft forever preferred_lft forever
```

When the floating IP is configured as a secondary network address on the `qg` interface, the router is able to respond to ARP requests to the floating IP.

A look at the iptables rules within the router namespace shows that rules have been added to perform the 1:1 NAT translation as follows:

```
[root@controller ~]# ip netns exec qrouter-1267aae4-6568-48cf-acef-5dbcf7ecb5db iptables-save
# Generated by iptables-save v1.4.7 on Wed Aug 13 23:49:32 2014
*nat
:PREROUTING ACCEPT [20:2714]
:POSTROUTING ACCEPT [31:2252]
:OUTPUT ACCEPT [45:3212]
:neutron-l3-agent-OUTPUT - [0:0]
:neutron-l3-agent-POSTROUTING - [0:0]
:neutron-l3-agent-PREROUTING - [0:0]
:neutron-l3-agent-float-snat - [0:0]
:neutron-l3-agent-snat - [0:0]
:neutron-postrouting-bottom - [0:0]
-A PREROUTING -j neutron-l3-agent-PREROUTING
-A POSTROUTING -j neutron-l3-agent-POSTROUTING
-A POSTROUTING -j neutron-postrouting-bottom
-A OUTPUT -j neutron-l3-agent-OUTPUT
-A neutron-l3-agent-OUTPUT -d 10.50.0.101/32 -j DNAT --to-destination 10.30.0.2
-A neutron-l3-agent-POSTROUTING ! -i qg-9ee818ab-1c ! -o qg-9ee818ab-1c -m conntrack ! --ctstate DNAT -j ACCEPT
-A neutron-l3-agent-PREROUTING -d 169.254.169.254/32 -p tcp -m tcp --dport 80 -j REDIRECT --to-ports 9697
-A neutron-l3-agent-PREROUTING -d 10.50.0.101/32 -j DNAT --to-destination 10.30.0.2
-A neutron-l3-agent-float-snat -s 10.30.0.2/32 -j SNAT --to-source 10.50.0.101
-A neutron-l3-agent-snat -j neutron-l3-agent-float-snat
-A neutron-l3-agent-snat -s 10.30.0.0/24 -j SNAT --to-source 10.50.0.100
-A neutron-postrouting-bottom -j neutron-l3-agent-snat
COMMIT
# Completed on Wed Aug 13 23:49:32 2014
# Generated by iptables-save v1.4.7 on Wed Aug 13 23:49:32 2014
```

With the proper routes in place on the client machine, traffic can be initiated directly to the instance via the floating IP as follows:

```
jamess-mbp:~ jdenton$ ssh cirros@10.50.0.101
The authenticity of host '10.50.0.101 (10.50.0.101)' can't be established.
RSA key fingerprint is de:4b:62:58:f0:d7:73:41:8a:65:70:5a:48:e5:89:11.
Are you sure you want to continue connecting (yes/no)? yes
Warning: Permanently added '10.50.0.101' (RSA) to the list of known hosts.
cirros@10.50.0.101's password:
$
```

Reassigning floating IPs

The idea behind a floating IP is that it is a NAT that can be quickly disassociated from an instance or other network resource and associated with another.

A listing of floating IPs shows the current association as follows:

```
[root@controller ~]# neutron floatingip-list
+--------------------------------------+-----------------+-------------------+--------------------------------------+
| id                                   | fixed_ip_address | floating_ip_address | port_id                              |
+--------------------------------------+-----------------+-------------------+--------------------------------------+
| ab0d44fd-ddcf-4804-a24f-c59bd94d5c20 | 10.30.0.2       | 10.50.0.101       | 3547dbf0-58e8-4645-b0ed-6f61747b77ba |
+--------------------------------------+-----------------+-------------------+--------------------------------------+
```

Using the Neutron `floatingip-disassociate` and `floatingip-associate` commands, disassociate the floating IP from `MyInstance1` and associate it with `MyInstance2`. The disassociation can be seen as follows:

```
[root@controller ~]# neutron floatingip-disassociate ab0d44fd-ddcf-4804-a24f-c59bd94d5c20
Disassociated floatingip ab0d44fd-ddcf-4804-a24f-c59bd94d5c20
```

The following screenshot using `floatingip-list` shows that the floating IP is no longer associated with any network resource:

```
[root@controller ~]# neutron floatingip-list
+--------------------------------------+-----------------+-------------------+---------+
| id                                   | fixed_ip_address | floating_ip_address | port_id |
+--------------------------------------+-----------------+-------------------+---------+
| ab0d44fd-ddcf-4804-a24f-c59bd94d5c20 |                 | 10.50.0.101       |         |
+--------------------------------------+-----------------+-------------------+---------+
```

Using the Neutron `floatingip-associate` command, associate the floating IP with the port of `MyInstance2` as follows:

```
[root@controller ~]# neutron floatingip-associate ab0d44fd-ddcf-4804-a24f-c59bd94d5c20 \
> $(neutron port-list | grep 10.30.0.4 | awk '{print $2}')
Associated floatingip ab0d44fd-ddcf-4804-a24f-c59bd94d5c20
```

In the following screenshot, observe the iptables rules within the `qrouter` namespace. The NAT relationship has been modified, and traffic from `MyInstance2` will now appear as the floating IP:

```
[root@controller ~]# ip netns exec qrouter-1267aae4-6568-48cf-acef-5dbcf7ecb5db iptables-save
# Generated by iptables-save v1.4.7 on Thu Aug 14 00:04:00 2014
*nat
:PREROUTING ACCEPT [21:2798]
:POSTROUTING ACCEPT [33:2380]
:OUTPUT ACCEPT [45:3212]
:neutron-l3-agent-OUTPUT - [0:0]
:neutron-l3-agent-POSTROUTING - [0:0]
:neutron-l3-agent-PREROUTING - [0:0]
:neutron-l3-agent-float-snat - [0:0]
:neutron-l3-agent-snat - [0:0]
:neutron-postrouting-bottom - [0:0]
-A PREROUTING -j neutron-l3-agent-PREROUTING
-A POSTROUTING -j neutron-l3-agent-POSTROUTING
-A POSTROUTING -j neutron-postrouting-bottom
-A OUTPUT -j neutron-l3-agent-OUTPUT
-A neutron-l3-agent-OUTPUT -d 10.50.0.101/32 -j DNAT --to-destination 10.30.0.4   The destination IP has changed from .2 to .4
-A neutron-l3-agent-POSTROUTING ! -i qg-9ee818ab-1c ! -o qg-9ee818ab-1c -m conntrack ! --ctstate DNAT -j ACCEPT
-A neutron-l3-agent-PREROUTING -d 169.254.169.254/32 -p tcp -m tcp --dport 80 -j REDIRECT --to-ports 9697
-A neutron-l3-agent-PREROUTING -d 10.50.0.101/32 -j DNAT --to-destination 10.30.0.4
-A neutron-l3-agent-float-snat -s 10.30.0.4/32 -j SNAT --to-source 10.50.0.101   The source IP has changed from .2 to .4
-A neutron-l3-agent-snat -j neutron-l3-agent-float-snat
-A neutron-l3-agent-snat -s 10.30.0.0/24 -j SNAT --to-source 10.50.0.100
-A neutron-postrouting-bottom -j neutron-l3-agent-snat
COMMIT
# Completed on Thu Aug 14 00:04:00 2014
# Generated by iptables-save v1.4.7 on Thu Aug 14 00:04:00 2014
```

As a result of the new association, attempting an SSH connection to the floating IP results in the following message:

```
jamess-mbp:~ jdenton$ ssh cirros@10.50.0.101
@@@@@@@@@@@@@@@@@@@@@@@@@@@@@@@@@@@@@@@@@@@@@@@@@@@@@@@@@@@
@    WARNING: REMOTE HOST IDENTIFICATION HAS CHANGED!     @
@@@@@@@@@@@@@@@@@@@@@@@@@@@@@@@@@@@@@@@@@@@@@@@@@@@@@@@@@@@
IT IS POSSIBLE THAT SOMEONE IS DOING SOMETHING NASTY!
Someone could be eavesdropping on you right now (man-in-the-middle attack)!
It is also possible that a host key has just been changed.
The fingerprint for the RSA key sent by the remote host is
2a:83:06:34:6c:9d:87:dc:7c:dc:9d:a4:3f:6a:5d:7d.
Please contact your system administrator.
```

The preceding message indicates that traffic is being sent to a different host. Clearing the key and logging into the instance reveals it to be MyInstance2 the following screenshot:

```
$ ip a
1: lo: <LOOPBACK,UP,LOWER_UP> mtu 16436 qdisc noqueue
    link/loopback 00:00:00:00:00:00 brd 00:00:00:00:00:00
    inet 127.0.0.1/8 scope host lo
    inet6 ::1/128 scope host
       valid_lft forever preferred_lft forever
2: eth0: <BROADCAST,MULTICAST,UP,LOWER_UP> mtu 1500 qdisc pfifo_fast qlen 1000
    link/ether fa:16:3e:de:fb:3d brd ff:ff:ff:ff:ff:ff
    inet 10.30.0.4/24 brd 10.30.0.255 scope global eth0
    inet6 fe80::f816:3eff:fede:fb3d/64 scope link
       valid_lft forever preferred_lft forever
```

Router management in the dashboard

From the Horizon dashboard, routers can be created and managed within the **Project** tab, as shown in the following screenshot:

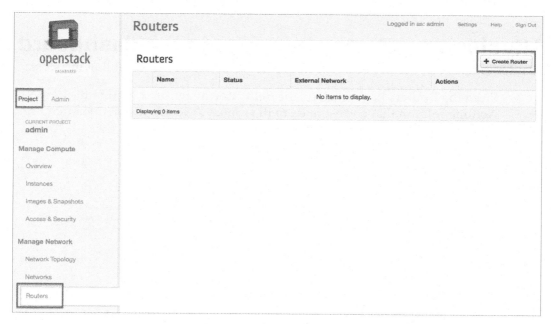

Creating a router in the dashboard

In order to create a router in the dashboard, perform the following steps:

1. From the **Routers** page, click on **Create Router** in the upper-right corner of the page. A window will pop up where the name of the router to be created should be specified as follows:

2. Enter the name of the router, and click on the blue **Create Router** button to complete the operation.

Attaching a gateway interface in the dashboard

In order to attach a gateway interface in the dashboard, perform the following steps:

1. From the **Routers** page, click on the **Set Gateway** button found in the **Actions** column that corresponds to the router. A window will open that allows you to set the external gateway network:

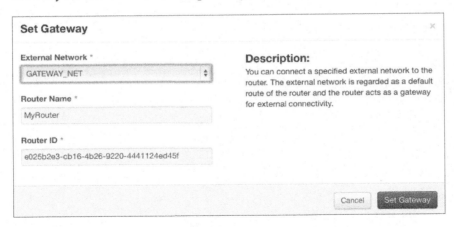

2. To confirm the gateway network selection, click on the blue **Set Gateway** button.

Attaching internal interfaces in the dashboard

In order to attach internal interfaces in the dashboard, perform the following steps:

1. To attach internal interfaces to routers in the dashboard, click on the router to reveal the **Router Details** page as follows:

2. Clicking on the **Add Interface** button will open a window that allows you to select details of the interface to be added as follows:

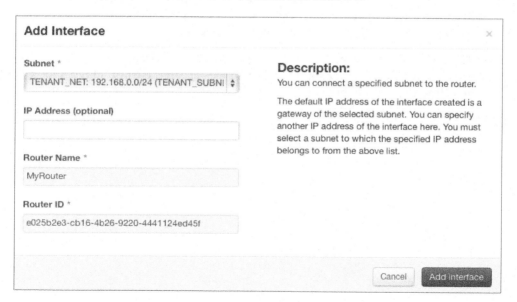

3. Select a tenant subnet you wish to attach to the router from the **Subnet** menu, and click on the blue **Add Interface** button to attach the interface:

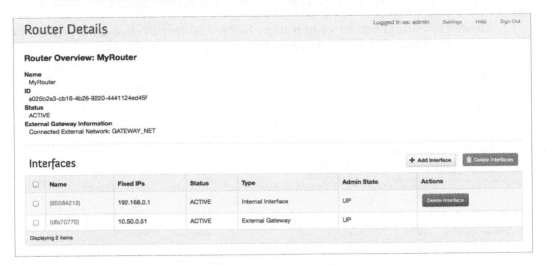

Viewing the network topology in the dashboard

From within the dashboard, users can view a logical topology of the network based on the network configuration managed by Neutron. In order to view the network topology in the dashboard, perform the following steps:

1. Click on **Network Topology** under the **Project** tab to find a logical diagram based on the networks, router, and instances created earlier. Have a look at the following screenshot:

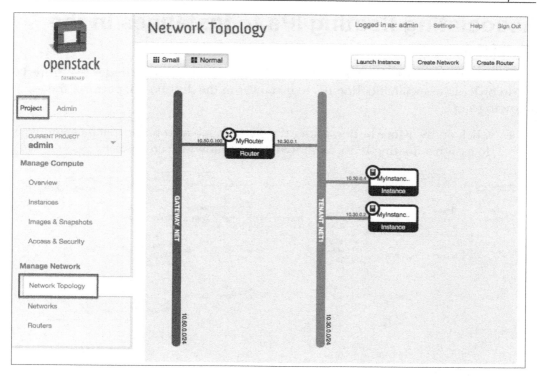

2. Hovering over the router icon reveals a window displaying details of the router such as connected ports, IPs, and port status as shown in the following screenshot:

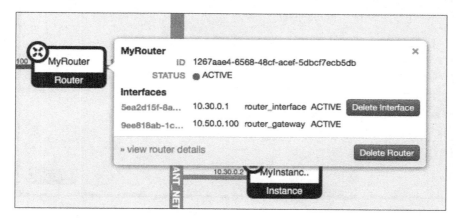

Associating floating IPs to instances in the dashboard

Floating IPs in the dashboard are managed on the **Instances** page under the **Project** tab. In order to associate floating IPs to instances in the dashboard, perform the following steps:

1. Click on the **More** button under the **Actions** tab next to the instance you wish to assign a floating IP to, as shown in the following screenshot:

2. Clicking on **Associate Floating IP** will open a window that allows you to manage floating IP allocations:

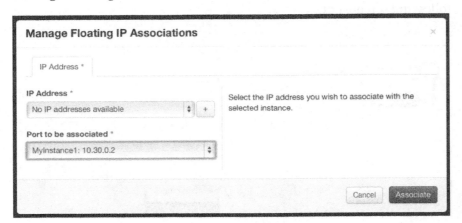

3. If there are no floating IP addresses available for allocation, click the plus **+** sign to create one. A new window will open that lists eligible floating IP pools, as shown in the following screenshot:

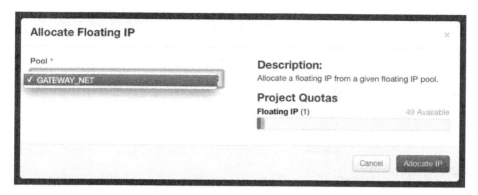

4. Since floating IPs are procured from provider networks, only provider networks whose `router:external` attribute is set to `True` will appear in the list. Click on the blue **Allocate IP** button to allow Neutron to procure the next available IP address:

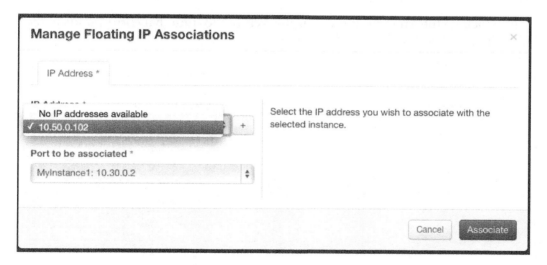

5. Once a floating IP has been selected, click on the blue **Associate** button to associate the floating IP with the instance as shown in the following screenshot:

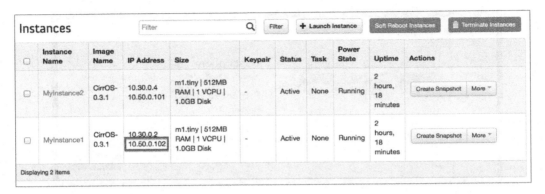

Disassociating floating IPs in the dashboard

To disassociate a floating IP from an instance in the dashboard, perform the following steps:

1. Click on the **More** button under the **Actions** column that corresponds to the instance as shown in the following screenshot:

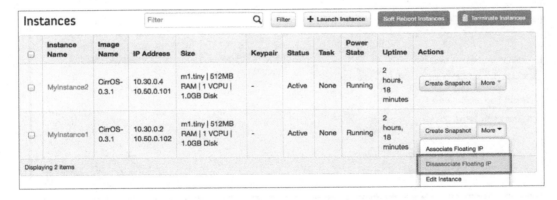

A window will open that warns you of the pending action as shown in the following screenshot:

2. Click on the blue **Disassociate Floating IP** button to proceed with the action as shown in the preceding screenshot.

 In Horizon, disassociating the floating IP from an instance has the unintended action of deleting the floating IP altogether.

Summary

Neutron routers are a core component of networking in OpenStack and provide tenants the flexibility to design the network to best suit their application. Floating IPs allow tenants to quickly and programmatically provide direct connectivity to applications through the use of network address translation. Icehouse offers improvements over Havana, including the ability to schedule multiple external networks to a single L3 agent or configure static routes on a router, but limitations still remain. The lack of a high-availability solution for Neutron routers is an issue that persists in Icehouse but is actively being worked on by the community.

In the next chapter, I will discuss OpenStack's **load-balancing-as-a-service (LBaaS)** solution that allows tenants to quickly scale their application while providing resiliency and availability.

7
Load Balancing Traffic in Neutron

The Neutron load balancing as a service extension, known as LBaaS, provides the ability to load balance traffic to applications running on virtual instances in the cloud. Neutron provides an API to manage virtual IPs, pools, pool members, and health monitors. First introduced in Grizzly, the Havana release of LBaaS offers numerous bug fixes and features over its predecessor but is not as polished as other Neutron services.

In this chapter, I will discuss fundamental load balancer concepts, including:

- Virtual IPs, pools, and pool members
- Load balancing algorithms
- Monitors
- Persistence
- Integrating load balancers in the network

LBaaS uses drivers to interact with hardware and software load balancers. In Havana, the default driver uses haproxy. Haproxy is a free, open source load balancer that is available for most Unix-based operating systems. Third-party drivers are supported by LBaaS but are outside the scope of this book.

Fundamentals of load balancing

There are three major components to a load balancer in Neutron:

- Pool member(s)
- Pool(s)
- Virtual IP(s)

A pool member is a layer 4 object and is composed of the IP address of a service and the listening port of the service. For example, a pool member might be a web server with a configured IP address, 10.30.0.2, listening on TCP port 80.

A pool is a group of pool members that typically serve identical content. A pool composed of web servers, for example, may resemble the following membership:

- **Server A**: 10.30.0.2:80
- **Server B**: 10.30.0.4:80
- **Server C**: 10.30.0.6:80

A virtual IP, or VIP, is an IP address that resides on the load balancer and listens for incoming connections. The load balancer then balances client connections among the members of the associated pool. A virtual IP is usually exposed to the Internet and is often mapped to a domain name.

Load balancing algorithms

In Havana, the following load balancing algorithms can be applied to a pool:

- Round robin
- Least connections
- Source IP

With the round robin algorithm, the load balancer passes each new connection to the next server in line. Over time, all connections will be distributed evenly across all machines being load balanced. Round robin is the least resource-intensive algorithm and has no mechanism to determine when a machine is overwhelmed by connections. To avoid overwhelming a pool member, all members should be equal in terms of processing speed, connection speed, and memory.

With the least-connections algorithm, the load balancer passes a new connection to a server that has the least number of current connections. It is considered a dynamic algorithm, as the system keeps track of the number of connections attached to each server and balances traffic accordingly. Pool members with higher specifications will likely receive more traffic, as they will be able to process connections quicker.

With the source IP algorithm, all connections originating from the same source IP address are sent to the same pool member. Connections are initially balanced using the round robin algorithm and are then tracked in a table for future lookup with subsequent connections from the same IP address. This algorithm is useful in cases where the application requires clients to use a particular server for all requests, such as an online shopping cart that stores session information on the local web server.

Monitoring

In Havana, LBaaS supports multiple monitor types, including TCP, HTTP, and HTTPS. The TCP monitor tests connectivity to pool members at layer 4, while the HTTP and HTTPS monitors test the health of pool members based on layer 7 HTTP status codes.

Session persistence

LBaaS supports session persistence on virtual IPs. Session persistence is a method of load balancing that forces multiple client requests of the same protocol to be directed to the same node. This feature is commonly used with many web applications that do not share application state between pool members.

The types of session persistence supported with the haproxy driver include the following:

- SOURCE_IP
- HTTP_COOKIE
- APP_COOKIE

Using the **SOURCE_IP** persistence type configures haproxy with the following settings within the backend pool configuration:

```
stick-table type ip size 10k
stick on src
```

The first time a client connects to the virtual IP, haproxy creates an entry in a sticky table based on the client's IP address and sends subsequent connections from the same IP address to the same backend pool member. Based on the configuration, up to 10,000 sticky entries can exist in the sticky table. This persistence method can cause a load imbalance between pool members if users connect from behind a proxy server that misidentifies multiple clients as a single address.

Using the **HTTP_COOKIE** persistence type configures haproxy with the following settings within the backend pool configuration:

```
cookie SRV insert indirect nocache
```

The first time a client connects to the virtual IP, haproxy balances the connection to the next pool member in line. When the pool member sends its response, haproxy injects a cookie named SRV into the response before sending it to the client. The value of the SRV cookie is a unique server identifier. When the client sends subsequent requests to the virtual IP, haproxy strips the cookie from the request header and sends the traffic directly to the pool member identified in the cookie. This persistence method is recommended over source IP persistence, as it is not reliant on the IP address of the client.

Using the **APP_COOKIE** persistence type configures haproxy with the following settings within the backend pool configuration:

```
appsession <CookieName> len 56 timeout 3h
```

When an application cookie is defined in a backend, haproxy will check when the server sets such a cookie, stores its value in a table, and associates it with the server's identifier. Up to 56 characters from the value will be retained. On subsequent client connections, haproxy will look for the cookie. If a known value is found, the client is directed to the pool member associated with the value. Otherwise, the load balancing algorithm is applied. Cookies are automatically removed from memory when they have gone unused for more than three hours.

Integrating load balancers into the network

When using the haproxy driver, load balancers are implemented in **one-arm** mode. In one-arm mode, the load balancer is not in the path of normal traffic to the pool members. The load balancer has a single interface for ingress and egress traffic to and from clients and pool members.

A logical diagram of a load balancer in one-arm mode can be seen in the following diagram:

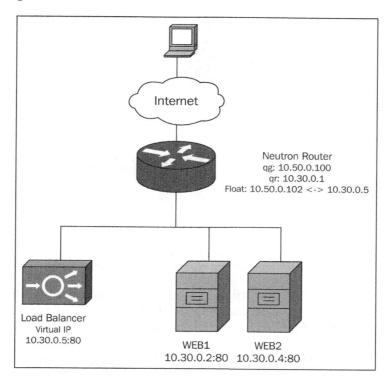

In the preceding diagram, a load balancer is configured in one-arm mode and resides on the same subnet as the servers it is balancing traffic to.

Because a load balancer in one-arm mode is not the gateway for pool members it is sending traffic to, it must rely on the use of source NAT to ensure that return traffic from the members to the client is sent back through the load balancer. An example of the traffic flow can be seen in the following diagram:

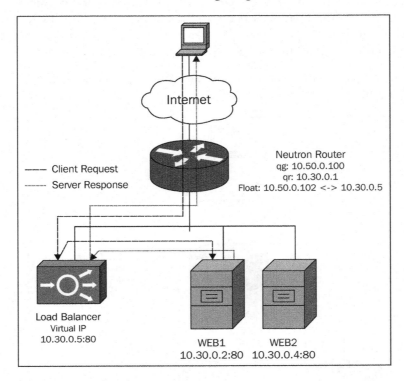

In the preceding diagram, the load balancer receives a request from the client and forwards it to Web1. The load balancer will modify the source IP of the request to its own address, 10.30.0.5, before forwarding the request to the server. This ensures the server sends the response to the load balancer, which will then rewrite the destination IP as the client address. If the server were to send the response directly to the client, the client would reject the packet.

Neutron configures haproxy to send an HTTP X-Forwarded-For header to the pool member, which allows the pool member to see the original client address. Without this header, all traffic will be identified as coming from the load balancer.

Alternatives to one-arm mode include routed mode and transparent mode. In **routed mode**, the load balancer acts as a gateway between the client and the pool member. The source addresses of packets do not need to be manipulated in most cases, as the load balancer serves as the gateway for pool members.

In **transparent mode**, the load balancer acts as a network bridge between two VLANS configured with the same subnet(s). Using this mode allows users to introduce a load balancer to the network with minimal disruption, as pool members do not need to change their gateway.

 There is currently no way to change the way a haproxy-based load balancer is integrated into the network. Some third-party drivers, however, may not be limited to the one-arm mode and can function in any mode.

Network namespaces

Neutron relies on network namespaces to provide individual load balancers when using the haproxy plugin. Load balancers are scheduled to LBaaS agents in the environment that are responsible for creating a corresponding network namespace and appropriate configuration. Namespaces used for load balancers are prefaced with qlbaas-* in the ip netns output.

Installing LBaaS

The neutron-lbaas-agent service was installed as part of the overall Neutron installation process documented in *Chapter 3, Installing Neutron*, and is typically installed on a dedicated network node or a controller node.

In Havana, haproxy is used as the default load balancer. To install haproxy, issue the following command on the controller node:

```
# yum -y install haproxy
```

Configuring the Neutron LBaaS agent service

Before the `neutron-lbaas-agent` service can be started, it must be configured. Neutron stores the LBaaS agent configuration in the `/etc/neutron/lbaas_agent.ini` file. The most common configuration options will be covered in the upcoming sections.

Define an interface driver

Like the previously installed agents, the Neutron LBaaS agent must be configured to use an interface driver that corresponds to the chosen networking plugin. In this configuration, there are two options:

- LinuxBridge
- Open vSwitch

Using `crudini`, configure the Neutron LBaaS agent to use one of the drivers.

For LinuxBridge, use the following command:

```
# crudini --set /etc/neutron/lbaas_agent.ini DEFAULT interface_driver
neutron.agent.linux.interface.BridgeInterfaceDriver
```

For Open vSwitch, use the following command:

```
# crudini --set /etc/neutron/lbaas_agent.ini DEFAULT interface_driver
neutron.agent.linux.interface.OVSInterfaceDriver
```

Define a device driver

To manage a load balancer, the Neutron LBaaS agent must be configured to use a device driver that provides the interface between the Neutron API and the programming of the load balancer itself.

Using `crudini`, define the haproxy device driver as follows:

```
# crudini --set /etc/neutron/lbaas_agent.ini DEFAULT device_driver
neutron.services.loadbalancer.drivers.haproxy.namespace_driver.
HaproxyNSDriver
```

Change the user group

On CentOS, Fedora, and RHEL-based systems, it is necessary to change the `user_group` value from its default of `nogroup` to `nobody`, as `nogroup` does not exist as a group on those systems.

Using `crudini`, set the user group to nobody:

```
crudini --set /etc/neutron/lbaas_agent.ini DEFAULT user_group nobody
```

All other configuration options can be left to their defaults or can be modified directly if the default values are not sufficient for your installation.

Define a service plugin

In addition to configuring the LBaaS agent, Neutron must be configured to use an LBaaS service plugin before the API can be utilized to create LBaaS objects.

Using a text editor, add the following service plugin to the `service_plugins` configuration option found in the `/etc/neutron/neutron.conf` file on the controller:

```
neutron.services.loadbalancer.plugin.LoadBalancerPlugin
```

Consider the following example:

```
service_plugins = neutron.services.loadbalancer.plugin.LoadBalancerPlugin
```

Close the file, and restart the `neutron-server` service as follows:

```
# service neutron-server restart
```

Starting the Neutron LBaaS agent service

To start the `neutron-lbaas-agent` service and configure it to start at boot, issue the following commands on the controller node:

```
# service neutron-lbaas-agent start
# chkconfig neutron-lbaas-agent on
```

Verify that the agent is running:

```
# service neutron-lbaas-agent status
```

The service should return output similar to the following:

```
[root@controller neutron]# service neutron-lbaas-agent status neutron-
lbaas-agent (pid  16496) is running...
```

If you encounter any issues, be sure to check the LBaaS agent log found at `/var/log/neutron/lbaas-agent.log` before proceeding.

Enabling LBaaS in Horizon

Before load balancers can be managed in the dashboard, the `enable_lb` setting in `/etc/openstack-dashboard/local_settings` file must be set to `True`. Use the following commands to change `enable_lb` from `false` to `true` and to restart the Apache web service:

```
# sed -i "/'enable_lb': False,/c\'enable_lb': True," /etc/openstack-dashboard/local_settings
# service httpd restart
```

Load balancer management in the CLI

Neutron offers a number of commands that can be used to create and manage virtual IPs, pools, pool members, and health monitors for load balancing purposes.

In the Havana implementation of LBaaS, the pool is the root object with which all other load balancer resources are associated. The workflow to create a functional load balancer starts with creating a pool and then continues with creating and associating pool members, health monitors, and a virtual IP.

Managing pools in the CLI

The following commands are used to manage pools in the CLI:

- `lb-pool-create`
- `lb-pool-delete`
- `lb-pool-list`
- `lb-pool-list-on-agent`
- `lb-pool-show`
- `lb-pool-stats`
- `lb-pool-update`

Creating a pool

A pool is a set of devices, such as web servers, that are grouped together to receive and process traffic. When traffic is sent to a virtual IP, the load balancer sends the request to any of the servers that are members of that pool.

To create a pool, use the Neutron `lb-pool-create` command as follows:

```
Syntax: lb-pool-create [--tenant-id TENANT_ID]
[--admin-state-down] [--description DESCRIPTION]
--lb-method {ROUND_ROBIN,LEAST_CONNECTIONS,SOURCE_IP}
--name NAME --protocol {HTTP,HTTPS,TCP}
--subnet-id SUBNET
```

The `--tenant-id` flag is optional; it allows you to associate the pool with the specified tenant.

The `--admin-state-down` attribute, when set, does not have any effect on the state of the pool. This is likely a bug or unimplemented feature.

The `--lb-method` attribute is used to specify the load balancing algorithm, which is used to distribute traffic amongst the pool members. The possible options include `ROUND_ROBIN`, `LEAST_CONNECTIONS`, and `SOURCE_IP`.

The `--name` attribute is used to specify a name for the pool.

The `--protocol` attribute is used to specify the type of traffic the pool will balance. `HTTP` and `HTTPS` are used to balance non-secure and secure web traffic, respectively. Use `TCP` for all other TCP traffic.

The subnet specified using the `--subnet-id` attribute should match the subnet of the pool members to be added to the pool.

Deleting a pool

To delete a load balancer pool, use the Neutron `lb-pool-delete` command as follows:

```
Syntax: lb-pool-delete POOL
```

The keyword `POOL` represents the ID of the pool that you want to delete.

> Before a pool can be deleted, any associated virtual IP must be disassociated.

Listing pools

To obtain a list of configured load balancer pools, use the Neutron `lb-pool-list` as follows:

```
Syntax: lb-pool-list
```

The returned list includes details of pools in the running tenant, such as ID, name, load balancing method, protocol, admin state, and status.

Showing pool details

To show the details of a pool, use the Neutron `lb-pool-show` command as follows:

`Syntax: lb-pool-show POOL`

The keyword `POOL` represents the ID of the pool. Details returned include the admin state, description, ID, load balancing method, members, protocol, provider, status, subnet ID, tenant ID, VIP ID, and health monitors associated with the pool.

Showing pool statistics

To display the statistics of a pool, use the Neutron `lb-pool-stats` command as follows:

`Syntax: lb-pool-stats POOL`

The keyword `POOL` represents the ID of the pool. Statistics returned include the number of active connections, total bytes in, total bytes out, and total connections.

> A pool must be in the ACTIVE state before statistics are collected, and even then, connection counters may be inaccurate. Attempting to return statistics on a pool in any other state may result in an error.

Updating a pool

To update the attributes of a pool, use the Neutron `lb-pool-update` command as follows:

`Syntax: lb-pool-update POOL [--description DESCRIPTION]`

`[--lb-method {ROUND_ROBIN,LEAST_CONNECTIONS,SOURCE_IP}]`

The `--lb-method` attribute is used to specify the load balancing algorithm used to distribute traffic among the pool members. The possible options are ROUND_ROBIN, LEAST_CONNECTIONS, and SOURCE_IP.

Listing pools associated with an agent

When a pool is created, it is scheduled to a load balancer agent. The idea is that multiple LBaaS agents can exist in an environment to provide high availability. To list the pools associated with an agent, use the Neutron `lb-pool-list-on-agent` command as follows:

```
Syntax: lb-pool-list-on-agent LBAAS_AGENT
```

The keyword `LBAAS_AGENT` represents the ID or name of an LBaaS agent. To determine the ID or name of load balancing agents known to Neutron, use the Neutron `agent-list` command.

Managing pool members in the CLI

The following commands are used to manage pool members in the CLI:

- `lb-member-create`
- `lb-member-delete`
- `lb-member-list`
- `lb-member-show`
- `lb-member-update`

Creating pool members

To create a pool member, use the Neutron `lb-member-create` command as follows:

```
Syntax: lb-member-create [--tenant-id TENANT_ID]
[--admin-state-down] [--weight WEIGHT]
--address <IP addr of member>
--protocol-port <application port number>
POOL
```

The `--tenant-id` flag is optional; it allows you to associate the pool member with the specified tenant.

The `--admin-state-down` attribute is a Boolean that, when set to `true`, places the pool member administratively down. In the down state, the pool member is not eligible to receive traffic. Pool members default to an administrative up state.

The `--weight` attribute allows you to associate a weight with the pool member. When set, a pool member may receive more or less traffic than other members in the same pool. For example, a pool member with a weight of 2 will receive twice the traffic as a pool member with a weight of 1, a pool member with a weight of 3 will receive three times the traffic as a pool member with a weight of 1, and so on.

The `--address` attribute is required; it is used to specify the IP address of the pool member.

The `--protocol-port` attribute is required; it is used to specify the listening port of the application being balanced. For example, if you are balancing HTTP traffic, the listening port specified would be 80. For SSL traffic, the port specified would be 443. In most cases, the VIP associated with the pool will utilize the same application port number.

Deleting pool members

To delete a pool member, use the Neutron `lb-member-delete` command as follows:

Syntax: `lb-member-delete MEMBER`

The keyword MEMBER represents the ID of the pool member to be deleted.

Listing pool members

To obtain a list of pool members, use the Neutron `lb-member-list` command as follows:

Syntax: `lb-member-list [--pool-id=<POOL ID>]`

The returned list of pool members includes member details, such as the ID, address, protocol port, admin state, and status. Use `--pool-id` to return pool members in the specified pool only.

Showing pool member details

To show the details of a pool member, use the Neutron `lb-member-show` command as follows:

Syntax: `lb-member-show MEMBER`

The keyword MEMBER represents the ID of the member to be shown. Returned details include the address, admin state, ID, pool ID, protocol port, status, description, tenant ID, and weight of the member.

Updating a pool member

To update the attributes of a pool member, use the Neutron `lb-member-update` command as follows:

```
Syntax: lb-member-update MEMBER [--weight WEIGHT]
```

The keyword MEMBER represents the ID of the pool member. In Havana, the only attribute of a pool member that can be updated is the weight. All other attributes are read-only.

Managing health monitors in the CLI

LBaaS in Neutron provides the ability to monitor the health of pool members as a method of ensuring the availability of an application. If a pool member is not in a healthy state, Neutron can pull a member out of rotation, limiting the impact of issues between the client and the application.

The following commands are used to manage health monitors in the CLI:

* `lb-healthmonitor-create`
* `lb-healthmonitor-delete`
* `lb-healthmonitor-associate`
* `lb-healthmonitor-disassociate`
* `lb-healthmonitor-list`
* `lb-healthmonitor-show`
* `lb-healthmonitor-update`

Creating a health monitor

To create a health monitor, use the Neutron `lb-healthmonitor-create` command as follows:

```
Syntax: lb-healthmonitor-create [--tenant-id TENANT_ID]
[--admin-state-down] [--expected-codes EXPECTED_CODES]
[--http-method HTTP_METHOD] [--url-path URL_PATH]
--delay DELAY --max-retries MAX_RETRIES
--timeout TIMEOUT --type {PING,TCP,HTTP,HTTPS}
```

The `--tenant-id` flag is optional; it allows you to associate the monitor with the specified tenant.

The `--expected-codes` attribute is optional; it allows you to specify the HTTP status code(s) that indicate that a pool member is working as expected when the monitor sends an HTTP request to the pool member for the specified URL. For example, if a `GET` request for a URL is sent to a pool member, the server is expected to return a `200 OK` status upon successful retrieval of the page. If `200` is listed as expected code, the monitor would mark the pool member as `UP`. As a result, the pool member would be eligible to receive connections. If a `500` status code were returned, it could indicate that the server is not properly processing connections. The health monitor would mark the pool member as `DOWN` and temporarily remove it from the pool. The default value is `200`.

The `--http-method` attribute is optional; it is used in conjunction with `--expected-codes` and `--url-path`. It is used to specify the type of HTTP request being made. Common types include `GET` and `POST`. There is no validation of this attribute, which may allow users to create monitors that don't work as expected. The default value is `GET`.

The `--url-path` attribute is optional; it is used in conjunction with `--expected-codes` and `--http-method`. When specified, the system will perform an HTTP request defined by `--http-method` for the URL against the pool member. The default value is root or `/`.

The `--delay` attribute is required; it is used to specify the period between each health check (in seconds). A common starting value is 5 seconds.

The `--max-retries` attribute is required; it is used to specify the maximum number of consecutive failures before a pool member is marked as `DOWN`. A common starting value is 3 retries.

The `--timeout` attribute is required; it is used to specify the number of seconds for a monitor to wait for a reply. A common value for this attribute is `(delay * max-retries) + 1` to ensure that a pool member is given adequate time to respond.

The `--type` attribute is required; it is used to specify the type of monitor being configured. The four types are as follows:

- **PING**: The simplest of all monitor types, PING uses ICMP to confirm connectivity to pool members.

 The PING type is not properly supported in the haproxy driver and results in the same behavior as the TCP type.

- **TCP**: This instructs the load balancer to send a TCP SYN packet to the pool member. Upon receiving a SYN ACK back, the load balancer resets the connection. This type of monitor is commonly referred to as a half-open TCP monitor.

- **HTTP**: This instructs the monitor to initiate an HTTP request to a pool member based on the `expected_codes`, `url_path`, and `http_method` attributes described here.

- **HTTPS**: This instructs the monitor to initiate an HTTPS request to a pool member based on the `expected_codes`, `url_path`, and `http_method` attributes described here.

Deleting a health monitor

To delete a health monitor, use the Neutron `lb-healthmonitor-delete` command as follows:

```
Syntax: lb-healthmonitor-delete HEALTH_MONITOR
```

The keyword `HEALTH_MONITOR` represents the ID of the health monitor to be deleted.

Associating a health monitor with a pool

To associate a health monitor with a pool, use the Neutron `lb-healthmonitor-associate` command as follows:

```
Syntax: lb-healthmonitor-associate HEALTH_MONITOR_ID POOL
```

The keyword `POOL` represents the ID of the pool to be associated with the monitor.

 More than one health monitor can be associated with a single pool. Also, a single monitor can be leveraged by multiple pools.

Disassociating a health monitor from a pool

To disassociate a health monitor from a pool, use the Neutron `lb-healthmonitor-disassociate` command as follows:

```
Syntax: lb-healthmonitor-disassociate HEALTH_MONITOR_ID POOL
```

The keyword `POOL` represents the ID of the pool to be disassociated from the monitor.

Listing health monitors

To obtain a list of health monitors, use the Neutron `lb-healthmonitor-list` command as follows:

```
Syntax: lb-healthmonitor-list
```

The list returned includes the ID, type, and admin status of all health monitors.

Showing health monitor details

To show the details of a health monitor, use the Neutron `lb-healthmonitor-show` command as shown below:

```
Syntax: lb-healthmonitor-show HEALTH_MONITOR
```

The details returned include delay, expected codes, HTTP method, ID, max retries, pools, tenant ID, timeout, type, and URL path.

Updating a health monitor

To update the attributes of a health monitor, use the Neutron `lb-healthmonitor-update` command as follows:

```
Syntax: lb-healthmonitor-update HEALTH_MONITOR_ID
```

Updateable attributes include delay, expected codes, HTTP method, max retries, timeout, and URL path.

Managing virtual IPs in the CLI

The following commands are used to manage virtual IPs in the CLI:

- `lb-vip-create`
- `lb-vip-delete`
- `lb-vip-list`
- `lb-vip-show`
- `lb-vip-update`

Creating a virtual IP

To create a virtual IP, use the Neutron `lb-vip-create` command as follows:

```
Syntax: lb-vip-create [--tenant-id TENANT_ID]
[--address ADDRESS] [--admin-state-down]
[--connection-limit CONNECTION_LIMIT]
[--description DESCRIPTION] --name NAME
--protocol-port PROTOCOL_PORT
--protocol {TCP,HTTP,HTTPS}
--subnet-id SUBNET
POOL
```

The `--tenant-id` flag is optional; it allows you to associate the monitor with the specified tenant.

The `--admin-state-down` attribute, when set, does not have any effect on the state of the load balancer.

The `--address` attribute is optional; it allows you to specify the IP address of the listener. A Neutron port will be created to reserve the address specified here.

The `--connection-limit` attribute is optional; it allows you to define a connection limit on the virtual IP. Once the limit has been reached, new client traffic will not be balanced.

The `--name` attribute is required; it is used to define the name of the virtual IP.

The `--protocol-port` attribute is required; it is used to specify the listening port of the application being balanced. For example, if you were balancing HTTP traffic, the port specified would be 80. For SSL traffic, this port specified would be 443. In most cases, the pool associated with the virtual IP would utilize the same application port number.

The `--protocol` attribute is required; it is used to specify the type of traffic being load balanced. The options are TCP, HTTP, and HTTPS. This value must match the protocol of the associated pool.

The `--subnet-id` attribute is required; it is used to provide the proper network configuration of the load balancer. Every load balancer exists in its own network namespace, and the subnet specified here is what is used to configure networking within the namespace, including the IP address and default route.

The keyword `POOL` represents the pool to be balanced by this virtual IP.

Deleting a virtual IP

To delete a virtual IP, use the Neutron `lb-vip-delete` command as follows:

Syntax: `lb-vip-delete VIP`

The keyword `VIP` represents the ID of the virtual IP to be deleted.

Listing virtual IPs

To obtain a list of virtual IPs, use the Neutron `lb-vip-list` command as follows:

Syntax: `lb-vip-list`

The output returned includes a list of virtual IPs and details, such as ID, name, address, protocol, and state.

Showing virtual IP details

To show the details of a virtual IP, use the Neutron `lb-vip-show` command as follows:

Syntax: `lb-vip-show VIP`

The keyword `VIP` represents the ID of the virtual IP. The details returned include the address, connection limit, description, ID, name, pool ID, port ID, protocol, protocol port, status, subnet ID, and tenant ID.

Updating a virtual IP

To update the attributes of a virtual IP, use the Neutron `lb-vip-update` command as follows:

Syntax: `lb-vip-update VIP [--connection-limit CONNECTION_LIMIT]`
`[--pool-id POOL] [--session-persistence`
`type={HTTP_COOKIE,SOURCE_IP,APP_COOKIE}]`

Session persistence is an attribute that is not directly exposed within the CLI but is available in the dashboard. You can, however, update this attribute with the `lb-vip-update` command in the following ways:

To enable `SOURCE_IP` or `HTTP_COOKIE` persistence, use the following syntax:

Syntax: `lb-vip-update VIP --session-persistence type=dict type={HTTP_COOKIE,SOURCE_IP}`

To enable `APP_COOKIE` persistence, use the following syntax:

```
Syntax: lb-vip-update VIP --session-persistence type=dict type=APP_
COOKIE,cookie_name=<application cookie name>
```

`APP_COOKIE` persistence requires the use of a specified cookie name unique to your application. A common example is the use of a `JSESSIONID` cookie in a JSP application.

 The `type=dict` mapping is needed for Python to properly process the subsequent key/value pairs.

Building a load balancer

To demonstrate the creation and use of load balancers in Neutron, this next section is dedicated to building a functional load balancer based on certain requirements.

A tenant has a simple Neutron network set up with a router attached to both an external provider network and an internal tenant network. The tenant would like to load balance HTTP traffic between two instances running a web server. Each instance has been configured with an `index.html` page containing a unique server identifier.

To eliminate the installation and configuration of a web server for this example, you can mimic the behavior of one by using the `SimpleHTTPServer` Python module on the instances as follows:

```
ubuntu@web1:~$ echo "This is Web1" > ~/index.html
ubuntu@web1:~$ sudo python -m SimpleHTTPServer 80
Serving HTTP on 0.0.0.0 port 80 ...
```

Repeat the aforementioned commands for the second instance, substituting `Web2` for `Web1` in the `index.html` file.

Creating a pool

The first step to building a functional load balancer is to create the pool. Using the Neutron `lb-pool-create` command, create a pool with the following attributes:

- Name: `WEB_POOL`
- Load balancing method: `Round robin`
- Protocol: `HTTP`
- Subnet ID: <Subnet ID of the pool members>

Have a look at the following screenshot:

```
[root@controller ~]# neutron lb-pool-create --description "The Web Pool" --lb-method ROUND_ROBIN \
> --name WEB_POOL --protocol HTTP --subnet-id 9e7f07bc-e194-4632-8558-4d81aa50ef16
Created a new pool:
+------------------------+--------------------------------------+
| Field                  | Value                                |
+------------------------+--------------------------------------+
| admin_state_up         | True                                 |
| description            | The Web Pool                         |
| health_monitors        |                                      |
| health_monitors_status |                                      |
| id                     | 393b994c-bb7c-4331-aedd-af1df196f133 |
| lb_method              | ROUND_ROBIN                          |
| members                |                                      |
| name                   | WEB_POOL                             |
| protocol               | HTTP                                 |
| provider               | haproxy                              |
| status                 | PENDING_CREATE                       |
| status_description     |                                      |
| subnet_id              | 9e7f07bc-e194-4632-8558-4d81aa50ef16 |
| tenant_id              | b1e5de8d1cfc45d6a15d9c0cb442a8ab     |
| vip_id                 |                                      |
+------------------------+--------------------------------------+
```

 The state of the pool will remain in PENDING_CREATE until a virtual IP has been associated with it.

Creating pool members

The next step to building a functional load balancer is to create the pool members that are to be balanced.

In this environment, there are two instances eligible for use in the pool, as shown in the following screenshot:

```
[root@controller ~]# nova list
+--------------------------------------+------+--------+------------+-------------+-----------------------+
| ID                                   | Name | Status | Task State | Power State | Networks              |
+--------------------------------------+------+--------+------------+-------------+-----------------------+
| a2b5c8fe-e3a0-4cf1-93ee-86ad4fb0ff35 | Web1 | ACTIVE | -          | Running     | TENANT_NET1=10.30.0.2 |
| eac1f201-76ca-488f-aaa8-d5c50d57c8f4 | Web2 | ACTIVE | -          | Running     | TENANT_NET1=10.30.0.4 |
+--------------------------------------+------+--------+------------+-------------+-----------------------+
```

Using the Neutron `lb-member-create` command, create two pool members with the following attributes:

- Member 1:
    - Name: `Web1`
    - Address: `10.30.0.2`
    - Protocol Port: `80`
    - Pool: `WEB_POOL`

- Member 2:
    - Name: `Web2`
    - Address: `10.30.0.4`
    - Protocol Port: `80`
    - Pool: `WEB_POOL`

The following screenshot demonstrates the process of creating the first pool member:

```
[root@controller ~]# neutron lb-member-create --address 10.30.0.2 --protocol-port 80 WEB_POOL
Created a new member:
+--------------------+--------------------------------------+
| Field              | Value                                |
+--------------------+--------------------------------------+
| address            | 10.30.0.2                            |
| admin_state_up     | True                                 |
| id                 | d55b787e-5cab-4dcb-ab7b-e58930988dba |
| pool_id            | 393b994c-bb7c-4331-aedd-af1df196f133 |
| protocol_port      | 80                                   |
| status             | PENDING_CREATE                       |
| status_description |                                      |
| tenant_id          | b1e5de8d1cfc45d6a15d9c0cb442a8ab     |
| weight             | 1                                    |
+--------------------+--------------------------------------+
```

Repeat the process shown in the preceding screenshot to create the second pool member.

The Neutron command `lb-member-list` returns a list showing the two pool members but does not list their associated pool(s). Have a look at the following screenshot:

```
[root@controller ~]# neutron lb-member-list
+--------------------------------------+-----------+---------------+----------------+----------------+
| id                                   | address   | protocol_port | admin_state_up | status         |
+--------------------------------------+-----------+---------------+----------------+----------------+
| 728c2508-6b43-403d-a32e-03041a85b8ec | 10.30.0.4 |            80 | True           | PENDING_CREATE |
| d55b787e-5cab-4dcb-ab7b-e58930988dba | 10.30.0.2 |            80 | True           | PENDING_CREATE |
+--------------------------------------+-----------+---------------+----------------+----------------+
```

As a workaround, you can include certain columns to be returned as shown in the following screenshot:

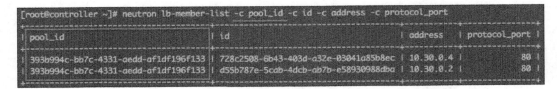

Creating a health monitor

To provide high availability of an application to clients, it is recommended that you create and apply a health monitor to a pool. Without a monitor, the load balancer will continue to send traffic to members that may not be available.

Using the Neutron `lb-healthmonitor-create` command, create a health monitor with the following attributes. This is shown in the screenshot following the attributes:

- Delay: 5
- Max retries: 3
- Timeout: 16 ((Delay * Max Retries) + 1)
- Type: TCP

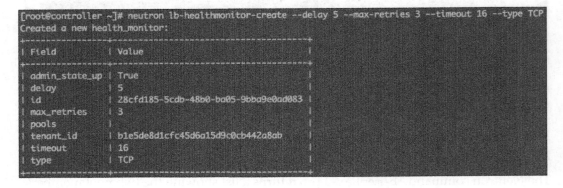

To associate the newly created health monitor with the pool, use the `lb-healthmonitor-associate` command as follows:

`Syntax: lb-healthmonitor-associate HEALTH_MONITOR_ID POOL`

Consider the following screenshot:

```
[root@controller ~]# neutron lb-healthmonitor-associate 28cfd185-5cdb-48b0-ba05-9bba9e0ad083 WEB_POOL
Associated health monitor 28cfd185-5cdb-48b0-ba05-9bba9e0ad083
```

Creating a virtual IP

The last step in creating a functional load balancer is to create the virtual IP, or VIP, which acts as a listener and balances traffic across pool members. Using the Neutron `lb-vip-create` command, create a virtual IP with the following attributes:

- Name: WEB_VIP
- Protocol Port: 80
- Protocol: HTTP
- Subnet ID: <Subnet ID of Pool>
- Pool: WEB_POOL

Have a look at the following screenshot:

```
[root@controller ~]# neutron lb-vip-create --description "The Web VIP" --name WEB_VIP \
> --protocol-port 80 --protocol HTTP --subnet-id 9e7f07bc-e194-4632-8558-4d81aa50ef16 WEB_POOL
Created a new vip:
+---------------------+--------------------------------------+
| Field               | Value                                |
+---------------------+--------------------------------------+
| address             | 10.30.0.5                            |
| admin_state_up      | True                                 |
| connection_limit    | -1                                   |
| description         | The Web VIP                          |
| id                  | cfd104cc-398d-4da5-a12e-6e3031e2cc94 |
| name                | WEB_VIP                              |
| pool_id             | 393b994c-bb7c-4331-aedd-af1df196f133 |
| port_id             | 4cd532f5-3188-4e2b-a77b-4c83c4a7128b |
| protocol            | HTTP                                 |
| protocol_port       | 80                                   |
| status              | PENDING_CREATE                       |
| status_description  |                                      |
| subnet_id           | 9e7f07bc-e194-4632-8558-4d81aa50ef16 |
| tenant_id           | b1e5de8d1cfc45d6a15d9c0cb442a8ab     |
+---------------------+--------------------------------------+
```

Once the virtual IP has been created, the state of the VIP and the pool will change to
ACTIVE as shown in the following screenshot:

```
[root@controller ~]# neutron lb-vip-list
+--------------------------------------+---------+------------+----------+----------------+--------+
| id                                   | name    | address    | protocol | admin_state_up | status |
+--------------------------------------+---------+------------+----------+----------------+--------+
| cfd104cc-398d-4da5-a12e-6e3031e2cc94 | WEB_VIP | 10.30.0.5  | HTTP     | True           | ACTIVE |
+--------------------------------------+---------+------------+----------+----------------+--------+
[root@controller ~]# neutron lb-pool-list
+--------------------------------------+----------+----------+-------------+----------+----------------+--------+
| id                                   | name     | provider | lb_method   | protocol | admin_state_up | status |
+--------------------------------------+----------+----------+-------------+----------+----------------+--------+
| 393b994c-bb7c-4331-aedd-af1df196f133 | WEB_POOL | haproxy  | ROUND_ROBIN | HTTP     | True           | ACTIVE |
+--------------------------------------+----------+----------+-------------+----------+----------------+--------+
```

The LBaaS network namespace

A listing of the network namespaces on the host running the LBaaS agent reveals a
network namespace that corresponds to the load balancer just created as shown in
the following screenshot:

```
[root@controller ~]# ip netns
qrouter-0f720e65-13b9-45f3-b750-d8a3a1b18672
qdhcp-a9fa092a-a412-4097-bb04-7f08fa5eb8e3
qlbaas-393b994c-bb7c-4331-aedd-af1df196f133
qdhcp-f92e9357-5070-42e1-916a-32bc11fd4c76
```

The IP configuration within the namespace reveals a tap interface that corresponds to
the subnet of the virtual IP as follows:

```
[root@controller ~]# ip netns exec qlbaas-393b994c-bb7c-4331-aedd-af1df196f133 ip a
22: lo: <LOOPBACK,UP,LOWER_UP> mtu 16436 qdisc noqueue state UNKNOWN
    link/loopback 00:00:00:00:00:00 brd 00:00:00:00:00:00
    inet 127.0.0.1/8 scope host lo
    inet6 ::1/128 scope host
       valid_lft forever preferred_lft forever
23: ns-4cd532f5-31: <BROADCAST,MULTICAST,UP,LOWER_UP> mtu 1500 qdisc pfifo_fast state UP qlen 1000
    link/ether fa:16:3e:92:92:72 brd ff:ff:ff:ff:ff:ff
    inet 10.30.0.5/24 brd 10.30.0.255 scope global ns-4cd532f5-31
    inet6 fe80::f816:3eff:fe92:9272/64 scope link
       valid_lft forever preferred_lft forever
```

Neutron creates a haproxy configuration file specific to every load balancer that is
created by users. The load balancer configuration files can be found in the /var/lib/
neutron/lbaas/ directory of the host running the LBaaS agent.

The configuration file for this load balancer built by Neutron can be seen in the following screenshot:

```
[root@controller ~]# cat /var/lib/neutron/lbaas/393b994c-bb7c-4331-aedd-af1df196f133/conf
global                                          Load balancer ID
        daemon
        user nobody
        group nobody
        log /dev/log local0
        log /dev/log local1 notice
        stats socket /var/lib/neutron/lbaas/393b994c-bb7c-4331-aedd-af1df196f133/sock mode 0666 level user
defaults
        log global
        retries 3
        option redispatch
        timeout connect 5000
        timeout client 50000
        timeout server 50000
frontend cfd104cc-398d-4da5-a12e-6e3031e2cc94
        option tcplog
        bind 10.30.0.5:80    The virtual IP
        mode http
        default_backend 393b994c-bb7c-4331-aedd-af1df196f133
        option forwardfor
backend 393b994c-bb7c-4331-aedd-af1df196f133
        mode http
        balance roundrobin
        option forwardfor
        timeout check 16s                    Pool Member IPs
        server 728c2508-6b43-403d-a32e-03041a85b8ec 10.30.0.4:80 weight 1 check inter 5s fall 3
        server d55b787e-5cab-4dcb-ab7b-e58930988dba 10.30.0.2:80 weight 1 check inter 5s fall 3
```

Confirming load balancer functionality

From within the router namespace, confirm connectivity to Web1 and Web2 over port 80 using `curl` as follows:

```
[root@controller ~]# ip netns exec qrouter-0f720e65-13b9-45f3-b750-d8a3a1b18672 curl http://10.30.0.2
This is Web1
[root@controller ~]# ip netns exec qrouter-0f720e65-13b9-45f3-b750-d8a3a1b18672 curl http://10.30.0.4
This is Web2
```

By opening multiple connections to the virtual IP 10.30.0.5 within the router namespace, you can observe round robin load balancing in effect:

```
[root@controller ~]# ip netns exec qrouter-0f720e65-13b9-45f3-b750-d8a3a1b18672 curl http://10.30.0.5
This is Web1
[root@controller ~]# ip netns exec qrouter-0f720e65-13b9-45f3-b750-d8a3a1b18672 curl http://10.30.0.5
This is Web2
[root@controller ~]# ip netns exec qrouter-0f720e65-13b9-45f3-b750-d8a3a1b18672 curl http://10.30.0.5
This is Web1
[root@controller ~]# ip netns exec qrouter-0f720e65-13b9-45f3-b750-d8a3a1b18672 curl http://10.30.0.5
This is Web2
```

With round robin load balancing, every connection is evenly distributed among the two pool members.

Observing health monitors

A packet capture on `Web1` reveals the load balancer is performing TCP health checks every 5 seconds. Have a look at the following screenshot:

```
root@web1:~# tcpdump -i any port 80 -n
tcpdump: verbose output suppressed, use -v or -vv for full protocol decode
listening on any, link-type LINUX_SLL (Linux cooked), capture size 65535 bytes

01:36:20.547583 IP 10.30.0.5.49533 > 10.30.0.2.80: Flags [S], seq 3636217985, win 14600,
01:36:20.547613 IP 10.30.0.2.80 > 10.30.0.5.49533: Flags [S.], seq 3716667043, ack 36362
01:36:20.547854 IP 10.30.0.5.49533 > 10.30.0.2.80: Flags [R.], seq 1, ack 1, win 115, op

01:36:25.549560 IP 10.30.0.5.49535 > 10.30.0.2.80: Flags [S], seq 1691059124, win 14600,
01:36:25.549586 IP 10.30.0.2.80 > 10.30.0.5.49535: Flags [S.], seq 1448956896, ack 16910
01:36:25.549816 IP 10.30.0.5.49535 > 10.30.0.2.80: Flags [R.], seq 1, ack 1, win 115, op

01:36:30.551589 IP 10.30.0.5.49537 > 10.30.0.2.80: Flags [S], seq 3689515567, win 14600,
01:36:30.551613 IP 10.30.0.2.80 > 10.30.0.5.49537: Flags [S.], seq 2737257391, ack 36895
01:36:30.551847 IP 10.30.0.5.49537 > 10.30.0.2.80: Flags [R.], seq 1, ack 1, win 115, op
```

In the preceding screenshot, the load balancer is sending a TCP SYN packet every 5 seconds and immediately sends an RST upon receiving the SYN ACK from the pool member.

To observe the monitor removing a pool member from eligibility, stop the web service on `Web1`, and observe the packet captures and logs as follows:

```
01:39:00.604726 IP 10.30.0.5.49604 > 10.30.0.2.80: Flags [S], seq 246239507, win 14600, op
01:39:00.604741 IP 10.30.0.2.80 > 10.30.0.5.49604: Flags [R.], seq 0, ack 246239508, win 0

01:39:05.606646 IP 10.30.0.5.49606 > 10.30.0.2.80: Flags [S], seq 1018504608, win 14600, o
01:39:05.606672 IP 10.30.0.2.80 > 10.30.0.5.49606: Flags [R.], seq 0, ack 1018504609, win

01:39:10.608178 IP 10.30.0.5.49608 > 10.30.0.2.80: Flags [S], seq 4134644631, win 14600, o
01:39:10.608193 IP 10.30.0.2.80 > 10.30.0.5.49608: Flags [R.], seq 0, ack 4134644632, win
```

In the preceding output, the web service is stopped, and connections to port 80 are refused. Immediately following the third failure, the load balancer marks the pool member as DOWN, as follows:

```
Aug 18 21:39:10 controller haproxy[9106]: Server 393b994c-bb7c-4331-aedd-af1df196f133/d55b787e-5cab-4dcb-ab7b-e58930988dba
is DOWN, reason: Layer4 connection problem, info: "Connection refused", check duration: 0ms. 1 active and 0 backup servers
left. 0 sessions active, 0 requeued, 0 remaining in queue.
```

Subsequent connections to the VIP are sent to WEB2 as follows

```
[root@controller ~]# ip netns exec qrouter-0f720e65-13b9-45f3-b750-d8a3a1b18672 curl http://10.30.0.5
This is Web2
[root@controller ~]# ip netns exec qrouter-0f720e65-13b9-45f3-b750-d8a3a1b18672 curl http://10.30.0.5
This is Web2
[root@controller ~]# ip netns exec qrouter-0f720e65-13b9-45f3-b750-d8a3a1b18672 curl http://10.30.0.5
This is Web2
```

After restarting the web service on Web1, the load balancer places the server back in the pool upon the next successful health check as follows:

```
Aug 18 21:44:35 controller haproxy[9106]: Server 393b994c-bb7c-4331-aedd-af1df196f133/d55b787e-5cab-4dcb-ab7b-e58930988dba
is UP, reason: Layer4 check passed, check duration: 0ms. 2 active and 0 backup servers online. 0 sessions requeued, 0 total
in queue.
```

Connecting to the virtual IP externally

To connect to a virtual IP externally, a floating IP must be associated with the Neutron port associated with the VIP, as the virtual IP exists within a subnet behind the router and is not reachable directly.

Using the Neutron `floatingip-create` command, assign a floating IP to be used with the virtual IP as follows:

```
[root@controller ~]# neutron floatingip-create GATEWAY_NET --port-id=$(neutron port-list | grep 10.30.0.5 | awk '{print $2}')
Created a new floatingip:
+---------------------+--------------------------------------+
| Field               | Value                                |
+---------------------+--------------------------------------+
| fixed_ip_address    | 10.30.0.5                            |
| floating_ip_address | 10.50.0.102    ◄──── External Virtual IP |
| floating_network_id | a9fa092a-a412-4097-bb04-7f08fa5eb8e3 |
| id                  | 10781e7e-7ec0-4ffb-8544-ded427da0016 |
| port_id             | 4cd532f5-3188-4e2b-a77b-4c83c4a7128b |
| router_id           | 0f720e65-13b9-45f3-b750-d8a3a1b18672 |
| tenant_id           | b1e5de8d1cfc45d6a15d9c0cb442a8ab     |
+---------------------+--------------------------------------+
```

A test from a workstation to the floating IP confirms external connectivity to the load balancer and its pool members. Have a look at the following screenshot:

```
jamess-mbp:~ jdenton$ curl http://10.50.0.102
This is Web1
jamess-mbp:~ jdenton$ curl http://10.50.0.102
This is Web2
jamess-mbp:~ jdenton$ curl http://10.50.0.102
This is Web1
jamess-mbp:~ jdenton$ curl http://10.50.0.102
This is Web2
```

Load balancer management in the dashboard

In the Horizon dashboard, load balancers can be managed from the **Project** panel by clicking on **Load Balancers** in the menu on the left-hand side of the screen. Have a look at the following screenshot:

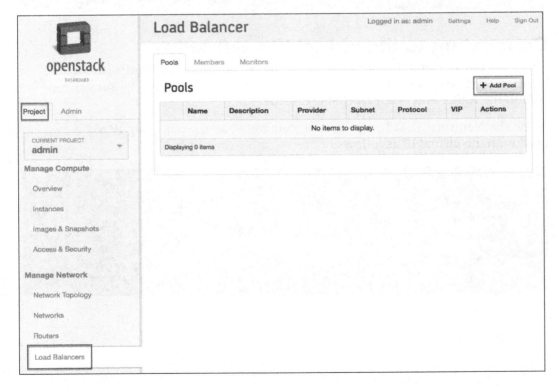

From the **Load Balancers** screen, pools, members, and monitors can be managed from their respective tabs.

Creating a pool in the dashboard

To create a pool, perform the following steps:

1. Click on the **Add Pool** button within the **Pools** section. A window will pop up that resembles the one shown in the following screenshot:

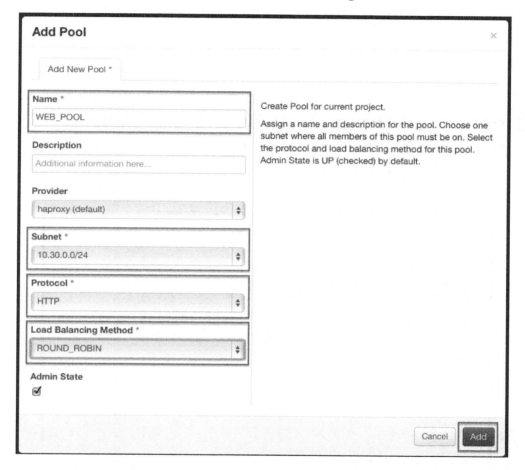

2. From the **Add Pool** window, you can specify a name for the pool and choose the subnet, protocol, and load balancing method.

3. To create the pool, click on the blue button labeled **Add**. Once created, the pool will be listed in the **Pools** section as follows:

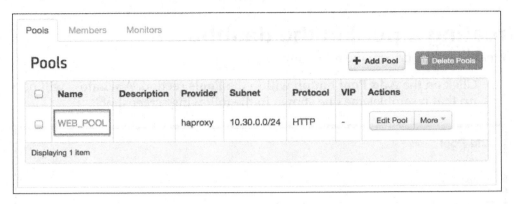

Creating pool members in the dashboard

To create a pool member, perform the following steps:

1. Click on the **Add Member** button within the **Members** section. A window will pop up that resembles the one shown in the following screenshot:

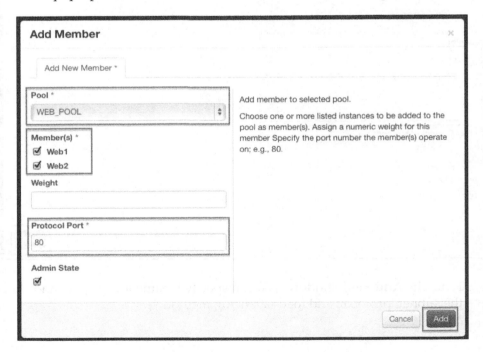

2. From the **Add Member** window, you can add multiple members to a pool simultaneously and set a common weight and protocol port for the chosen pool members.

3. To create pool members, click on the blue button labeled **Add**:

4. To edit a particular pool member, click on the **Edit Member** button under the **Actions** column next to the pool member:

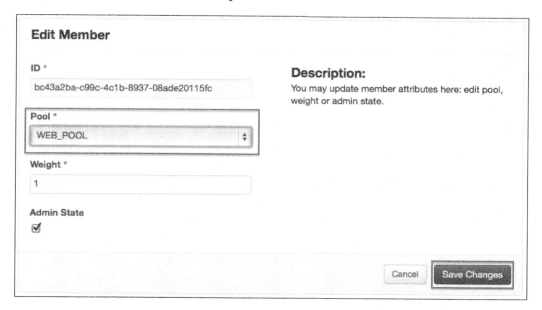

5. From the **Edit Member** screen, you can move the member to another pool, change the weight, or mark the member as administratively down. To save your changes, click on the blue **Save Changes** button.

Creating health monitors in the dashboard

To create a health monitor, perform the following steps:

1. Click on **Add Monitor** from the **Monitors** tab on the **Load Balancers** screen. A window will pop up similar to the one shown in the following screenshot:

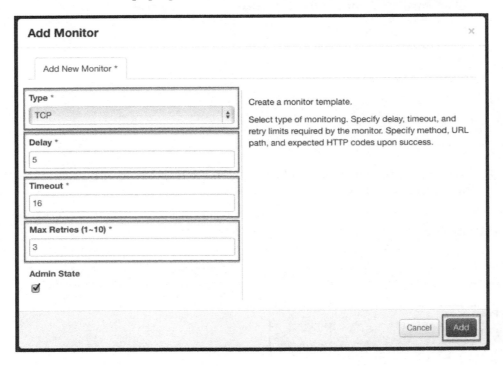

2. From the **Add Monitor** window, you can choose the type of monitor to be created as well as specify the delay, timeout, and max retries for the monitor. To add the monitor, click on the blue **Add** button.

3. To associate a monitor with a pool, navigate to the list of pools by clicking on the **Pools** tab in the **Load Balancers** section. Choose **Add a Health Monitor** from the **More** menu under **Actions** next to the pool as shown in the following screenshot:

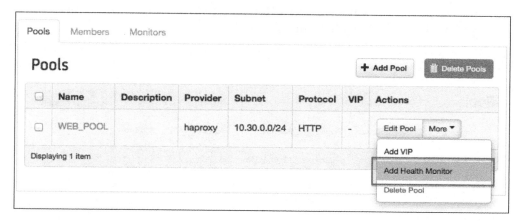

4. Choose a monitor from the menu, and click the blue **Add** button to associate it with the pool. Have a look at the following screenshot:

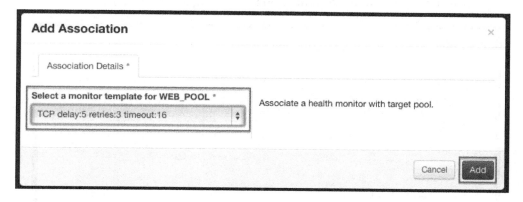

Creating a virtual IP in the dashboard

To create a virtual IP, perform the following steps:

1. Navigate to the list of pools by clicking on the **Pools** tab in the **Load Balancers** section. Choose **Add VIP** from the **More** menu next to the pool as shown in the following screenshot:

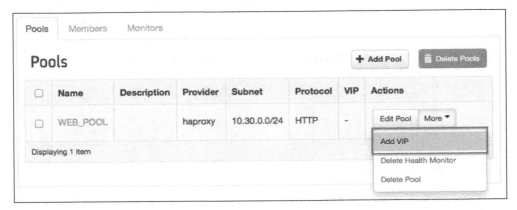

A window will pop up similar to the following screenshot:

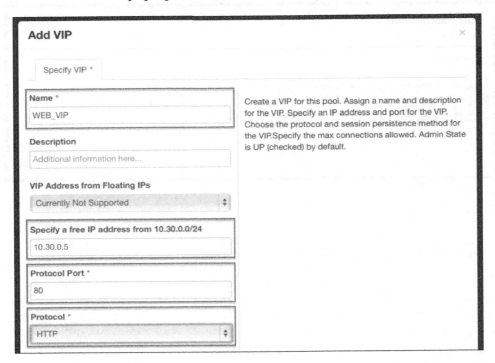

2. From the **Add VIP** window, you can assign a name to the VIP, specify an IP address, specify the protocol and listener port, define a type of session persistence, and set the connection limit. Information on session persistence types can be found earlier in this chapter.

3. Once configured, click on the blue **Add** button to associate the VIP with the pool.

One limitation found in the dashboard is the inability to have Neutron automatically assign an IP address from the subnet for use as the virtual IP. You must specify a free IP address from the subnet associated with the pool, otherwise the VIP creation process will fail.

Connecting to the virtual IP externally

In Havana and Icehouse, the ability to assign a floating IP to the virtual IP from the **Add VIP** window is not functional. Instead, you must perform the following steps:

1. Navigate to the **Instances** pane, and choose **Associate Floating IP** from any of the instances listed as follows:

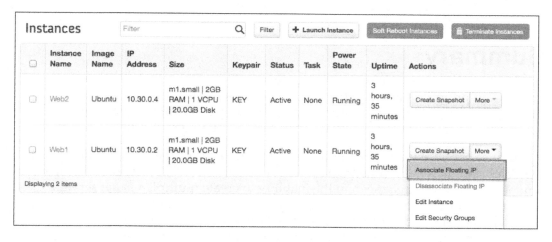

A window will pop up similar to the one pictured below:

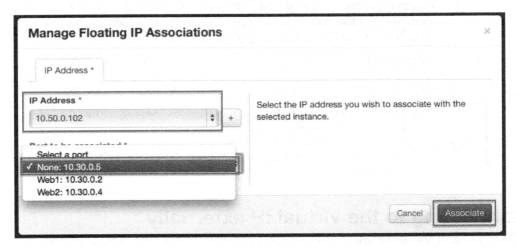

2. From the **Manage Floating IP Associations** window, select a floating IP from the **IP Address** menu, and choose the address utilized by the virtual IP from the **Port To Be Associated** menu. Click on the blue **Associate** button to associate the floating IP with the virtual IP.

Summary

Load balancing as a service provides tenants with the ability to scale their application programmatically through the Neutron API. Users can balance traffic to pools consisting of multiple application servers and can provide high availability of their application through the use of intelligent health monitors.

The user experience varies greatly between the CLI and the dashboard with regard to LBaaS, and there is not much difference in the Icehouse release either. A major limitation to LBaaS can be seen in the inability to create multiple virtual servers using the same IP address and different layer 4 ports. This limits the ability to send SSL and non-SSL traffic to the same pool of servers. Advanced features, such as SSL offloading and layer 7 load balancing, are not available in either the Havana or the Icehouse release. The community is looking to address many functional and performance concerns in the Juno release of OpenStack, and beyond.

In the next chapter, I will discuss the two methods of securing instances in an OpenStack cloud: Neutron security groups and firewall as a service.

8
Protecting Instances on the Network

Neutron includes two methods of providing network-level security to instances. The first method is using security groups that leverage iptables rules to filter traffic on the compute node hosting the instance. The second method is a feature known as **Firewall-as-a-Service (FWaaS)** that provides filtering at the perimeter of the network on a Neutron router. First introduced in the Havana release of OpenStack as a technical preview, FWaaS serves as a complement to Neutron security groups, not a replacement.

In this chapter, we will discuss some fundamental security features of Neutron, such as:

- Managing security groups
- Demonstrating how security groups leverage iptables
- Managing Neutron firewalls
- Demonstrating how Neutron firewalls leverage iptables

Security groups in OpenStack

Prior to Neutron, the Nova (Compute) service handled the securing of network traffic to and from instances through the use of security groups. A **security group** is a collection of network access rules that limit the types of traffic an instance can send or receive. Neutron provides an API to create, modify, apply, and delete security group rules.

When a port is created in Neutron, it is associated with a default security group unless a specific security group is specified. The default security group drops all ingress traffic and allows all egress traffic from instances. In addition, standard rules are applied to every instance that prohibit IP, DHCP, and MAC address spoofing. Rules can be added to the default security group to change its behavior. Once a security group has been applied to a Neutron port, the corresponding security group rules are translated by Neutron into iptables rules that are then applied to the respective compute node hosting the instances.

Firewall-as-a-service

FWaaS is an extension for Neutron that provides users with the ability to deploy perimeter firewalls to protect their networks. The FWaaS extension enables you to do the following things:

- Apply firewall rules on traffic entering and leaving tenant networks attached to Neutron routers
- Create and share firewall policies that hold an ordered collection of the firewall rules
- Audit firewall rules and policies

The FWaaS extension introduces the following network resources:

- **Firewall**: This represents a logical firewall resource that a tenant can instantiate and manage. A firewall is associated with one firewall policy.
- **Firewall policy**: This is an ordered collection of firewall rules that can be shared across tenants.
- **Firewall rule**: This represents a collection of attributes, such as layer 4 ports and IP addresses, that define match criteria and perform an action to be taken on the matched data traffic.

Like security group rules, firewalls in Neutron utilize iptables to perform traffic filtering. Rather than being configured on every compute node, however, firewall rules are implemented using iptables within a Neutron router namespace. Future improvements may allow the use of third-party drivers and plugins that allow Neutron to interact with other hardware or software firewalls.

Introducing iptables

Both security groups and Neutron firewalls leverage iptables rules to perform traffic filtering. Iptables is a built-in firewall in Linux that allows a system administrator to define tables containing chains of rules that determine how network packets should be treated. Packets are processed by sequentially traversing rules in chains within the following tables:

- **Raw**: This is a default table that filters packets before any other table. It is mainly used to configure exemptions from connection tracking and is not used by security groups or FWaaS.

- **Filter**: This is a default table used to filter packets.

- **NAT**: This is a default table used for network address translation.

- **Mangle**: This is a default table used for specialized packet alteration and is not used by security groups or FWaaS.

A rule in a chain can cause a jump to another chain, and this behavior can be repeated to whatever level of nesting is required. The system recalls the point at which a jump occurs and can return to that point for further processing. When iptables is enabled, every network packet arriving at or leaving from the computer traverses at least one chain.

There are five default chains, and the origin of the packet determines which chain it will initially traverse. The five default chains are as follows:

- PREROUTING: Packets will enter this chain before a routing decision is made. This chain is not used for security group rules, but instead for floating IP functionality within a router namespace. The PREROUTING chain is used by the raw, mangle, and NAT tables.

- INPUT: This is used when a packet is going to be locally delivered (that is, meant for the host machine). The INPUT chain is used by the mangle and filter tables.

- FORWARD: All packets that have been routed and were not for local delivery will traverse this chain. The FORWARD chain is used by the mangle and filter tables.

- OUTPUT: Packets sent from the host machine itself will traverse this chain. The OUTPUT chain is used by the raw, mangle, NAT, and filter tables.

- POSTROUTING: Packets will enter this chain when a routing decision has been made. This chain is not used for security group rules, but is used for floating IP functionality within a router namespace. The POSTROUTING chain is used by the mangle and NAT tables.

Each rule in a chain contains criteria that packets can be matched against. The rule may also contain a target (another chain) or a verdict, like DROP or ACCEPT. As a packet traverses a chain, each rule is examined. If a rule does not match the packet, the packet is passed to the next rule. If a rule does match the packet, the rule takes the action indicated by the target or verdict. Possible verdicts include the following:

- ACCEPT: This indicates that the packet is accepted and sent to the application for processing
- DROP: This indicates that the packet is dropped silently
- REJECT: This indicates that the packet is dropped and an error message is sent to the sender
- LOG: This indicates that the packet details are logged
- DNAT: This indicates that the destination IP of the packet is rewritten
- SNAT: This indicates that the source IP of the packet is rewritten
- RETURN: This indicates that the processing returns to the calling chain

The ACCEPT, DROP, and REJECT verdicts are often used by the filter table. Common rule criteria include the following:

- -p <protocol>: This matches protocols such as TCP, UDP, ICMP, and more
- -s <ip_addr>: This matches the source IP address
- -d <ip_addr>: This matches the destination IP address
- --sport: This matches the source port
- --dport: This matches the destination port
- -i <interface>: This matches the interface from which the packet entered
- -o <interface>: This matches the interface from which the packet exits

The difference in the application of iptables rules between security groups and FWaaS will be discussed later in this chapter.

For more information on iptables, please visit the following resources:

- https://access.redhat.com/documentation/en-US/Red_Hat_Enterprise_Linux/6/html/Security_Guide/sect-Security_Guide-IPTables.html
- http://rlworkman.net/howtos/iptables/iptables-tutorial.html

Working with security groups

Security groups can be managed in either the Neutron CLI or the Horizon dashboard. Both offer a pretty complete experience and are broken down in the following sections.

Managing security groups in the CLI

From within the Neutron command-line client, a number of commands can be used to manage security groups, such as:

- `security-group-create`
- `security-group-delete`
- `security-group-list`
- `security-group-rule-create`
- `security-group-rule-delete`
- `security-group-rule-list`
- `security-group-rule-show`
- `security-group-show`
- `security-group-update`

Creating security groups in the CLI

To create a security group within the CLI, use the Neutron `security-group-create` command as follows:

`Syntax: security-group-create [--tenant-id TENANT_ID]`

`[--description DESCRIPTION] NAME`

> By default, security groups in Neutron are prepopulated with two egress rules that allow all outbound traffic over IPv4 and IPv6. Inbound traffic is not permitted by default.

Deleting security groups in the CLI

To delete a security group within the CLI, use the Neutron `security-group-delete` command as follows:

`Syntax: security-group-delete SECURITY_GROUP`

The keyword `SECURITY_GROUP` can be the ID or name of the security group to be deleted.

> A security group must be removed from all ports before it can be deleted.

Listing security groups in the CLI

To obtain a listing of security groups within the CLI, use the Neutron `security-group-list` command as follows:

Syntax: `security-group-list`

The output returned includes the ID, name, and description of all security groups within the tenant where the command was run. If run as an administrator, all security groups across all tenants will be listed.

Showing the details of a security group in the CLI

To display the details of a security group, use the Neutron `security-group-show` command as follows:

Syntax: `security-group-show SECURITY_GROUP`

The keyword `SECURITY_GROUP` can be the ID or name of the security group to show. The output returned includes the description, ID, name, associated tenant ID, and individual rules within the security group.

Updating security groups in the CLI

To update the attributes of a security group, use the Neutron `security-group-update` command as follows:

Syntax: `security-group-update [--description DESCRIPTION]`

`[--name NAME]`

> It is not possible to change the name of the default security groups provided by Neutron.

Creating security group rules in the CLI

To create a security group rule, use the Neutron `security-group-rule-create` command as follows:

```
Syntax: security-group-rule-create [--tenant-id TENANT_ID][--direction {ingress,egress}]
[--ethertype ETHERTYPE][--protocol PROTOCOL][--port-range-min PORT_RANGE_MIN]
[--port-range-max PORT_RANGE_MAX][--remote-ip-prefix REMOTE_IP_PREFIX]
[--remote-group-id REMOTE_GROUP] SECURITY_GROUP
```

The `--direction` flag is optional; it allows you to specify the direction of traffic that should be affected. Specifying `ingress` means the rule applies to incoming traffic, while specifying `egress` means the rule applies to outgoing traffic from the instance. The default value is `ingress`.

The `--ethertype` flag is optional; it allows you to specify whether the rule applies to IPv4 or IPv6 traffic. The default value is `IPv4`.

The `--protocol` flag is optional; it allows you to specify the type of traffic the rule applies to. Possible options include ICMP, TCP, UDP, or an IP number.

The `--port-range-min` flag is optional; it allows you to specify the starting port of a range of ports. If this option is specified, a protocol must also be defined.

The `--port-range-max` flag is optional; it allows you to specify the ending port of a range of ports. If this option is specified, a protocol must also be defined.

The `--remote-ip-prefix` flag is optional; it allows you to specify the source address or network the rule applies to. The address or network should be defined in CIDR format.

The `--remote-group-id` flag is optional; it allows you to specify the ID of a security group the rule should apply to rather than individual IP addresses or networks. For example, when creating a rule to allow inbound SQL traffic to database servers, you can specify the ID of a security group that application servers are a member of without having to specify their individual IP addresses.

The `SECURITY_GROUP` keyword is used to specify the ID of the security group the rule should be placed in.

Deleting security group rules in the CLI

To delete a security group rule, use the Neutron `security-group-rule-delete` command as follows:

Syntax: `security-group-rule-delete SECURITY_GROUP_RULE_ID`

> While it is possible to delete the rules within the default security group, it is not possible to delete the group itself.

Listing security group rules in the CLI

To list the security group rules within a security group, use the Neutron `security-group-rule-list` command as follows:

Syntax: `security-group-rule-list`

The output returned includes details of individual security group rules such as their ID, associated security group, direction, protocol, remote IP prefix, and remote group name.

Showing the details of a security group rule in the CLI

To display the details of a particular security group rule, use the Neutron `security-group-rule-show` command as follows:

Syntax: `security-group-rule-show SECURITY_GROUP_RULE_ID`

The output returned includes the ID, direction, ethertype, port range, protocol, remote group IP, remote IP prefix, tenant ID, and associated security group ID of the specified security group rule.

Applying security groups to instances in the CLI

Applying security groups to instances within the CLI can be accomplished in one of two ways. The first method involves specifying the security group when creating an instance:

Example: `nova boot --flavor <flavor_id> --image <image_id> --nic net-id=<network_id> --security-group <SECURITY_GROUP_ID> INSTANCE_NAME`

The second method involves updating the security group attribute of the Neutron port associated with the instance:

```
Example: (neutron) port-update <neutron_port_id> --security-group
<SECURITY_GROUP_ID>
```

> Using port-update to assign security groups to a port will overwrite the existing security group associations.

Multiple security groups can be associated with a Neutron port simultaneously. To apply multiple security groups to a port, use the --security-group flag before each security group:

```
Example: (neutron) port-update <neutron_port_id> --security-group
<SECURITY_GROUP_ID1> --security-group <SECURITY_GROUP_ID2>
```

To remove all security groups from a port, use the --no-security-groups flag as shown in the following command:

```
Example: (neutron) port-update <neutron_port_id> --no-security-groups
```

> In Havana, it is not possible to remove single security groups from a port using the port-update command. All security groups should be removed from the port and then selected groups can be added back.

Implementing security group rules

To demonstrate how security group rules are implemented on a compute node, check out the following WEB_SERVERS security group:

```
[root@controller ~]# neutron security-group-list
+--------------------------------------+-------------+----------------------------------+
| id                                   | name        | description                      |
+--------------------------------------+-------------+----------------------------------+
| 39cb6ec7-561a-4257-8b19-d4124b483cf1 | default     | default                          |
| 3a69c841-5f9d-4be7-bc40-5d247923e86f | WEB_SERVERS | Allows access to web services    |
| 6b555da5-da47-4563-985e-78f1bdca6ff5 | default     | default                          |
| 763d3dc3-775c-4e11-a37b-4254b7901d4a | default     | default                          |
+--------------------------------------+-------------+----------------------------------+
```

In the following screenshot, you can see that two security group rules are being added that allow inbound connections on ports 80 and 443 from any host:

```
[root@controller ~]# neutron security-group-rule-create --protocol tcp --port-range-min 80 \
> --port-range-max 80 --remote-ip-prefix 0.0.0.0/0 3a69c841-5f9d-4be7-bc40-5d247923e86f
Created a new security_group_rule:
+-------------------+--------------------------------------+
| Field             | Value                                |
+-------------------+--------------------------------------+
| direction         | ingress                              |
| ethertype         | IPv4                                 |
| id                | de24e92b-7601-4a2a-96f1-39f6aa092d4f |
| port_range_max    | 80                                   |
| port_range_min    | 80                                   |
| protocol          | tcp                                  |
| remote_group_id   |                                      |
| remote_ip_prefix  | 0.0.0.0/0                            |
| security_group_id | 3a69c841-5f9d-4be7-bc40-5d247923e86f |
| tenant_id         | b1e5de8d1cfc45d6a15d9c0cb442a8ab     |
+-------------------+--------------------------------------+
[root@controller ~]# neutron security-group-rule-create --protocol tcp --port-range-min 443 \
> --port-range-max 443 --remote-ip-prefix 0.0.0.0/0 3a69c841-5f9d-4be7-bc40-5d247923e86f
Created a new security_group_rule:
+-------------------+--------------------------------------+
| Field             | Value                                |
+-------------------+--------------------------------------+
| direction         | ingress                              |
| ethertype         | IPv4                                 |
| id                | 690e67aa-fdff-4fbb-b427-806cea37c17f |
| port_range_max    | 443                                  |
| port_range_min    | 443                                  |
| protocol          | tcp                                  |
| remote_group_id   |                                      |
| remote_ip_prefix  | 0.0.0.0/0                            |
| security_group_id | 3a69c841-5f9d-4be7-bc40-5d247923e86f |
| tenant_id         | b1e5de8d1cfc45d6a15d9c0cb442a8ab     |
+-------------------+--------------------------------------+
```

Using the Neutron `port-update` command, I applied the WEB_SERVERS security group to the Neutron port of the Web1 instance, as shown in the following screenshot:

```
[root@controller ~]# neutron port-update c2a46367-100c-4d87-b2a5-e1ad7aa12324 \
> --security-group WEB_SERVERS
Updated port: c2a46367-100c-4d87-b2a5-e1ad7aa12324
```

Alternatively, the Nova client can be used to associate security groups to running instances using the following syntax:

```
# nova add-secgroup <server> <securitygroup>
```

> The Nova client proxies security group commands to Neutron when `security_group_api` is equal to `neutron` in the `nova.conf` file.

Once a security group has been applied to the corresponding Neutron port of an instance, a series of iptables rules and chains are implemented on the compute node hosting the instance.

Stepping through the chains

On `compute01`, the iptables rules can be observed using the `iptables-save` command as follows:

```
[root@compute01 ~]# iptables-save
```

For readability, only the `filter` table is shown in the following screenshot:

```
*filter
:INPUT ACCEPT [0:0]
:FORWARD ACCEPT [0:0]
:OUTPUT ACCEPT [17:2586]
:neutron-filter-top - [0:0]
:neutron-linuxbri-FORWARD - [0:0]
:neutron-linuxbri-INPUT - [0:0]
:neutron-linuxbri-OUTPUT - [0:0]
:neutron-linuxbri-ic2a46367-1 - [0:0]
:neutron-linuxbri-local - [0:0]
:neutron-linuxbri-oc2a46367-1 - [0:0]
:neutron-linuxbri-sc2a46367-1 - [0:0]
:neutron-linuxbri-sg-chain - [0:0]
:neutron-linuxbri-sg-fallback - [0:0]
-A INPUT -j neutron-linuxbri-INPUT
-A INPUT -m state --state RELATED,ESTABLISHED -j ACCEPT
-A INPUT -p icmp -j ACCEPT
-A INPUT -i lo -j ACCEPT
-A INPUT -p tcp -m state --state NEW -m tcp --dport 22 -j ACCEPT
-A FORWARD -j neutron-filter-top
-A FORWARD -j neutron-linuxbri-FORWARD
-A OUTPUT -j neutron-filter-top
-A OUTPUT -j neutron-linuxbri-OUTPUT
-A neutron-filter-top -j neutron-linuxbri-local
-A neutron-linuxbri-FORWARD -m physdev --physdev-out tapc2a46367-10 --physdev-is-bridged -j neutron-linuxbri-sg-chain
-A neutron-linuxbri-FORWARD -m physdev --physdev-in tapc2a46367-10 --physdev-is-bridged -j neutron-linuxbri-sg-chain
-A neutron-linuxbri-INPUT -m physdev --physdev-in tapc2a46367-10 --physdev-is-bridged -j neutron-linuxbri-oc2a46367-1
-A neutron-linuxbri-ic2a46367-1 -m state --state INVALID -j DROP
-A neutron-linuxbri-ic2a46367-1 -m state --state RELATED,ESTABLISHED -j RETURN
-A neutron-linuxbri-ic2a46367-1 -p tcp -m tcp --dport 443 -j RETURN
-A neutron-linuxbri-ic2a46367-1 -p tcp -m tcp --dport 80 -j RETURN
-A neutron-linuxbri-ic2a46367-1 -s 10.30.0.3/32 -p udp -m udp --sport 67 --dport 68 -j RETURN
-A neutron-linuxbri-ic2a46367-1 -j neutron-linuxbri-sg-fallback
-A neutron-linuxbri-oc2a46367-1 -p udp -m udp --sport 68 --dport 67 -j RETURN
-A neutron-linuxbri-oc2a46367-1 -j neutron-linuxbri-sc2a46367-1
-A neutron-linuxbri-oc2a46367-1 -p udp -m udp --sport 67 --dport 68 -j DROP
-A neutron-linuxbri-oc2a46367-1 -m state --state INVALID -j DROP
-A neutron-linuxbri-oc2a46367-1 -m state --state RELATED,ESTABLISHED -j RETURN
-A neutron-linuxbri-oc2a46367-1 -j RETURN
-A neutron-linuxbri-oc2a46367-1 -j neutron-linuxbri-sg-fallback
-A neutron-linuxbri-sc2a46367-1 -s 10.30.0.2/32 -m mac --mac-source FA:16:3E:BC:9A:A0 -j RETURN
-A neutron-linuxbri-sc2a46367-1 -j DROP
-A neutron-linuxbri-sg-chain -m physdev --physdev-out tapc2a46367-10 --physdev-is-bridged -j neutron-linuxbri-ic2a46367-1
-A neutron-linuxbri-sg-chain -m physdev --physdev-in tapc2a46367-10 --physdev-is-bridged -j neutron-linuxbri-oc2a46367-1
-A neutron-linuxbri-sg-chain -j ACCEPT
-A neutron-linuxbri-sg-fallback -j DROP
COMMIT
# Completed on Fri Aug 22 19:25:47 2014
```

Network traffic to or from an instance will first traverse the FORWARD chain, as follows:

```
-A FORWARD -j neutron-filter-top
-A FORWARD -j neutron-linuxbri-FORWARD
```

The first rule causes iptables to jump to the neutron-filter-top chain for further processing:

```
-A neutron-filter-top -j neutron-linuxbri-local
```

Iptables then jumps to the neutron-linuxbri-local chain for further processing. Because there are no rules defined in that chain, iptables returns to the calling chain, neutron-filter-top. Once all rules have been processed, iptables returns to the previous calling chain, FORWARD.

Then there is the next rule in the FORWARD chain that is processed:

```
-A FORWARD -j neutron-linuxbri-FORWARD
```

This rule causes iptables to jump to the neutron-linuxbri-FORWARD chain as follows:

```
-A neutron-linuxbri-FORWARD -m physdev --physdev-out tapc2a46367-10 --physdev-is-bridged -j neutron-linuxbri-sg-chain
-A neutron-linuxbri-FORWARD -m physdev --physdev-in tapc2a46367-10 --physdev-is-bridged -j neutron-linuxbri-sg-chain
```

The -m flag followed by physdev is a directive to iptables to use an extended packet-matching module that supports devices enslaved to a bridge device. When the LinuxBridge plugin is used, tap devices for instances are members of network bridges prefaced with brq-*. The packet will match one of the two rules based on the direction the packet is headed through the interface. In both cases, iptables jumps to the neutron-linuxbri-sg-chain chain as follows:

```
-A neutron-linuxbri-sg-chain -m physdev --physdev-out tapc2a46367-10 --physdev-is-bridged -j neutron-linuxbri-ic2a46367-1
-A neutron-linuxbri-sg-chain -m physdev --physdev-in tapc2a46367-10 --physdev-is-bridged -j neutron-linuxbri-oc2a46367-1
-A neutron-linuxbri-sg-chain -j ACCEPT
```

The direction of the packet will again dictate which rule is matched. Traffic entering the tapc2a46367-10 interface from an outside network will be processed by the neutron-linuxbri-ic2a46367-1 chain as follows:

```
-A neutron-linuxbri-ic2a46367-1 -m state --state INVALID -j DROP
-A neutron-linuxbri-ic2a46367-1 -m state --state RELATED,ESTABLISHED -j RETURN
-A neutron-linuxbri-ic2a46367-1 -p tcp -m tcp --dport 443 -j RETURN
-A neutron-linuxbri-ic2a46367-1 -p tcp -m tcp --dport 80 -j RETURN
-A neutron-linuxbri-ic2a46367-1 -s 10.30.0.3/32 -p udp -m udp --sport 67 --dport 68 -j RETURN
-A neutron-linuxbri-ic2a46367-1 -j neutron-linuxbri-sg-fallback
```

The name of a security group chain corresponds to the first nine characters of the UUID of the Neutron port to which it is associated.

In this rule, iptables uses the `state` module to determine the state of the packet. Combined with connection tracking, iptables is able to track the connection and determine the following states of the packet: INVALID, NEW, RELATED, or ESTABLISHED. The state of the packet results in an appropriate action being taken. The `-s` flag instructs iptables to match the source address of the packet against the address defined in the rule. The UDP rule allows inbound DHCP response traffic from the DHCP server at 10.30.0.3/32. Traffic not matched by any rule is dropped by the `neutron-linuxbri-sg-fallback` chain:

```
-A neutron-linuxbri-sg-fallback -j DROP
```

Traffic exiting the `tapc2a46367-10` interface and headed towards an outside network is processed by the `neutron-linuxbri-oc2a46367-1` chain as follows:

```
-A neutron-linuxbri-oc2a46367-1 -p udp -m udp --sport 68 --dport 67 -j RETURN
-A neutron-linuxbri-oc2a46367-1 -j neutron-linuxbri-sc2a46367-1
-A neutron-linuxbri-oc2a46367-1 -p udp -m udp --sport 67 --dport 68 -j DROP
-A neutron-linuxbri-oc2a46367-1 -m state --state INVALID -j DROP
-A neutron-linuxbri-oc2a46367-1 -m state --state RELATED,ESTABLISHED -j RETURN
-A neutron-linuxbri-oc2a46367-1 -j RETURN
-A neutron-linuxbri-oc2a46367-1 -j neutron-linuxbri-sg-fallback
```

The first UDP rule allows the instance to send DHCP Discover and DHCP Request broadcast packets. All other traffic is then processed by the `neutron-linuxbri-s c2a46367-1` chain as follows:

```
-A neutron-linuxbri-sc2a46367-1 -s 10.30.0.2/32 -m mac --mac-source FA:16:3E:BC:9A:A0 -j RETURN
-A neutron-linuxbri-sc2a46367-1 -j DROP
```

The rule above prevents an instance from performing IP and MAC address spoofing. Any traffic exiting the `tapc2a46367-10` interface must be sourced from 10.30.0.2/32 and the MAC address FA:16:3E:BC:9A:A0. To permit traffic from additional IP or MAC addresses, use the Neutron `allowed-address-pairs` extension, as discussed in *Chapter 5, Creating Networks with Neutron*.

When traffic is returned to the calling chain, the next UDP rule prohibits the instance from acting as a rogue DHCP server. Further processing includes verifying the state of the packet and performing the appropriate action. Traffic eventually returns to the `neutron-linuxbri-sg-chain` calling chain and is allowed through:

```
-A neutron-linuxbri-sg-chain -j ACCEPT
```

Working with security groups in the dashboard

Within the Horizon dashboard, security groups are managed in the **Access & Security** section under the **Project** tab:

To create a security group, perform the following steps:

1. Click on the **Create Security Group** button in the upper right-hand corner of the screen. A window will appear that will allow you to create a security group:

2. Both the **Name** and **Description** fields are required. When you are ready to proceed, click on the blue **Create Security Group** button to create the security group.

3. Once it is created, you will be directed to the **Access & Security** section again, where you can add rules to the security group:

4. To add rules, click on the **Edit Rules** button next to the security group. You will be directed to a page where you can add or delete rules within the security group:

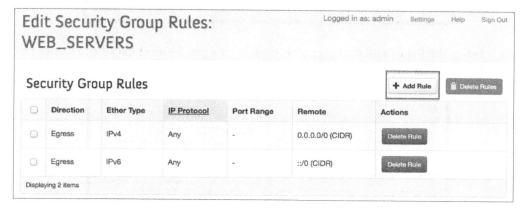

5. To add a rule, click on the **Add Rule** button in the upper right-hand corner. A window will appear that will allow you to create rules:

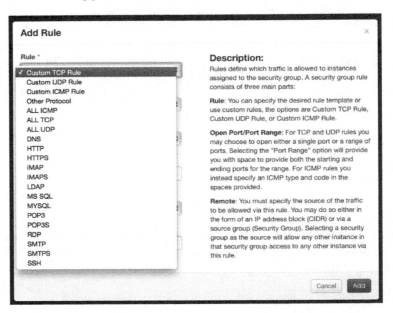

6. From the list of rules, you can choose from a predefined list of protocols or create a custom rule, as follows:

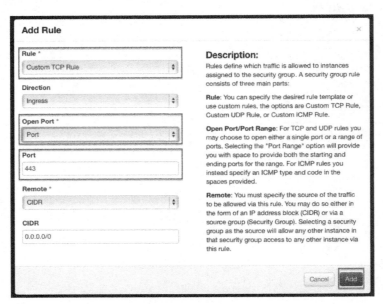

7. To complete the rule creation, click on the blue **Add** button.

8. To apply the security group to an instance, return to the **Instances** section of the **Project** tab. Click on the **More** menu next to the instance and choose **Edit Security Groups**:

9. A window will appear that allows you to apply or remove security groups from an instance:

10. Click on the blue **Save** button to apply the changes.

Working with FWaaS

Like LBaaS, FWaaS requires a specific workflow to properly implement firewall policies. First, firewall rules are created and inserted into policies. Then, a firewall is created and associated with a firewall policy. Once a firewall policy has been applied, the rules are immediately put in place on all routers that exist within the tenant. In Havana, a hard-set quota exists that allows only one active firewall policy per tenant.

Firewall policies can be shared amongst tenants, which means that whenever a policy is updated, it results in the immediate updating of any firewall that is associated with the policy. The FWaaS API is considered experimental in Havana and Icehouse, and it may exhibit unexpected behavior. Therefore, it cannot be recommended for production use.

Preparing Neutron for FWaaS

To properly implement FWaaS, some changes must be made to the Neutron configuration files on the controller node. There is no dedicated agent required to implement FWaaS; all firewall rules are implemented by the Neutron L3 agent.

Configuring the FWaaS driver

To enable FWaaS, the FWaaS driver configuration file must be configured appropriately. Using `crudini`, update the `/etc/neutron/fwaas_driver.ini` file on the controller node to specify the iptables FWaaS driver:

```
# crudini --set /etc/neutron/fwaas_driver.ini fwaas driver neutron.
services.firewall.drivers.linux.iptables_fwaas.IptablesFwaasDriver

# crudini --set /etc/neutron/fwaas_driver.ini fwaas enabled true
```

Defining a service plugin

Before Neutron `firewall-*` commands will work, the FWaaS plugin must be defined in the `/etc/neutron/neutron.conf` configuration file of the controller node. Edit the file to specify the following service plugin:

```
neutron.services.firewall.fwaas_plugin.FirewallPlugin
```

Service plugins should be comma separated if there are more than one:

```
Example: service_plugins = neutron.services.loadbalancer.plugin.
LoadBalancerPlugin,neutron.services.firewall.fwaas_plugin.FirewallPlugin
```

Save your changes and restart `neutron-server` and `neutron-l3-agent`:

```
# service neutron-server restart
# service neutron-l3-agent restart
```

Enabling FWaaS in the dashboard

To enable the management of firewall resources in the Horizon dashboard, the `enable_firewall` parameter must be set to `True` in the `/etc/openstack-dashboard/local_settings` configuration file. Use the following commands to set the parameter and restart the Apache web service:

```
# sed -i "/'enable_firewall': False,/c\'enable_firewall': True," /etc/
openstack-dashboard/local_settings
# service httpd restart
```

Working with firewalls in the CLI

The primary commands associated with FWaaS in the Neutron CLI are as follows:

- `firewall-create`
- `firewall-delete`
- `firewall-list`
- `firewall-policy-create`
- `firewall-policy-delete`
- `firewall-policy-insert-rule`
- `firewall-policy-list`
- `firewall-policy-remove-rule`
- `firewall-policy-show`
- `firewall-policy-update`
- `firewall-rule-create`
- `firewall-rule-delete`
- `firewall-rule-list`
- `firewall-rule-show`
- `firewall-rule-update`
- `firewall-show`
- `firewall-update`

Creating a firewall rule in the CLI

The first step in creating a firewall is to create a firewall rule and apply it to a policy. To create a firewall rule in the CLI, use the Neutron `firewall-create` command as follows:

```
Syntax: firewall-rule-create [--tenant-id TENANT_ID][--name NAME] [--description DESCRIPTION]
[--shared] [--source-ip-address SOURCE_IP_ADDRESS] [--destination-ip-address DESTINATION_IP_ADDRESS]
[--source-port SOURCE_PORT] [--destination-port DESTINATION_PORT] [--disabled] --protocol {tcp,udp,icmp,any}
--action {allow,deny}
```

The `--tenant-id` flag is optional; it allows you to associate the firewall rule with the specified tenant.

The `--name` flag is optional; it allows you to provide a name to the rule. If a name isn't specified, Neutron uses the first eight characters of the rule's UUID as its name.

The `--description` flag is optional; it allows you to provide a description of the firewall rule.

The `--shared` flag is optional; it allows the rule to be shared amongst other tenants.

The `--source-ip-address` flag is optional; it allows you to specify the source host or network the rule should apply to.

The `--destination-ip-address` flag is optional; it allows you to specify the destination host or network the rule should apply to.

The `--source-port` flag is optional; it allows you to specify a source port or range of ports the rule should apply to. If specifying a range of ports, use a colon between the start and end port (`a:b`).

The `--destination-port` flag is optional; it allows you to specify a destination port or range of ports the rule should apply to. If specifying a range of ports, use a colon between the start and end port (`a:b`).

The `--disabled` flag is optional; it allows you to specify whether or not the rule is inserted into the firewall.

The `--protocol` flag is required; it is used to specify the type of traffic the rule applies to; possible options include `tcp`, `udp`, `icmp`, and so on.

The `--action` flag is required; it allows you to specify the action that takes place when traffic matches the rule's criteria; possible options include `allow` or `deny`.

Deleting a firewall rule in the CLI

To delete a firewall rule in the CLI, use the Neutron `firewall-rule-delete` command as follows:

```
Syntax: firewall-rule-delete FIREWALL_RULE_ID
```

The keyword `FIREWALL_RULE_ID` is used to represent the ID of the firewall rule to be deleted.

Listing firewall rules in the CLI

To list all firewall rules within the CLI, use the Neutron `firewall-rule-list` command as follows:

```
Syntax: firewall-rule-list
```

The returned output includes the ID, name, summary, and associated firewall policy of firewall rules within the tenant.

Showing the details of a firewall rule in the CLI

To show the details of a firewall rule within the CLI, use the Neutron `firewall-rule-show` command as follows:

```
Syntax: firewall-rule-show FIREWALL_RULE_ID
```

The returned output includes the name, description, action, destination IP address, destination port, source IP address, source port, associated firewall policy, position, protocol, and tenant ID of the specified firewall rule.

Updating a firewall rule in the CLI

Many of the attributes of a firewall rule can be edited at any time. To update an attribute of a firewall rule in the CLI, use the Neutron `firewall-rule-update` command as follows:

```
Syntax: firewall-rule-update
[--source-ip-address SOURCE_IP_ADDRESS] [--destination-ip-address DESTINATION_IP_ADDRESS]
[--source-port SOURCE_PORT] [--destination-port DESTINATION_PORT] [--protocol {tcp,udp,icmp,any}]
[--action {allow,deny}] [--name NAME] [--description DESCRIPTION] [--shared]
FIREWALL_RULE_ID
```

Creating a firewall policy in the CLI

The next step in creating a firewall is to create a firewall policy that contains one or more firewall rules. To create a firewall policy, use the Neutron `firewall-policy-create` command as follows:

```
Syntax: firewall-policy-create [--tenant-id TENANT_ID] [--description DESCRIPTION]
[--shared] [--firewall-rules FIREWALL_RULES] [--audited] NAME
```

The `--tenant-id` flag is optional; it allows you to associate the firewall rule with the specified tenant.

The `--description` flag is optional; it allows you to provide a description of the firewall policy.

The `--shared` flag is optional; it allows the policy to be shared amongst other tenants.

 Shared policies are not supported within Horizon.

The `--firewall-rules` flag is optional; it is used to add firewall rules to the policy during creation. If multiple rules are specified, they should be enclosed in quotes and separated by spaces. In the following example, two firewall rules are added to the policy named EXAMPLE_POLICY during creation:

```
Example: firewall-policy-create --firewall-rules "a7a03a5f-ecda-4471-
92db-7a1c708e20e1 a9dd1195-f6d9-4942-b76a-06ff3bac32e8" EXAMPLE_POLICY
```

 Neutron always adds a default deny-all rule at the lowest precedence of each policy. As a result, a firewall policy with no rules blocks all traffic by default.

The `--audited` flag is optional; it is used to reflect whether or not a policy has been audited by an external resource. There are no audit logs or auditing mechanisms within Neutron.

Deleting a firewall policy in the CLI

To delete a firewall policy within the CLI, use the Neutron `firewall-policy-delete` command as follows:

```
Syntax: firewall-policy-delete FIREWALL_POLICY_ID
```

Listing firewall policies in the CLI

To list all firewall policies within a tenant in the CLI, use the Neutron `firewall-policy-list` command as follows:

Syntax: `firewall-policy-list`

The returned output includes the ID, name, and associated firewall rules of firewall policies.

Showing the details of a firewall policy in the CLI

To show the details of a firewall policy in the CLI, use the Neutron `firewall-policy-show` command as follows:

Syntax: `firewall-policy-show FIREWALL_POLICY_ID`

The returned output includes the ID, name, description, tenant ID, audited status and associated firewall rules of the specified tenant.

Updating a firewall policy in the CLI

To update the attributes of a firewall policy, use the Neutron `firewall-policy-update` command as follows:

Syntax: `firewall-policy-update FIREWALL_POLICY_ID`

`[--name NAME] [--description DESCRIPTION] [--shared]`

`[--firewall-rules list=true RULES]`

> Multiple rules should be separated by a space. The `list=true` attribute is required to help Python interpret the data being passed as multiple entries.

Inserting rules into firewall policies in the CLI

Using the Neutron `firewall-policy-insert-rule` command, it is possible to insert firewall rules into an existing policy before or after the existing rules. The syntax to insert a rule into a policy is as follows:

```
Syntax: firewall-policy-insert-rule [--insert-before FIREWALL_RULE]
[--insert-after FIREWALL_RULE] FIREWALL_POLICY_ID NEW_FIREWALL_RULE_ID
```

The `--insert-before` flag is optional; it allows you to insert a new firewall rule before the specified firewall rule.

The `--insert-after` flag is optional; it allows you to insert a new firewall rule after the specified firewall rule.

> The `--insert-before` and `--insert-after` flags are mutually exclusive and cannot be used at the same time.

The keyword `FIREWALL_POLICY_ID` is used to represent the ID of the firewall policy to be updated.

The keyword `NEW_FIREWALL_RULE_ID` is used to represent the ID of the firewall rule to be added to the policy.

Removing rules from firewall policies in the CLI

Using the Neutron `firewall-policy-remove-rule` command, it is possible to remove firewall rules from a firewall policy. The syntax to remove a rule from a policy is as follows:

```
Syntax: firewall-policy-remove-rule FIREWALL_POLICY_ID
FIREWALL_RULE_ID
```

The keyword `FIREWALL_POLICY_ID` is used to represent the ID of the firewall policy to be updated.

The keyword `NEW_FIREWALL_RULE_ID` is used to represent the ID of the firewall rule to be removed from the policy.

Creating a firewall in the CLI

To create a firewall within the CLI, use the Neutron `firewall-create` command as follows:

```
Syntax: firewall-create [--tenant-id TENANT_ID] [--name NAME]
[--description DESCRIPTION] [--admin-state-down] POLICY
```

The `--tenant-id` flag is optional; it allows you to associate the firewall with the specified tenant.

The `--name` flag is optional; it allows you to provide a name to the firewall. If a name is not specified, the default value is blank or null.

The `--description` flag is optional; it allows you to provide a description of the firewall.

The `--admin-state-down` flag is optional; it allows you to create the firewall in a DOWN state. In a DOWN state, the firewall rules are not applied.

The POLICY keyword is used to represent the ID of the policy that should be applied to the firewall. Only one policy can be associated with a firewall at a time, and a policy cannot be associated with multiple firewalls simultaneously.

 Due to a bug in the Havana release of OpenStack, firewalls cannot be created in the admin tenant if another tenant already has a firewall. If the admin user attempts to create a firewall an error will occur. For more information on this bug, please refer to the following URL:

https://bugs.launchpad.net/neutron/+bug/1258438

Deleting a firewall in the CLI

To delete a firewall within the CLI, use the Neutron `firewall-delete` command as follows:

`Syntax: firewall-delete FIREWALL_ID`

Listing firewalls in the CLI

To list all firewalls within a tenant in the CLI, use the Neutron `firewall-list` command as follows:

`Syntax: firewall-list`

The returned output includes a list of firewalls containing the ID, name, and associated firewall policy for each firewall within the tenant.

Showing the details of a firewall in the CLI

To show the details of a firewall within the CLI, use the Neutron `firewall-show` command as follows:

`Syntax: firewall-show FIREWALL_ID`

The output returned includes the ID, admin state, name, description, status, tenant ID, and associated firewall policy ID of the specified firewall.

Updating a firewall in the CLI

To update the attributes of a firewall within the CLI, use the Neutron `firewall-update` command as follows:

```
Syntax: firewall-update FIREWALL_ID [--name NAME]
[--firewall-policy-id FIREWALL_POLICY_ID]
[--admin-state-up]
```

The `--name` flag is optional; it allows you to update the name of the firewall.

The `--firewall-policy-id` flag is optional; it allows you to associate a different policy with the firewall.

The `--admin-state-up` flag is a Boolean that when set to FALSE, puts the firewall in a DOWN state. When a firewall is in a DOWN state, all rules are removed from the Neutron router.

Working with firewalls in the dashboard

Within the Horizon dashboard, firewalls are managed within the **Firewalls** section under the **Project** tab. In the dashboard, the workflow to create functional firewalls is similar to the CLI. First the firewall rules must be created, and then a firewall policy and the firewall itself should be created. To create a firewall rule, perform the following steps:

1. Click on the **Add Rule** button under the **Firewall Rules** tab:

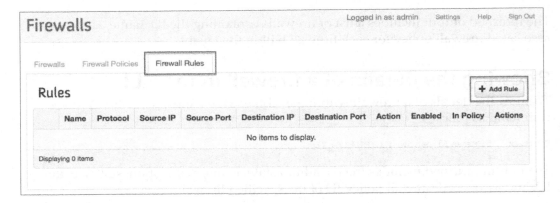

A window will appear that will allow you to specify the details of the firewall rule:

2. In this window, you can specify the source and destination addresses, source and destination ports, protocol, and the desired action: **ALLOW** or **DENY**. To create the rule, click on the blue **Add** button.

3. To create a firewall policy that will contain the rule(s), click on the **Add Policy** button under the **Firewall Policies** tab:

A window will appear that will allow you to specify the details of the firewall policy:

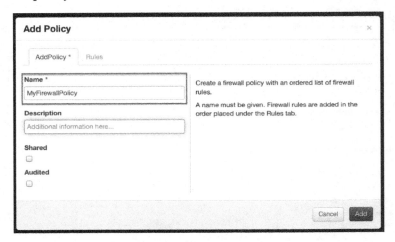

4. In the **Add Policy** window, the **Name** field has to be filled. Then, click on the **Rules** tab to insert rules into the policy:

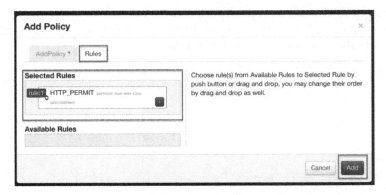

5. Once the desired rules have been moved from the **Available Rules** section to the **Selected Rules** section, click on the blue **Add** button to complete the policy creation process.

6. Lastly, click on the **Create Firewall** button under the **Firewalls** tab to create the firewall:

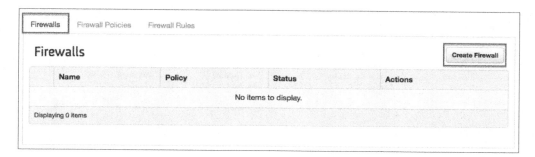

7. A window will appear, allowing you to specify the details of the firewall, including the name, description, and associated policy:

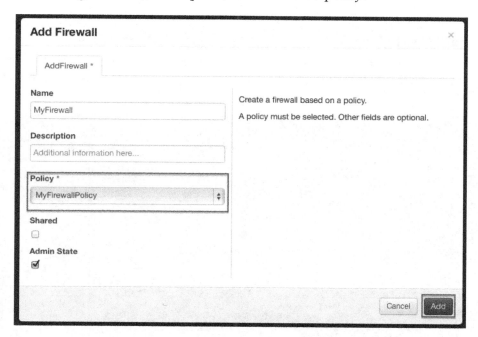

8. Click on the blue **Add** button to complete the firewall creation process. The firewall status will remain in **PENDING_CREATE** until the rules have been applied to the Neutron routers within the tenant, at which time the status will turn to **ACTIVE**:

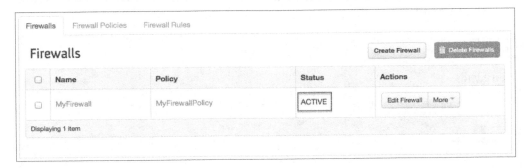

 A change in status may require the page to be refreshed.

Firewall rules – behind the scenes

To demonstrate how firewall policies are applied to a Neutron router, check out the following firewall rule that allows HTTP traffic from any remote host to any instance on TCP port 80:

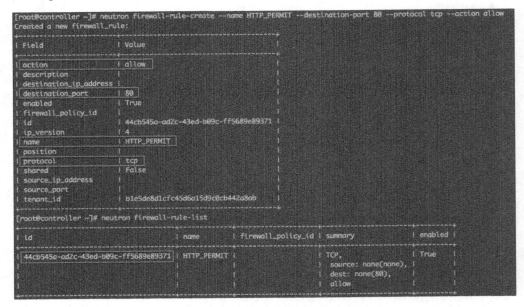

Using the Neutron `firewall-policy-create` command, I have created a policy that contains the preceding rule:

Using the Neutron `firewall-create` command, I have created a firewall using the policy `MyFirewallPolicy`:

```
[root@controller ~]# neutron firewall-create --name MyFirewall \
> a49c8073-fbc8-4b6c-8621-d27969f73dd2
Created a new firewall:
+----------------------+--------------------------------------+
| Field                | Value                                |
+----------------------+--------------------------------------+
| admin_state_up       | True                                 |
| description          |                                      |
| firewall_policy_id   | a49c8073-fbc8-4b6c-8621-d27969f73dd2 |
| id                   | 01ea5b3a-e265-4c8a-9103-9200ed80b46a |
| name                 | MyFirewall                           |
| status               | PENDING_CREATE                       |
| tenant_id            | b1e5de8d1cfc45d6a15d9c0cb442a8ab     |
+----------------------+--------------------------------------+
```

The firewall status will remain in `PENDING_CREATE` until the rules have been applied to the Neutron routers within the tenant, at which time the status will turn to `ACTIVE`:

```
[root@controller ~]# neutron firewall-show 01ea5b3a-e265-4c8a-9103-9200ed80b46a
+----------------------+--------------------------------------+
| Field                | Value                                |
+----------------------+--------------------------------------+
| admin_state_up       | True                                 |
| description          |                                      |
| firewall_policy_id   | a49c8073-fbc8-4b6c-8621-d27969f73dd2 |
| id                   | 01ea5b3a-e265-4c8a-9103-9200ed80b46a |
| name                 | MyFirewall                           |
| status               | ACTIVE                               |
| tenant_id            | b1e5de8d1cfc45d6a15d9c0cb442a8ab     |
+----------------------+--------------------------------------+
```

Stepping through the chains within the firewall

As a result of creating the firewall, the rules within the firewall policy have been implemented on all routers within the tenant. This is not a desired behavior; rather, it is a limitation of FWaaS.

Running `iptables-save` within a router namespace reveals the iptables rules in place. For readability, only the filter table is shown in the following screenshot:

```
[root@controller init.d]# ip netns exec qrouter-0f720e65-13b9-45f3-b750-d8a3a1b18672 \
> iptables-save | sed -e '1,/*filter/d'
:INPUT ACCEPT [0:0]
:FORWARD ACCEPT [13466:12225870]
:OUTPUT ACCEPT [0:0]
:neutron-filter-top - [0:0]
:neutron-l3-agent-FORWARD - [0:0]
:neutron-l3-agent-INPUT - [0:0]
:neutron-l3-agent-OUTPUT - [0:0]
:neutron-l3-agent-fwaas-defau - [0:0]
:neutron-l3-agent-iv401ea5b3a - [0:0]
:neutron-l3-agent-local - [0:0]
:neutron-l3-agent-ov401ea5b3a - [0:0]
-A INPUT -j neutron-l3-agent-INPUT
-A FORWARD -j neutron-filter-top
-A FORWARD -j neutron-l3-agent-FORWARD
-A OUTPUT -j neutron-filter-top
-A OUTPUT -j neutron-l3-agent-OUTPUT
-A neutron-filter-top -j neutron-l3-agent-local
-A neutron-l3-agent-FORWARD -o qr-+ -j neutron-l3-agent-iv401ea5b3a
-A neutron-l3-agent-FORWARD -i qr-+ -j neutron-l3-agent-ov401ea5b3a
-A neutron-l3-agent-FORWARD -o qr-+ -j neutron-l3-agent-fwaas-defau
-A neutron-l3-agent-FORWARD -i qr-+ -j neutron-l3-agent-fwaas-defau
-A neutron-l3-agent-INPUT -d 127.0.0.1/32 -p tcp -m tcp --dport 9697 -j ACCEPT
-A neutron-l3-agent-fwaas-defau -j DROP
-A neutron-l3-agent-iv401ea5b3a -m state --state INVALID -j DROP
-A neutron-l3-agent-iv401ea5b3a -m state --state RELATED,ESTABLISHED -j ACCEPT
-A neutron-l3-agent-iv401ea5b3a -p tcp -m tcp --dport 80 -j ACCEPT
-A neutron-l3-agent-ov401ea5b3a -m state --state INVALID -j DROP
-A neutron-l3-agent-ov401ea5b3a -m state --state RELATED,ESTABLISHED -j ACCEPT
-A neutron-l3-agent-ov401ea5b3a -p tcp -m tcp --dport 80 -j ACCEPT
COMMIT
# Completed on Sat Aug 23 22:27:41 2014
```

Like security groups, the FORWARD chain is used since traffic is being forwarded through the namespace rather than directed at the namespace itself:

```
-A FORWARD -j neutron-filter-top
-A FORWARD -j neutron-l3-agent-FORWARD
```

A `neutron-filter-top` chain does not exist, so traffic moves to the `neutron-l3-agent-FORWARD` chain as follows:

```
-A neutron-l3-agent-FORWARD -o qr-+ -j neutron-l3-agent-iv401ea5b3a
-A neutron-l3-agent-FORWARD -i qr-+ -j neutron-l3-agent-ov401ea5b3a
-A neutron-l3-agent-FORWARD -o qr-+ -j neutron-l3-agent-fwaas-defau
-A neutron-l3-agent-FORWARD -i qr-+ -j neutron-l3-agent-fwaas-defau
```

The first rule matches all traffic exiting any `qr-*` interface attached to the router and sends it to the `neutron-l3-agent-iv401ea5b3a` chain:

```
-A neutron-l3-agent-iv401ea5b3a -m state --state INVALID -j DROP
-A neutron-l3-agent-iv401ea5b3a -m state --state RELATED,ESTABLISHED -j ACCEPT
-A neutron-l3-agent-iv401ea5b3a -p tcp -m tcp --dport 80 -j ACCEPT
```

Packets that are invalid are dropped, while established connections are accepted without further processing. New connections destined to any instance on port 80 are allowed.

The next rule in the `neutron-l3-agent-FORWARD` chain matches all traffic entering any `qr-*` interface attached to the router and sends it to the `neutron-l3-agent-ov401ea5b3a` chain:

```
-A neutron-l3-agent-ov401ea5b3a -m state --state INVALID -j DROP
-A neutron-l3-agent-ov401ea5b3a -m state --state RELATED,ESTABLISHED -j ACCEPT
-A neutron-l3-agent-ov401ea5b3a -p tcp -m tcp --dport 80 -j ACCEPT
```

Like the previous chain, packets that are invalid are dropped, while established connections are accepted without further processing. New connections destined to any outside network on port 80 are allowed.

Traffic that does not match rules in either of the mentioned chains is dropped by the `neutron-l3-agent-fwaas-defau` chain:

`-A neutron-l3-agent-fwaas-defau -j DROP`

Unlike security group rules, there is no way to differentiate the direction of traffic when creating firewall rules with FWaaS. As a result, firewall rules are unnecessarily applied to both incoming and outgoing traffic in an identical manner.

Summary

It is important to know the differences between the two methods of securing network traffic to instances. Where security group rules are implemented at the network bridge connected to an instance on a compute node, firewall rules created with FWaaS are implemented on a Neutron router at the edge of the tenant network. FWaaS is not intended to replace security group functionality, and it serves more as a complement to security groups, especially in its current state. FWaaS is currently lacking functionality that security groups provide, including the inability to specify the direction of traffic that should be filtered. The opposite can said for security groups, too, as they lack the ability to create specific deny rules as all traffic is denied by default.

FWaaS is considered experimental in the Icehouse release of OpenStack and possibly beyond, and it lacks features and functionalities that could make it useable and reliable in a production setting. Like other OpenStack projects, FWaaS will become more mature in future releases.

A
Additional Neutron Commands

In the book, we covered core Neutron commands related to building networks, routers, firewalls, and load balancers. Neutron is capable of much more, provided the appropriate extension or plugin is installed. In this appendix, you will find Neutron commands that didn't quite have a home in other chapters or are used in network solutions outside the scope of this book. Commands used to manage the following are discussed in this appendix:

- VPN-as-a-service
- Quotas
- Cisco 1000V
- VMware NSX / Nicira NVP

Neutron extensions

Neutron extensions allow a plugin to extend the Neutron API to provide advanced functionality or to expose a capability before it has been incorporated into an official Neutron API.

Listing Neutron API extensions

To list the extensions available in Neutron, use the Neutron `ext-list` command as follows:

```
Syntax: ext-list
```

The returned output includes the `alias` and `name` of the available extensions:

```
[root@controller ~]# neutron ext-list
+----------------------+--------------------------------------------+
| alias                | name                                       |
+----------------------+--------------------------------------------+
| security-group       | security-group                             |
| l3_agent_scheduler   | L3 Agent Scheduler                         |
| external-net         | Neutron external network                   |
| ext-gw-mode          | Neutron L3 Configurable external gateway mode |
| binding              | Port Binding                               |
| quotas               | Quota management support                   |
| agent                | agent                                      |
| dhcp_agent_scheduler | DHCP Agent Scheduler                       |
| provider             | Provider Network                           |
| router               | Neutron L3 Router                          |
| extraroute           | Neutron Extra Route                        |
+----------------------+--------------------------------------------+
```

Showing the details of an API extension

To show the details of an API extension, use the Neutron `ext-show` command as follows:

Syntax: ext-show EXTENSION_ALIAS

The `EXTENSION_ALIAS` keyword represents `alias` of the extension provided in the `ext-list` output. The returned output includes the alias, description, name, namespace, and updated date of the specified extension.

To find more information on creating Neutron API extensions, please visit the Neutron development wiki at `https://wiki.openstack.org/wiki/NeutronDevelopment`.

Virtual private networks

Using methods of encryption and authentication, a **virtual private network** provides secure access to a remote computer or network over the Internet. In Havana, Neutron supports the creation and use of virtual private networks based on IPSec. In both the Havana and Icehouse releases of OpenStack, **Virtual Private Network as a Service (VPNaaS)** is considered experimental.

For your reference, the following Neutron commands are used to manage VPN connections in OpenStack:

- `ipsec-site-connection-create`
- `ipsec-site-connection-delete`
- `ipsec-site-connection-list`
- `ipsec-site-connection-show`
- `ipsec-site-connection-update`
- `vpn-ikepolicy-create`
- `vpn-ikepolicy-delete`
- `vpn-ikepolicy-list`
- `vpn-ikepolicy-show`
- `vpn-ikepolicy-update`
- `vpn-ipsecpolicy-create`
- `vpn-ipsecpolicy-delete`
- `vpn-ipsecpolicy-list`
- `vpn-ipsecpolicy-show`
- `vpn-ipsecpolicy-update`
- `vpn-service-create`
- `vpn-service-delete`
- `vpn-service-list`
- `vpn-service-show`
- `vpn-service-update`

The installation and configuration of VPNaaS is outside the scope of this book. For more information on the service, please refer to the official OpenStack documentation at `http://docs.openstack.org/api/openstack-network/2.0/content/vpnaas_ext.html`.

Per-tenant quotas

To prevent system resources from being exhausted, Neutron supports per-tenant quota limits via the `quotas` extension. Every tenant is bound to a default quota that is set by the administrator in the Neutron configuration file:

```
[quotas]
# resource name(s) that are supported in quota features
# quota_items = network,subnet,port
```

```
# number of networks allowed per tenant, and minus means unlimited
# quota_network = 10


# number of subnets allowed per tenant, and minus means unlimited
# quota_subnet = 10


# number of ports allowed per tenant, and minus means unlimited
# quota_port = 50


# number of security groups allowed per tenant, and minus means unlimited
# quota_security_group = 10


# number of security group rules allowed per tenant, and minus means
unlimited
# quota_security_group_rule = 100
```

To change the default settings, change the value and uncomment the line associated with the quota you want to change. Restarting neutron-server is necessary for changes to take effect.

You can also set a quota to limit the number of routers and floating IPs per tenant by adding the following to the [quotas] section:

```
[quotas]
# number of routers allowed per tenant, and minus means unlimited
quota_router = 10


# number of floating IPs allowed per tenant, and minus means unlimited
quota_floatingip = 50
```

The following Neutron commands can be used to manage per-tenant quotas:

- quota-delete
- quota-list
- quota-show
- quota-update

Listing the default quotas

To see a list of the default quotas, use the Neutron `quota-show` command as follows:

Syntax: `quota-show`

The listed output will contain the default per-tenant Neutron quotas:

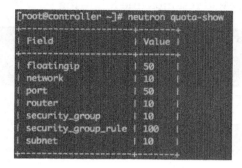

Updating tenant quotas

To update a quota for a specified tenant, use the Neutron `quota-update` command as follows:

```
Syntax: quota-update --tenant-id <ID of tenant> [--network NUM_OF_
NETWORKS] [--port NUM_OF_PORTS] [--subnet NUM_OF_SUBNETS] [--floatingip
NUM_OF_FLOATIP] [--security_group NUM_OF_SECGROUPS] [--security_group_
rule NUM_OF_SECGRP_RULES] [--router NUM_OF_ROUTERS]
```

The attributes in brackets are optional and allow you to specify new values for the respective quota. You can update multiple attributes simultaneously, as shown in the following screenshot:

```
[root@controller ~]# neutron quota-update --tenant-id b1e5de8d1cfc45d6a15d9c0cb442a8ab \
> --floatingip 6 --network 12 --port 23 --router 2 --subnet 5
+---------------------+-------+
| Field               | Value |
+---------------------+-------+
| floatingip          | 6     |
| network             | 12    |
| port                | 23    |
| router              | 2     |
| security_group      | 10    |
| security_group_rule | 100   |
| subnet              | 5     |
+---------------------+-------+
```

Listing tenant quotas

To list the quotas of a tenant, use the Neutron `quota-list` command as follows:

`Syntax: quota-list --tenant-id <ID of tenant>`

If a tenant is using default quotas, no output will be provided. If the quotas have been modified, the output will resemble the following screenshot:

Deleting tenant quotas

To revert tenant quotas to their default values, use the Neutron `quota-delete` command as follows:

`Syntax: quota-delete --tenant-id <ID of tenant>`

 The `quota-delete` command results in all per-tenant quotas being reverted to default values. It is not possible to revert a single quota.

Cisco Nexus 1000V command reference

OpenStack Networking supports the Cisco Nexus 1000V switch through the use of an API extension and plugin. The following commands enable you to manage network profiles, policy profiles, profile binding, and credentials:

- `cisco-credential-create`
- `cisco-credential-delete`
- `cisco-credential-list`
- `cisco-credential-show`
- `cisco-network-profile-create`
- `cisco-network-profile-delete`
- `cisco-network-profile-list`
- `cisco-network-profile-show`
- `cisco-network-profile-update`

- `cisco-policy-profile-list`
- `cisco-policy-profile-show`
- `cisco-policy-profile-update`

The `cisco-network-profile` commands enable you to create, modify, list, delete, and show details of Cisco Nexus 1000V network profiles.

The `cisco-policy-profile` commands enable you to list and show details of Cisco Nexus 1000V policy profiles, as well as associate or disassociate profiles with tenants.

The `cisco-credential` commands enable you to create, update, delete, and show details of Cisco Nexus 1000V credentials.

For more information on configuring a Cisco Nexus 1000V with KVM in OpenStack, please refer to the official Cisco release guide at `http://www.cisco.com/c/en/us/td/docs/switches/datacenter/nexus1000/kvm/config_guide/network/521sk122/b-Cisco-N1KV-KVM-Virtual-Network-Config-521SK122.html`.

VMware/Nicera command reference

OpenStack Networking supports VMware NSX and Nicera NVP through the use of API extensions and plugins. These plugins leverage standard and extended Neutron commands to manage networks. The following Neutron commands are specific to the NSX extension:

- `net-gateway-connect`
- `net-gateway-create`
- `net-gateway-delete`
- `net-gateway-disconnect`
- `net-gateway-list`
- `net-gateway-show`
- `net-gateway-update`
- `queue-create`
- `queue-delete`
- `queue-list`
- `queue-show`

For more information on configuring Neutron with the NSX/NVP plugin, please refer to the OpenStack Cloud administrator guide at `http://docs.openstack.org/admin-guide-cloud/content/nsx_plugin.html`.

B
ML2 Configuration

The **Modular Layer 2 (ML2)** plugin is a framework that allows OpenStack Networking to simultaneously utilize a variety of layer 2 networking technologies that are found in data centers. The ML2 plugin works with existing Open vSwitch and LinuxBridge agents and is intended to replace the monolithic plugins associated with those agents. The ML2 framework greatly simplifies adding support for new L2 networking technologies, as less effort is required to add functionality compared to creating a new monolithic core plugin.

In Havana, ML2 can be configured to support the following network types:

- Flat
- VLAN
- Local
- GRE
- VXLAN

The ML2 plugin has its own configuration file that must be used in conjunction with the Open vSwitch or LinuxBridge configuration file. The configuration of ML2 is documented in the upcoming sections.

Installing the ML2 plugin

RHEL-based distributions, such as CentOS, require the installation of the `openstack-neutron-ml2` package on all nodes as follows:

```
# yum install openstack-neutron-ml2
```

Creating a database for ML2

The ML2 plugin attempts to use a common database and schema that can be shared amongst multiple layer 2 agents. On the controller node, create a new database specifically for use with the ML2 plugin using the MySQL client:

```
# mysql -u root -p
```

Use the password set earlier in the OpenStack installation. In this guide, the password was set to openstack.

At the mysql> prompt, execute the following commands to create a database named neutron_ml2 and to grant permissions to the existing neutron user:

```
CREATE DATABASE neutron_ml2;
GRANT ALL PRIVILEGES ON neutron_ml2.* TO 'neutron'@'localhost'
IDENTIFIED BY 'neutron';
GRANT ALL PRIVILEGES ON neutron_ml2.* TO 'neutron'@'%';
QUIT;
```

Use crudini to overwrite the existing database connection string in the Neutron configuration file with the new string on all hosts as follows:

```
# crudini --set /etc/neutron/neutron.conf database connection mysql://
neutron:neutron@controller/neutron_ml2
```

Configuring Neutron to use ML2

Before the ML2 plugin can be used, changes, which include specifying the core plugin and database options, must be made to the Neutron configuration on all hosts.

The core_plugin configuration must be set to use the ML2 plugin. Use the following crudini command to make this change on all hosts:

```
# crudini --set /etc/neutron/neutron.conf DEFAULT core_plugin neutron.
plugins.ml2.plugin.Ml2Plugin
```

In addition to configuration file changes, a symbolic link named plugin.ini must be created in the /etc/neutron/ directory that points to the appropriate plugin configuration file before neutron-server will start. For ML2, the link can be created with the following command:

```
# ln -s /etc/neutron/plugins/ml2/ml2_conf.ini /etc/neutron/plugin.ini
```

If you previously used the LinuxBridge or Open vSwitch plugin and are switching to ML2, be sure to remove the corresponding symbolic link prior to creating a new one for ML2.

The Neutron database must be stamped as the havana release before neutron-server starts. Use the neutron-db-manage command to accomplish this task only on the controller:

```
# neutron-db-manage --config-file /etc/neutron/plugin.ini --config-file /
etc/neutron/neutron.conf stamp havana
```

Configuring service plugins

When the ML2 plugin is used, the L3 router plugin must be defined as a service plugin in the neutron.conf configuration file in addition to the FWaaS and LBaaS service plugins. The following are the service plugins for each of the services:

- **Routing**: neutron.services.l3_router.l3_router_plugin. L3RouterPlugin
- **Load balancing**: neutron.services.loadbalancer.plugin. LoadBalancerPlugin
- **Firewalling**: neutron.services.firewall.fwaas_plugin. FirewallPlugin

To add support for the aforementioned services, add them to the service_plugins configuration option in /etc/neutron/neutron.conf using a text editor as follows:

```
service_plugins= neutron.services.l3_router.l3_router_plugin.
L3RouterPlugin, neutron.services.loadbalancer.plugin.LoadBalancerPlugin,
neutron.services.firewall.fwaas_plugin.FirewallPlugin
```

Configuring the ML2 plugin

The ML2 plugin has its own configuration file, which can be found at /etc/ neutron/plugins/ml2/ml2_conf.ini. The LinuxBridge and Open vSwitch agents continue to rely on their respective configuration files, which were configured previously in this book.

To implement ML2 with the LinuxBridge agent based on prior configuration documented in earlier chapters, use the following configuration in /etc/neutron/ plugins/ml2/ml2_conf.ini:

```
[ml2]
type_drivers = local,flat,vlan
```

```
tenant_network_types = vlan
mechanism_drivers = linuxbridge


[ml2_type_flat]
flat_networks = physnet1


[ml2_type_vlan]
network_vlan_ranges = physnet1:30:33


[database]
connection = mysql://neutron:neutron@controller/neutron_ml2


[securitygroup]
firewall_driver = dummyValue
```

The `firewall_driver` parameter must be defined in the ML2 configuration to enable the `securitygroup` extension. However, the actual value set for `firewall_driver` in the `ml2_conf.ini` file is irrelevant. Each L2 agent configuration file, such as `ovs_neutron_plugin.ini` or `linuxbridge_conf.ini`, should set the actual value for the `firewall_driver` parameter for that agent. Those values were set previously in this book.

For information on configuring ML2 with the Open vSwitch agent, please refer to the following URL:

`http://openstack.redhat.com/ML2_plugin`

Restarting Neutron services

Neutron services must be restarted before the aforementioned changes can take effect.

On the controller node, restart the Neutron server API:

```
# service neutron-server restart
```

On all nodes, restart the LinuxBridge agent:

```
# service neutron-linuxbridge-agent restart
```

Any networks previously created under a monolithic plugin will need to be recreated, as a new database has been built for use with ML2. Instances connected to those networks will need to be deleted and recreated as well.

Index

Symbols

--type attribute
  HTTP 199
  HTTPS 199
  PING 198
  TCP 199

A

admin-state-down switch 112
admin-state-up attribute 151
admin-state-up switch 117
Advanced Message Queue Protocol (AMQP) 30
allocation-pool attribute 123
allowed-address-pairs extension 137
API endpoints
  defining 33, 38
API network 12
APP_COOKIE persistence type 186

B

brctl show command 78
bridge mappings, Open vSwitch plugin
  bridges, configuring 101
bug
  URL 245

C

CentOS 6.5
  URL 22
CIDR argument 124
cisco-credential commands 261

cisco-network-profile commands 261
Cisco Nexus 1000V
  command reference 260, 261
cisco-policy-profile commands 261
classless inter-domain routing (CIDR) 121
CLI
  load balancer management 192
components, load balancer
  pool 184
  pool member 184
  virtual IP 184
components, Open vSwitch
  database server 83
  kernel module 83
  vSwitch daemon 83
compute node components
  configuring 43-45
  installing 43-45
Compute service
  communication, verifying 45, 46
  compute node components, configuring 43-45
  compute node components, installing 43-45
  controller node components, configuring 40-43
  controller node components, installing 40-43
configuration, Neutron LBaaS agent service
  about 190
  device driver, defining 190
  interface driver, defining 190
  user group, modifying 190
configuration, NIC bonding on hosts
  references 15

G

gateway attribute 123
gateway_external_network_id option
  configuring 146
gateway_ip attribute 127
Glance 36
Glance image service installation
  verifying 39, 40
Glance service
  defining 38
GRE network 75, 76
guest network 12

H

haproxy 189
health monitors, CLI
  associating, with pool 199
  commands 197
  creating 197-199
  deleting 199
  details, displaying 200
  disassociating, from pool 199
  listing 200
  managing 197
  updating 200
Horizon
  LBaaS, enabling in 192
Horizon dashboard
  URL 46
hostnames
  setting 27
host-route attribute 123
host-routes attribute 127
HTTP_COOKIE persistence type 186

I

Identity service
  configuring 30-32
  installing 30-32
image service
  configuring 36-38
  Glance image service installation,
    verifying 39, 40

Glance service, defining 38
  installing 36-38
installation, LBaaS 189
installation, OpenStack
  about 29
  Compute service, installing 40
  Identity service, installing 30, 31
  image service, installing 36-38
  messaging server, installing 30
  MySQL database client, installing 30
  MySQL database server, installing 29
  OpenStack dashboard, installing 46
  URL 21
instances
  associated IP address, obtaining 138-140
  attaching, to networks 135
  attaching, to networks with nova boot 135
  layer 2 connectivity, providing to 71
  metadata, retrieving 140
  network interfaces, attaching 136
  network interfaces, detaching 136
  secondary addresses, adding to
    interfaces 137, 138
integration bridge 85, 104
interface
  configuration 25
internal network connections, LinuxBridge
  about 77
  flat network 79-81
  local network 82
  VLAN 77, 78
internal network connections,
    Open vSwitch
  about 84-86
  local VLANs, identifying 88, 89
  ports, identifying on virtual switch 86, 87
ip netns command 53
iptables
  about 223
  filter 223
  mangle 223
  NAT 223
  raw 223
  references 224
iptables rules
  removing 27

Thank you for buying
Learning OpenStack Networking (Neutron)

About Packt Publishing

Packt, pronounced 'packed', published its first book "*Mastering phpMyAdmin for Effective MySQL Management*" in April 2004 and subsequently continued to specialize in publishing highly focused books on specific technologies and solutions.

Our books and publications share the experiences of your fellow IT professionals in adapting and customizing today's systems, applications, and frameworks. Our solution based books give you the knowledge and power to customize the software and technologies you're using to get the job done. Packt books are more specific and less general than the IT books you have seen in the past. Our unique business model allows us to bring you more focused information, giving you more of what you need to know, and less of what you don't.

Packt is a modern, yet unique publishing company, which focuses on producing quality, cutting-edge books for communities of developers, administrators, and newbies alike. For more information, please visit our website: www.packtpub.com.

About Packt Open Source

In 2010, Packt launched two new brands, Packt Open Source and Packt Enterprise, in order to continue its focus on specialization. This book is part of the Packt Open Source brand, home to books published on software built around Open Source licenses, and offering information to anybody from advanced developers to budding web designers. The Open Source brand also runs Packt's Open Source Royalty Scheme, by which Packt gives a royalty to each Open Source project about whose software a book is sold.

Writing for Packt

We welcome all inquiries from people who are interested in authoring. Book proposals should be sent to author@packtpub.com. If your book idea is still at an early stage and you would like to discuss it first before writing a formal book proposal, contact us; one of our commissioning editors will get in touch with you.

We're not just looking for published authors; if you have strong technical skills but no writing experience, our experienced editors can help you develop a writing career, or simply get some additional reward for your expertise.

OpenStack Cloud Computing Cookbook
Second Edition

ISBN: 978-1-78216-758-7   Paperback: 396 pages

Over 100 recipes to successfully set up and manage your OpenStack cloud environments with complete coverage of Nova, Swift, Keystone, Glance, Horizon, Neutron, and Cinder

1. Learn how to install, configure, and manage all of the OpenStack core projects, including new topics such as block storage and software defined networking.

2. Learn how to build your Private Cloud utilizing DevOps and Continuous Integration tools and techniques.

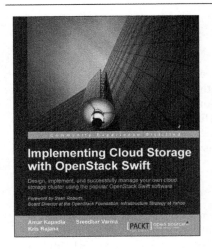

Implementing Cloud Storage with OpenStack Swift

ISBN: 978-1-78216-805-8   Paperback: 140 pages

Design, implement, and successfully manage your own cloud storage cluster using the popular OpenStack Swift software

1. Learn about the fundamentals of cloud storage using OpenStack Swift.

2. Explore how to install and manage OpenStack Swift along with various hardware and tuning options.

3. Perform data transfer and management using REST APIs.

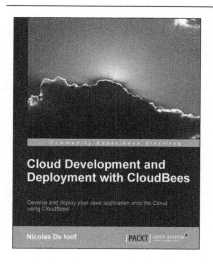

CPSIA information can be obtained at www.ICGtesting.com
Printed in the USA
LVOW03s0527280415

436304LV00010B/66/P